Loving Your Marriage in Retirement

Keep The Music Playing

Sally Strosahl
With Contributions by Tom Johnson

IN THE
ROUND
PUBLISHING

Published by In the Round Publishing

Cover design: Stephanie Warner - stephwarner.com
Back cover photo: Donnell Collins - donnellcollinsphotography.com

ISBN: 978-0692163207

Library of Congress Cataloging-in-Publication Data Pending

Printed in the United States of America.

First Printing, 2018 In the Round Publishing

Contents

Introduction

This book is the product of two series of events. The first was my husband Tom's retirement six years ago after four decades in the newspaper business. The second was a series of discussions in my counseling office, spread over many years, in which couples worked through the changes retirement had brought to their marriage.

We had boarded an early evening flight from Chicago to Sarasota, Fla., where we had booked a condo on Anna Maria Island for the week before Christmas. The Boeing 717 had what is known as 2-plus-3 seating, and we had a pair of seats to ourselves, which felt to us like flying first-class. An exquisite full moon was visible off to the left.

The next day we were sitting on beach chairs, watching a shimmering sunset, listening to the waves, when Tom told me he had decided to retire at that moment aloft the previous night, sailing smoothly along in the moonlight at 31,000 feet. He had been contemplating ending his career for awhile, watching colleagues being offered buyouts, keeping track of newspapers' shrinking circulation and payrolls, and wondering about his own future. He loved his job as news editor of our local newspaper — which was still making money. However, he knew when he was ready to leave. We returned from our week of bliss to our full-time jobs. He told a couple of close colleagues he would be retiring in July, and waited a few months before officially putting in his notice.

Right before we left for Florida we had a huge birthday party, celebrating his 65th. It also felt like an early retirement party. He was bested and roasted and there were good stories and good fun.

After he retired, he very wisely gave himself six months before he made any commitments. He wanted to find his natural rhythm again after so many years of shift work and deadlines. He slept as long as his body clock would allow. He napped when he wanted. He found a new workout routine at the health club.

With the help of a former college roommate, he tried new golf courses.

It shifted our dynamic also. After 40-plus years of marriage, he had a lot more free time and I was still working, seeing clients in my private practice, some weeks full-time. Five years younger, I had no plans to retire, even though several of our friends and some of my colleagues had. A matter of fact, not only was I not interested in retiring, I felt like I had never done better work. The older I get, the more laser-focused I am. I want people to be happier and more satisfied with their lives, faster and better. And I'm probably a little impatient. I do feel like we are all running out of time, not just us older folks but the whole planet, too. We need more positivity now, ASAP, and yesterday, please.

I am cutting back as we travel more and as I ease into retirement in a few years. I trust I'll know when I'm ready. Right now as long as folks want to make appointments and I feel I still have something to offer, I'm enjoying working. We're finding our way with each other with our schedules. Tom will often ask after I've had my coffee what my schedule is that day and when he can expect to see me for dinner.

Growing up I loved reading books. Since we moved so much, the public libraries (and the librarians) were havens. My imagination was vivid. The words on the page would transport me on adventures to new countries or continents yet to explore. I'm sure I read adult fiction which went right over my head, but my carry-away was that the world was much bigger than the streets of my neighborhoods in southeast Wisconsin.

As an adult, books have been important resources. As a psychotherapist I have always recommended books, called bibliotherapy. As I worked with more couples facing the issues of retirement I went searching the bookstores and online to find books to recommend. I found books on finance and travel and tips for fun-filled retirement, but I found very little written for couples about their marriages. While I have been writing this book a few volumes focusing on relationships have been published. I expect there will be a boom in such titles soon, since many of us Baby Boomers are also avid readers.

I heard someone say, "Everyone has a book in them." I couldn't relate. I had watched colleagues write books, and I had not been tempted. My husband was the writer, not me. I was most comfortable doing a workshop or being in the consultation room working with a couple. And then I started noticing I was waking up with whole paragraphs being written for me, in my mind. Very clearly. At first I resisted, and then I understood this to be a spiritual challenge — an invitation to be a channel. Not in an egotistical way but in a heart-to-heart, listening way. Tom and I were in the midst of this transition to retirement and so were many of my clients and good friends. Others had forged a path for us. We could learn from them and from research and from sharing our stories. I finally realized I needed to surrender to the process already unfolding. I decided to open to the possibility of writing a book and seeing where it would take me. And what an adventure it has been!

It's been an amazing experience, life-changing. And sometimes frustrating and agonizing. And exciting and revealing. And I'm grateful. First I had to learn to get very quiet. And listen. I upped my meditation practice. I prayed a lot and called on the guidance of my loved ones who have passed. I learned I couldn't write after a day of clients or even early in the morning before going to work. I learned I write best away from home or office in a place of beauty, preferably with a view of water. My favorite place has been on the balcony of the beachside condo we rent for a week each December on Marco Island. The almost daily visits from the dolphins bring inspiration.

We sent out the first draft of the book to 10 volunteer readers, of various backgrounds and careers. They gave us encouragement. We got feedback that it was actually three books: one for couples, one for academia and one to teach therapists how to work with couples. We took out the parts that were the last two to focus on the first. I got more clear and found my voice, realizing what I really want to say about marriage and retirement — and keeping the music playing so we can love our marriages in retirement.

That became the vision for this book: to help couples create the marriage and the life we want now and provide practical and effective solutions to achieve our mutual goals as we transition into retirement. As we get older, the time together becomes even more precious. We kept hearing the message, "Don't waste another moment. Do it now."

It has also been good for our marriage. We've learned even more about ourselves and about what we want moving forward. I hope you have a similar experience. Thank you for picking up the book. I am glad and honored to share this journey with you.

Facing the Challenges

01 - Loving Your Marriage in Retirement

"If we can be the best of lovers
Yet be the best of friends
If we can try with every day to make it better as it grows
With any luck, then I suppose, the music never ends"

Lyrics by Marilyn and Alan Bergman

I recently read a billboard along an expressway that read in large letters: "We spend more time clicking 'Like' than we do planning for retirement." Of course, the ad was referring to financial and estate planning. I read the billboard to my husband, who was driving, and added the thought, "Yes, and we spend even less time planning how retirement affects our marriage and other relationships."

The billboard was also referencing the amount of time many of us spend on Facebook reading posts about other people's lives and clicking "Like." Some complain that the Facebook connection feels more meaningful than our real-time connections with our partner, family or friends.

As a marriage and family therapist I get a front-row seat to the real-time connections couples are making with each other as they adjust to the changes brought on by retirement or with couples who have started to anticipate what might happen when one or both retire and as they continue to experience the challenges of aging bodies, minds and spirits.

So Many Questions

Maybe you are starting to plan for your retirement or your partner's and are looking for guidance. You might feel excited to retire and are wondering how this will affect your marriage and other aspects of your life. Or maybe you are already retired and are feeling bored and discontented and lonely. Maybe you have been married for decades and are wondering, "Is this all there is?" Or you may feel lost now that you are no longer working and have dropped the connections to work friends or colleagues. "How does my life have meaning now? What is my value? What do I want to do with myself and this supposed free time? Why does my partner feel so driven and have purpose and is so excited while I feel left behind?"

Or maybe you feel invisible. As you are aging you are aware that fewer people look at you or ask you about your life or even say hello. Are you also becoming invisible to yourself and your partner? Do your children and grandchildren really care about who you are and who you were?

Maybe you are suffering with unhappiness in your marriage and are concerned about what growing older and spending more time together means. What do you share? What do you enjoy doing together? How do you resolve conflicts? How well do you listen to each other? Perhaps you have some health challenges.

You may be wondering what you need to get unstuck and move forward. Do you need to go for help? Would counseling or a workshop or a book help guide the way?

Couples Caught Off-Guard

That is what this book is about. As a marriage and family therapist in private practice for 40-plus years, I have witnessed so many couples who got caught off-guard by the changes and challenges that happened when one or both retired. Or maybe the couples have been retired for years and a major health crisis like a stroke or cancer diagnosis threw the whole equilibrium off and the relationship is challenged. Marital issues left neglected or unresolved over the years suddenly blew up in their faces. Intense feelings exploded, making them feel blindsided. Irritations simmering under the surface came out in unexpected or nasty ways. Instead of looking forward to retirement, the couples argue more or become overwhelmed and pull away from each other. There is more conflict, distress and increasing unhappiness.

Couples who had enjoyed years of relative calm and happiness started looking at their partners and wondering, "Who am I married to? And how did this happen? Can my marriage survive retirement?"

They might even decide that their marriage is over or can't be saved. We know from research that there is a spike in the number of divorces corresponding with "empty nest" — and then again with retirement.

Spending More Time Together

Spending more time together becomes a mixed blessing. It can create more tension or expose a lack of ability to resolve conflict or an imbalance about who is in charge or which tasks get done by whom, when and how. The husband who has not "touched a dish in decades" becomes intent on instructing his wife on proper placement protocols for the dishwasher, repeatedly reminding her when she is not compliant. Or the wife complains about her husband, "acting like Velcro. He follows me around the house and goes wherever I go. I'm used to only seeing each other after work and on weekends. Now it is too much time together."

Having more time together and more choices about how to spend the time can be stressful in retirement. It also presents more opportunities for pleasure of all varieties, increasing your quality of life and making the retirement years possibly the best years of your marriage.

We came up with the title *Loving Your Marriage In Retirement: Keep the Music Playing* from the song *How Do You Keep the Music Playing?*

We have loved this song since we first heard Tony Bennett sing it live decades ago. The lyrics, by Alan and Marilyn Bergman, give a template for how to keep your marriage tuned up and resonating to each other as you both adapt to the changes which come year after year. The Bergmans, married for 60 years, are a husband-wife writing team who have written lyrics to songs for numerous TV shows, movies and stage musicals. They have won three Academy Awards. *How Do You Keep the Music Playing?* was written for the 1983 film *Best Friends*. The music was composed by Michel Legrand.

As you read the lyrics printed here, take a moment to pull up one of the many YouTube versions of this song. (Versions by Tony Bennett, Johnny Mathis, Barbra Streisand and Celine Dion are readily available.) Allow yourself to imagine dancing with your partner, looking into his/her eyes. Or better yet, swoop your partner into your arms and let yourselves swoon for a few minutes. Even if your joints are aching!

How do you keep the music playing?
How do you make it last?
How do you keep the song from fading too fast?

How do you lose yourself to someone?
And never lose your way
How do you not run out of new things to say?

And since we're always changing
How can it be the same?
And tell me how year after year
You're sure your heart will fall apart
Each time you hear his name
I know the way I feel for you
It's now or never
The more I love the more that I'm afraid
That in your eyes I may not see forever ...
Forever ...

If we can be the best of lovers
Yet be the best of friends
If we can try with every day to make it better as it grows
With any luck, then I suppose
The music never ends

Lyrics by Marilyn and Alan Bergman
Lyrics reprinted with permission
Music by Michel Legrand

Getting Older Together Is a Challenge
— As Is Retirement

Our focus is not only about retirement. Some folks reach official retirement age and continue working in some form or another. Each change comes with its own challenges. Just getting older together is a challenge. We're hoping you will find guidance in this book as you read stories of other couples. You may recognize your own story, with your own unique spin, of course. Our hope is you will carry away some ideas as you find what works for you.

If you're already retired, you might commit to using tools in this book to enrich your marriage and make it even better. If you are getting ready to retire, you might use the suggestions to assess your marriage and introduce the strategies to ensure a smoother transition into retirement with a stronger, more loving relationship.

For those contemplating retirement, the book works through some recurring questions: When to retire? One or both? How will we handle all the extra time with each other? What do I want to do with myself now that I'm not working? How do we want to spend our money? Will we have enough money? Where do we want to live? What about caring for our parents? How close do we want to live to our adult kids and our grandkids? What is still on our "bucket lists?" What about our friendships? What happens if one of us gets ill or is already impaired? What will give our lives meaning? How can we feel happier?

For couples who have already retired, it might be a good idea to revisit the questions listed above and update the information from your new perspective. We don't know what we don't know until we know it.

Every marriage needs a tune-up, just like when we take our cars in for regular maintenance or get annual physical checkups.

We Learn From Each Other's Stories

When contacted for marriage therapy I request to meet with the couple together the first session. I want to hear their story with both of them listening to how the other portrays themselves and describes the marriage. I consider the first session a chance for all of us, the couple and me, to check out whether we are a good fit for the work ahead. If I start with the wife and the husband joins us after a few sessions, or vice versa if the husband contacts me first, I take precautions to make sure the other feels safe and that they know I will not take sides nor place blame. I appreciate getting feedback, especially from men, who tell me that they feel safe with me, even though I am a female therapist. Sometimes they expect to be piled on or as one guy told me, "I expected you to pin me to the wall and tell me what a jerk I am." Hopefully this safety comes across in the book. We don't learn when we feel threatened. We become open to growth when we feel safe. Some of the stories in this book come from my clients — with their permission — presented in composite form to protect confidentiality.

In addition, I interviewed several couples to get their suggestions of what helped them navigate these waters of retirement and aging and to share their wisdom with others going through this life stage. I interviewed couples who were able to transition with relative ease, as well as those who needed to overhaul their marriages after retirement. I call them my Wise Married Elders (WME). Some of the couples wanted to be named. Some wanted to protect their adult children or loved ones from some of the painful truths revealed and asked to have the interviews remain anonymous.

Over the years it has been important to me to be culturally sensitive as I work with couples and families of another race and religion and class, including LBGT individuals, couples and families. Some of their stories are in the book. Unless I refer to he-he or she-she, assume the couples are heterosexual.

The stories also represent a range of income levels. Some couples are barely making it living on Social Security and modest savings, where others are wealthy enough to own multiple homes and travel the world. What we own or how much money we each have is only one parameter by which we measure ourselves and our happiness. The ideas presented in *Loving Your Marriage in Retirement: Keep The Music Playing* are applicable for any budget. A long happy life is not dependent on wealth. Positive, hopeful thoughts and kind actions do not cost even a dime. Although I may give you a penny for your thoughts.

As a marriage therapist, after a day of working with couples I feel so blessed to come home to my husband. In my opinion, I have married the best guy in the world. My friends call him "Saint Thomas." I reference my marriage through the book as illustration and also to reinforce the idea that we are all in this together, just trying to work it out day by day. What works for us might not work for you. We are navigating these same waters. We are walking the talk as we move into retirement and as our minds, spirits and bodies age. I've included the stories — mine and others — because that is the way many of us learn the best: from each other.

My husband is five years older. He retired at age 65-1/2 after 40 years as a reporter, writer and editor for our local newspaper. He was drafted out of graduate school and served 34 months in the Army (thankfully, all stateside) during the Vietnam War. I am still working. I love my work. I plan to keep working as long as I feel I have something to offer and as long as people keep making appointments. I will work less as we travel more. I trust I will know when it is time to close my practice. Not right now.

Writing this book about marriage and retirement has been part of our journey in our own transition from two careers, working full time, into what retirement looks like for us now and as we envision the future. Learning from my clients' experiences, doing the Wise Married Elder interviews, as well as a lot of research, has expanded my understanding of the issues and the remedies. Tom's, too. In some of the chapters he has added his own thoughts, which we call "Tom's notes." They are set off in shaded boxes. We've worked together as an author-editor team. I appreciate his male/husband/journalist perspective as a counterbalance to mine. Plus, he has a low tolerance for psycho-babble.

Live the Process

We teach what we have to learn. I am writing this book as we are living this transition. And I am so grateful for all the teachers in my life. As one of my good friends, Dr. Sue Ross, who is a retired professor of social work and gerontology, says, "It is not enough to have the knowledge. We also have to live the process. There is no bypass. Knowing about aging doesn't protect us from the effects of aging. It may just give us some ideas about how to cope with the changes."

The late Dr. Richard Eastman, former dean of North Central College and Tom's favorite English professor (and the man who first introduced us), wrote in his book called *Style,* "Writing is not just putting down what one knows. Writing is the means by which one comes to know." Writing this book is a re-examination of years of experience and clinical practice. It is my hope that it will offer some help to you and your partner as you find your own truth in your marriage.

Find Your Own Truth

Getting ready for retirement, couples contemplate what having extra time together will mean for them. Does this stir excitement and fantasy? Smiles and anticipation? Or does it settle in the body as boredom, dread or fear?

In a counseling session, Suzanne, 49, has many questions as she imagines her future with Gary, 55. They have spent their marriage focused on careers and raising their children. They both are conflict-avoidant and sidestep issues they disagree about. They are superior at compromise. However, they back away from sharing from the heart. Suzanne, the youngest of three, was 6 years old when her parents divorced. She is used to being the "accommodator," her needs being invisible. She brought this pattern into her marriage to Gary, who was the only son of parents who married late and were thrilled to have a son.

After the business of living and meeting the kids' needs, their own exercise programs and grocery shopping, not much is left over for their marriage. Nor do they choose to go there. Attaining more satisfaction would need to start with conversation and a commitment to really know each other. Suzanne's tears show both her desire for more and her fears at taking the risk. I wondered how Gary might have responded if he had been in the session.

This retirement guide is for them. It is also for the couple who have a pretty good marriage and want some guidance for the changes they anticipate as one or both retire.

This book is also for couples who have retired years ago and are more acutely feeling the changes in their marriage as they face the issues related to getting older.

Choose the Life and the Marriage You Desire

We Baby Boomers are blessed with better circumstances, longer life, and the potential for greater health and happiness than our parents' generation and their forebears. This blessing also becomes our challenge.

As we age we become more free to choose the life we desire. And the marriage we desire. Or not, if you are in a marriage you don't desire. Please do not waste another moment of your precious time being less than or settling for less than you desire — for yourself and for your loved ones.

If you are already in a marriage that is working well and you feel good about yourself, this book may help validate what you and your partner are already doing and may offer a few ideas to help you stay on the path of increasing health and satisfaction.

If you are experiencing stress as you think about retirement or you have a marriage that falls short of what you desire, you may recognize your story in these chapters and may read suggestions and learn skills to help improve your situation with yourself and your partner. This might be the time to reboot your marriage.

Marlo Thomas, actress and author, has written a book called

It Ain't' Over ... Till it's Over: Reinventing Your life — and Realizing Your Dreams." She interviewed 60 women who redefine growing older. Some have called the book *Free to Be You and Me* for older adults. Thomas writes:

"*The trick is not to view every change as a deficit. You have to learn to roll with the changes or you're always going to be in a state of loss. When you lose your parents, you're in a state of loss. When your kids go to college, you're in a state of loss. When your house is suddenly empty and too big, you're in a state of loss. Life changes, and we're not ready for it, even though there have been signs all along the way. So we have to reinvent ourselves as individuals, reinvent our marriages, reinvent our careers.*"

There is no more perfect time than right now to be the person you want to be, to create the life you want, and to be in the marriage you desire from this day forward. In *Loving Your Marriage In Retirement: Keep the Music Playing,* each chapter helps bring you to a clearer picture of what that might look like for you and how to get there from here.

I use this favorite quotation as a guide for relationships, written by Virginia Satir, one of the founders of family systems therapy:

Goals For Me

I want to love you without clutching,
appreciate you without judging,
join you without invading,
invite you without demanding.

Leave you without guilt,
criticize you without blaming,
and help you without insulting

If I can have the same from you
then we can truly meet and enrich each other.

Virginia Satir, *Making Contact*

~~~~Reflection~~~~

Read this poem stanza by stanza and reflect on how this relates to your marriage. How do you feel appreciated? How do you appreciate your spouse? Record your thoughts, maybe in a special journal or workbook. Decide what you want to share with your partner.

Each chapter of the book has at least one Reflection. This is a time to quiet yourself, take a few deep breaths and shift your focus to reflecting on the questions proposed. Be aware of both your thoughts and your feelings. You may wish to write your thoughts down or make a drawing. You may set up your own workbook or journal. The worksheets are also available to be downloaded on the website www.sallystrosahl.com or you can order for purchase a workbook of all the worksheets.

Tom's Note:

We look in the mirror as we begin another day. The face looking back at us is a bit more wrinkled. The hair is a bit grayer and thinner — and we're fine with that. Retirement is in view, and our checklist begins rolling:

- *Ready to leave work? Check.*
- *Work ready for us to leave? Check.*
- *Kids on their own? Check.*
- *Investments in place? Check.*
- *Home equity growing? Check.*
- *Debt manageable? Check.*
- *Wills executed? Check.*
- *"Bucket list" nailed? Check*
- *Hearing? Check.*
- *Exercise? Check.*
- *Sex? Well, not quite a "check," but ...*

Our partner's face appears in the mirror, peeking over our shoulder. We exchange smiles and greetings, and our inventory continues.

- *Marriage ready for next step? Well ... we haven't talked about it in THAT way.*

We have become a culture of list-makers, but Sally's many decades as an individual and marriage therapist and my own experiences have shown that many people approaching retirement have not thought to give their marriage a check-up.

Sally invites you to take that inventory. What works well? What needs work? What do we expect of each other in retirement? How is aging affecting our marriage?

This book shares many stories. Perhaps you will find your own situation reflected and take heart. This process is work, but it can be fun. You will gain tools which will be useful in building the marriage you want as retirement gives you more time together.

02 – *Keep The Music Playing*

As the two of you retire, many aspects of your lives change. This can be stressful and put a strain on your marriage. It can also be a window, a place in time, where you are invited to focus more closely on each other and your relationship, looking at what works and what your struggles or challenges are. It can be a time of active and creative problem-solving, a time of appreciation and gratitude. All of this requires careful listening and tuning in to your own needs and your partner's needs. That is why this book has 20 chapters. We had to stop ourselves from making it even longer!

Someone asked me what I would identify as the top five issues facing married and retired seniors and what were the top five suggestions to deal with these challenges. The answer reflects the information from the interviews and experiences with couples in my office rather than published surveys, listed not necessarily in order of importance.

The top five issues for married retired seniors:
- Getting used to having so much time together.
- Deciding how to spend the time together in satisfying, meaningful ways.
- Dealing with limitations due to health and aging.
- Planning financially and determining if they have enough money to support retirement.
- Redefining who they are, now that they are retired, and how to make a difference.

The top five suggestions for married retired seniors:
- Talk and listen to each other about what you are feeling, your dreams, your fears, your hopes, your needs.
- Find a way to keep falling in love with your partner.
- Laugh whenever you can. Use your sense of humor to change your frame of mind.
- Use gratitude, especially if feeling challenged.
- Do it now!

Each chapter in the book expands on this information.

Facing the Challenges

Loving Your Marriage in Retirement: Keep the Music Playing offers practical solutions to the issues many couples face during the transitions presented by retirement. His, hers or both. And the challenges presented by aging, whether you or your spouse are still working. The first section of the book focuses on facing the challenges which have been generally addressed in the Introduction and Chapter 1. This chapter, "Keep the Music Playing," expands and describes the layout of the book and how to navigate the chapters to best meet the needs of your relationship. It ends with a reflection and a script for a guided visualization. For the full experience, go to the website www.sallystrosahl.com and play the guided visualization called, "Imagine your marriage in retirement."

I've included *Reflections* in each chapter. These are opportunities to quiet yourself and reflect or think about the information being presented as well as tune into the feelings that may be coming up as you reflect. You may be tempted to skip these exercises, especially if you are skimming the chapter or looking for sections addressing your specific concerns. When you have time later you may wish to go back and sit with yourself and see what comes up or go further and ask your partner to do the exercise together. If you were in the office having a session with me, I might lead you through one of these exercises to deepen and enrich the content and connect on a mind-body-spirit level. You can do this for yourself as you go through the book. The Reflection called "Ground In Strength and Goodness" in Chapter 3 is important to do as you examine your marriage.

After I worked with a chapter for awhile, Tom would edit using the skills he practiced for over 40 years at our local newspaper as a reporter, city editor, features editor and news editor. Sometimes he was moved to add his perspective called "Tom's Notes," which are in shaded boxes.

Chapter 3, called "Retirement and Aging: Building Resilience," makes a distinction between changes, which occur by our choice or are imposed on us, and transition, which is the process of adjusting to the changes. The chapter discusses some of the minor irritations as well as the more important issues which couples face and includes suggestions for coping with the stress. *The Four-Fold Way* by Angeles Arrien is presented as a helpful lens through which we can explore the changes happening to us during this transition into retirement and as we age. They are: show up, pay attention, tell the truth (or keep noble silence) and stay open but not attached to the outcome. The chapter ends with two reflections for further discussion.

Chapter 4, "The Wise Married Elders Speak," profiles some of the couples we interviewed and is a compilation of their suggestions. As I began writing this book I decided to search out and interview couples who had already retired and had some years of success in loving their marriage in retirement. I wanted to know what they went through and how they coped and what helped them. I asked them what they wish they had known then and what wisdom they had to pass on to younger couples going through the transition now. Their ideas are presented in this chapter as well as sprinkled through the rest of the book.

Chapter 5, "Can Your Marriage Survive Retirement?," focuses on marriages that are not working and where one or both spouses are very unhappy. It was not originally part of the plan for the book, but as I listened to the interviews and my counseling clients I decided a book about marriage and retirement would not be complete without addressing these issues. It is important to honor the courage and the desire for a better life in retirement. The stories in this chapter reflect people who did not give up on themselves even though they had to give up on their marriage. Some couples were able to do this amicably and are able to gather for family events and share adult children and grandchildren, spreading the love around. Everyone benefits. If you already have serious doubts about spending another day — much less the rest of your life — with your spouse, read this chapter with courage and find the strength to make the decision to either make things work by investing in the possibility of change — or let go and start to discover who you can be when free of a marriage that is not healthy for you and quite possibly for your spouse.

Enhancing Togetherness

The next section of five chapters, called "Enhancing Togetherness," focuses on the skills and strategies of using the time of retirement to make your marriage even better.

Chapter 6, called "One Talks; One Listens," gives instruction for keeping connection, communication and listening skills and enhancing emotional intimacy. It explains how to come from your "higher self," how to give criticism, and how to use love languages to give and receive love.

Chapter 7, "Strengthening Emotional Intimacy With Couple Check-ins," describes the steps for the recommended weekly couple check-in which puts the listening skills in practice and lays the groundwork for continued emotional intimacy and healthy connection. Even though it may seem stilted or forced at first, couples who commit to this routine feel closer and more trusting over the long run. You may not call it something formal like "couple check-in," but my hunch is that if you are in a healthy long-term marriage you are already doing some form of this ritual.

Chapter 8, called "Can We Both Be Right?" focuses on conflict resolution and fair fighting, skills essential in any healthy marriage. Retirement and spending more time together is an excellent time to get better at both. Resentment is not good. Understanding and resolution are. Most issues can be talked through with loving kindness. This chapter includes pointers for resolving conflicts, examining expectations, healing from shame and being "good enough" partners. It concludes with a list of the "Ten Most Common Bad Habits" and a Reflection.

More time and occasion to have sex is a common expectation I hear, especially from husbands, and especially if both spouses retire at the same time. The stress of childrearing or caring for aging parents, added to the normal stresses of jobs and schedules plus health concerns, often results in a diminished sex life. A couple times a week reduces to a couple times a month reduces to a couple times a year and then only on holidays or getaways. Maybe one of you lost interest years ago, or has been bored with the same foreplay and routine positions. Your flame has gone out and you may be too tired or disinterested to even get it going again. Or maybe one of you does. Well, you have a lot of company.

Explore Chapter 9, called "Sex 1: Naked Nightly and Afternoon Delight," to find suggestions for re-igniting the flame or enhancing what is already good and making it better and understanding how aging affects our sex life.

Chapter 10, "Sex 2: If Sex Has Stopped," is for couples who are no longer having sex for various reasons with suggestions for those who desire to rekindle romance. The chapter also offers information for those whose sex life is impacted by chronic pain or has stopped because of infidelity.

Being Your Best Self

The next section of four chapters focuses on "Being Your Best Self" and includes discussions about personal development, health, and spirituality. We've also included the prospect of facing serious illness and death in this section because of the challenges to the concept of being our best self when confronted with sickness and death, and yet how often this happens to our loved ones and our friends at this age.

Retiring from paid work frees us to explore parts of ourselves which we have left neglected or have put on the shelf in our busy lives. Having fun discovering what floats our boats at this time in our lives can make us each feel more alive, more vital, humming and singing with a new tune and dancing with a lighter step. That lightness of being can translate into feeling healthier and even more sexy. It gets our nitric oxide going.

Chapter 11, called "Personal Development: Rediscovering Yourself and Each Other," includes suggestions and exercises for this adventure in self-exploration.

Several of the couples I interviewed spoke about retirement affording them the time and resources to focus on improving their emotional and physical health and fitness through exercise, regulating their sleep patterns, receiving correct medical and dental care, taking supplements, preparing nutritious food, doing yoga or tai chi, and communing with nature. Management of chronic pain is another major concern. These topics are addressed in Chapter 12, "Health: Laugh, Move, and Green Smoothies."

Chapter 13, "Spirituality: Be Here Now," focuses on what we believe about God or a Higher Power or Source or whatever concept you embrace. As Jesuit philosopher Pierre Teilhard de Chardin says, "We are not humans being having a spiritual experience. We are spiritual beings having a human experience." Taking the time to define who we are and what we believe spiritually — versus what we believe about religion — is part of this phase in our lives, centering and nourishing our souls and helping us prepare for what is ahead. As a couple, being mindful and sharing about our beliefs can deepen our relationship and may have some health benefits as well.

Facing serious health issues, and more sadly the loss of our loved ones, is the focus of Chapter 14. Knowing the older we get the more likely one of us will live without the other can be an incentive to live more intentionally during the years we have together. The bucket lists become more important. Whispering those sweet nothings and giving that unasked-for hug brings the awareness of the precious into each moment. Mutually facing the paperwork of advanced directives and assigning powers of attorney *before* the health crisis can open up an important discussion about our own mortality and what we need from each other right now.

Enjoying Retirement

Retirement, and the extended personal time it affords, can accommodate a wide variety of lifestyles, highlighted in Chapter 15, "Lifestyle Choices — Do it Now!" Some of the options were ones the couples interviewed had not even considered before they started preparing for retirement. Of course, how much money we have affects how much we can do and what choices we have in retirement and even affects when we might retire. It is important to have a good understanding about how much money you have and how you want to spend it. Getting a good handle on your financial circumstances is recommended but not covered in detail. We leave that to other experts in other books.

Chapter 16, "Other Generations: Grandparents, Adult Children and Elderly Parents," recognizes the many roles we play at this life stage. We may feel like the name given to us, the "Sandwich Generation," caught between juggling the needs of our children and grandchildren while still caring for our elderly parents. We face many questions: How does caring for elderly parents affect your marriage and your finances? What is your value system? What are the cultural expectations? When our parents die, are we left to be the patriarch or matriarch of the family? You're now the oldest or part of the generation that is the oldest. What does that mean? What if our adult children still live at home or need support financially? How do you decide your role in grandchildren's lives? What if you live next door? What if you live across the country? What if you have no grandchildren? How do we establish effective boundaries? We examine some answers in this chapter.

The research about longevity and having friends is compelling. It is not the number of friends but the quality of the relationships that can add vitality, spark and years to our lives. Chapter 17, "Friendships: Enriching the Quality of Life," examines this correlation and includes the many faces of friendship for retired couples as well as differences related to gender.

It is recommended to have a plan for retirement, his, hers,

both, when and how. Ideally, financial planning occurs through-out adulthood, with discussion of other issues beginning at least a decade before a couple's first retirement day. In Chapter 18, "Retirement Choices," you'll meet some couples who were able to do just that and read their suggestions. In the same chapter you'll meet other folks who were laid off, fired or catapulted into retirement with no plan or with no choice — and discovered surprising resilience to face the storms.

Chapter 19, "Designing Your Retirement Plan," concludes with a set of questions to help you create your own plan for retirement. Explore the answers together. Keep revising the plan as you find out what works best. Bringing intention enhances the adventure.

In Chapter 20, "Grow Old Along With Me," the ideas are pulled together with concluding thoughts including another guided visualization.

For each reflection and guided visualization exercise there are worksheets available to record your answers. Some folks like to just think about the answers while others like to put pen to paper. Since the format of the book doesn't lend itself to tearing out pages you can visit the website www.sallystrosahl.com to download each worksheet or order a workbook.

It is a privilege to meet you through this book and share some of the stories and ideas as we journey through this retirement transition. We are walking this talk, too. We would love to hear your comments, questions and your stories as you read *Loving Your Marriage In Retirement: Keep the Music Playing.*

~~~~Reflection~~~~

So, before we move on, take a moment and reflect on your own marriage:
- *How is it going?*
- *What is working well?*
- *What is not working so well?*
- *What do you need more of?*
- *What do you need less of?*

- *How do you feel about all of this?*
- *How do you think your spouse feels?*
- *Is it time to set up a check-in?*
- *Is it time to do more intentional planning for retirement or beyond?*
- *How hopeful do you feel about creating the relationship you both desire?*

You may want to write down your answers or speak into a voice recorder. You may be curious what your spouse answered and decide to share with each other your responses. Check these questions periodically to check in with how your marriage is going and what you may want to tweak to make it even better.

Guided Visualization: Your Marriage In Retirement

If you are interested in going deeper, set aside 15-30 minutes and do the following guided visualization. You can find a recording of this script on the website www.sallystrosahl.com.

Pick a quiet time where you won't be interrupted. Put on some relaxing music if you choose. Have a notepad and pen ready. Or a voice recorder. Get comfortable. Take a few deep breaths, exhaling completely. Bring yourself into the moment. Close your eyes and get a picture of you and your spouse in a place of beauty and relaxation. Now visualize your retirement. Create a picture or a vision in your mind's eye. What does it look like? Where are you? What are the sights and sounds, the sensations, tastes and smells of this place of beauty and adventure? How do you feel? What are you wearing? What is your spouse wearing? What do you notice around you? Heighten the experience by making all your senses more vivid. See the colors brighter. Feel the sensations sharper. Turn up the volume. Use your imagination to flesh out this vision of retirement.

Enjoy the vision. When you are ready, take another deep breath and return to here and now, this time and place. Take a few moments to write down this vision and record your experience.

Now, read what you've written or recorded. Write a list of five things you need to do to make this vision a reality. Now write five things your partner needs to do to make this happen.

If you choose, share this experience with each other. See how close (or far apart) your visions are. Discuss. Repeat as you choose. It's your imagination. It's your creation. You are in charge of the manifestation.

Tom's Note:

A veteran actor in community theater once told us that acting is the process of spreading out your identity, then finding which portions of your identity can be applied to the experience of the character you're playing.

Sally's book is a form of this exercise. By reading the distillation of her decades as a therapist, you will meet many people. You'll be invited to see whether the experiences of other couples resonate with your own life as you work through the many variables of your relationships.

If you recognize parts of yourself in the lives of others, it might become easier to identify what works and what needs work.

03 - Retirement and Aging: Building Resilience

"Grow old along with me; the best is yet to be" is the opening line to a well-loved Robert Browning poem, popularized by the Beatles' John Lennon. I see this image of Tom and me holding on tightly to each other as we walk a path into a woods with the sunlight streaming through the trees. It gives me a warm and loving feeling.

Examining our marriages as we prepare for retirement requires courage, as well as a good sense of humor and a belief that it is worth the effort. I believe that's one of the reasons you picked up this book and have read this far. As the saying goes, "Growing old is not for sissies." And growing old with your spouse is not for sissies either. Allowing ourselves to take a good look at how we relate to each other in marriage strengthens our connection and opens the way to being more clear about our choices, bringing more satisfaction and happiness into our lives.

Marriages often hold together with unspoken agreements about whose needs get priority or how conflicts get resolved. The unspoken is sometimes unconscious, without intent: "That's just what we do." Retirement, with all its changes, shakes this up, forcing the healthy couple to become more aware of the patterns in their marriage. Some patterns help sustain and nurture the relationship. Other patterns cause unhappiness, resentment and frustration. This next story illustrates this dynamic:

"I am not going to listen ..."

The couple came into my office already arguing. Gina was fuming. She looked at her husband, John, with disgust and said, "I'm telling you right now. I am not going to listen to you go on and on every moment of the day about when and what is going on in the bathroom, how your back feels, how your knees hurt, and hear every belch, cough and sneeze with your commentary. If this is what retirement is going to be like, I'm going to tell the School Board to rip up my resignation letter."

John, sitting on the couch next to her, probably a little too closely for her comfort, wisely let her keep talking without interrupting. I encouraged her to say more and complimented him for doing a good job listening.

This couple returned for marital counseling after a trip to visit their oldest son and his family. They barely spoke to each other on the plane ride home. When they did start talking, both agreed they had been arguing more, feeling more tense and not sleeping well. They knew they needed to figure out what was going on. They had worked with me several years before during a crisis with their younger son. Their marriage was in pretty good shape then, and they needed only a few sessions to improve their communication and learn the skill of detachment with love and support. Now they were seeking guidance through this time of transition.

John, 66, had retired from a management job when he was 60. Gina, 62, a high school teacher, was planning to retire at the end of the school year. She had mixed feelings about leaving. She was aware that she had already started to grieve the loss of what she loved about being in the classroom and thought she might greatly miss the daily contact with her students and colleagues. She put on a happy face for others and saved her grief, which was taking the form of increased irritation, for her husband. John, on the other hand, was excited about her retirement, already planning trips for extended times away now that they would both be "free." He had relaxed into a comfortable retirement routine, sleeping later, going out to exercise and meeting his buddies at the local coffee shop, spending several hours a week volunteering. His biggest stressor was his 87-year-old mother, who had recently moved into a nursing home in a neighboring community.

With support, they both were able to identify what they were feeling and what they needed. Quickly the tension level decreased and the arguing lessened. They agreed to learn some better ways to resolve conflicts, including how to lighten up and laugh more. They decided that John would limit himself to 10 minutes each morning for an update on his bodily functions and Gina would listen. If he brought it up later in the day, she would remind him, "Tell me tomorrow."

They also recommitted to more quality time together, taking a break from their long to-do lists and having what they called "snuggle-

cuddle time." A few sessions later, they left the office a happier couple, agreeing that they would call again if needed.

Gina, like many wives I've interviewed, was afraid her husband would expect her to be available for him 24/7. She was used to working full time and having her own free time as well as her own income. When she retired, she was looking forward to unstructured time. She resisted John or her adult children or anyone else scheduling her or locking her into any obligations — even travel. She decided to ask John to hold off on any extended time away from home together until after she had been retired for six months.

More Time, Same Tasks

Some marriages survive by sidestepping the annoyances, both big and small. The problems don't get addressed. However, they don't go away — and when husband or wife retires, the couple has to face what happens when they spend more time together. Work no longer provides the escape or reprieve. Tasks once done alone are witnessed — and criticized — by the other partner. Individual desires and schedules are more transparent and sometimes open to discussion, resulting in resentment and defensiveness. This is often the number one irritant noted by couples after retirement.

One challenge of retirement is figuring out how to spend your time and how much you want to be together. Another major challenge is the distribution of chores and how they get done. The executive, male or female, who retires from a job managing people, might be accustomed to telling people what to do and how to do it. Now, he or she is at home and — without even thinking about it — starts managing the spouse. After years of never paying attention to loading the dishwasher or separating the colors for laundry, the partner tries to redesign the tasks with the fervor of an entrepreneur.

Over the years of counseling couples who express resentment about how much each spouse is doing, I've suggested the following exercise: Make a list of every chore, including ones not done frequently or only quarterly. Be sure to include laundry, cleaning out the refrigerator, mowing the lawn, weeding the garden, maintaining the car, paying bills, doing the taxes, arranging travel, notifying the post office of absences. Discuss preferences, divvying up the chores in a way that feels equitable. Try it for a few months and discuss the list again.

But of course, it's never about the dishes or the laundry. It's about acceptance, feeling loved and trusting that we will get our needs met by our partner. It's about communication and respect. It's about figuring out what is really important.

The Messy Cook

Here's an example from my own marriage of a small irritant that got bigger after Tom retired and I am still working. He is a messy cook! He cooks delicious food, and I have enjoyed his many creations over the years. Our adult kids compliment us when they call for our recipes. We've had an agreement for our whole 46-year marriage: whoever cooks, doesn't do the dishes. The one who doesn't cook cleans the kitchen. Sometimes when we leave the dishes and go to bed early, we joke with each other the next morning that the maid did not come last night!

When I cook, I clean as I go. When Tom cooks, he leaves the kitchen in complete disarray. Pans, spice bottles, spatulas and lids are everywhere. Packaging and litter are strewn about on the counters (even if the garbage can is a foot away).

As Tom retired and did even more of the cooking, this difference became more annoying. What was a small irritant before became bigger. How could I complain when he made such yummy meals? Often now he volunteers to both cook and clean up saying, "You have to work, honey, and I have all day tomorrow to do the dishes."

In this case, I have chosen not to complain. It is minor. Instead I chuckle and have a moment of gratitude that I'm lucky to be married to this amazing man even if he does mess up the kitchen. In this case, what would complaining get me? He cooks with a style, and bringing his awareness to the mess might cramp his style. The outcome is delicious, and I can take a few more minutes to wipe up the stovetop or the floor.

(Full disclosure: In the months since he read the first draft of this book, Tom has become a bit less messy in the kitchen. And he rarely goes to bed without at least loading and running the dishwasher.)

Up Or Down?

Another example of something minor: When we were raising our two sons and daughter, the males in the family respectfully and very kindly put the toilet seat down after they did their business. As they left home and Tom got older, he started leaving the seat up more often. For awhile, especially when I was crabby about something else, I would feel annoyed. If it happened in the middle of the night and I hadn't turned on the light, I could be nasty (or at least think nasty thoughts)! After a particularly poignant client session with a recent widow who missed her husband so deeply, I shifted my attitude. I decided to reframe those toilet-seat-up times with smiles of gratitude. My husband was still here to leave the toilet seat up. I could deal with the cold porcelain. As funny as it sounds, I'm actually a little disappointed when he remembers to put it down now.

Major Concerns

Both these examples are minor irritants. In healthy marriages, they are sources for laughter or teasing or humor. However, minor irritants can add up to major resentments. In other instances, it is important to find a way to express the irritation and ask for change. Examples: interrupting each other, repeating stories, forgetting to pass on messages, perhaps neglecting to pay attention to or comment about the small niceties in everyday life your spouse does, being rude or unconsciously unkind.

Behaviors or idiosyncrasies that build resentment need to be attended to. Let resentment be your cue. If you are unable to ignore the irritant, and using gratitude to reframe it doesn't take care of it for you, find a way to talk about it and come up with a mutually agreed solution.

Some behaviors need to be addressed quickly and decisively. Leaving a stove burner on is a safety issue. Leaving doors or windows open when the furnace is running is a money issue. Failing to close the garage door is a security issue. Discuss each issue, reach an agreement and hold each other accountable.

Making It Better

Over the years I have met with hundreds of couples with similar problems. Some faced the challenges and restructured their marriages, getting more satisfaction and probably feeling healthier in mind, body and spirit. Others were too far gone over the cliff of separation, with resentment, bitterness and hurts unhealed. They ended up divorced — or worse, stayed married but continued to hurt each other.

Another group of couples long ago gave up on their marriages as a source of friendship, comfort, joy, fun or pleasure, and have been living separate lives for a long time. This book does not address them. They have settled for the status quo and make it work for themselves and their kids and grandkids.

This book is for the couples who want to reinvent or improve their marriage and themselves as they face retirement — or are already into the transition and want to enhance the quality of their relationship.

If your marriage is not in good shape when you retire, it will only get worse because of the stress of change. You do not have to settle for worse. If you have been retired for a long time and your marriage has hit a rocky place because of events you were not prepared for, please know from the experiences of others that it can get better. You can make it better. It might be simpler than you think. As the Bergman lyric goes, just "try with every day to make it better as it grows."

~~~~Reflection I~~~~

Take a moment to think about the changes you are experiencing in your marriage right now. What are the changes related to the process of aging? What are the changes due to retirement for yourself or your spouse or both of you? Are some of the rough places in your marriage ones you have experienced for decades and are just now becoming more intolerable? Do you want to talk about these issues? What ideas do you have to bring resolution? Or harmony? Is this a time to apply the strategy of acceptance? Or forgiveness?

Changes and Transitions

As I wrote in the beginning of this chapter, growing old requires courage and humor to face the changes that are an inevitable part of living. Retirement contributes to both the stress and the blessings of these major changes. It bears repeating, "Growing old is not for sissies." And growing old with your spouse is not for sissies either. It requires resilience. It involves constant change, sometimes at a pace much quicker than we would choose.

Some of the changes which happen to us are self-imposed, by our choice. Some are decided for us or externally imposed. Choosing to leave a job feels very different than being let go, fired or laid off. Choosing to downsize and move to a smaller home feels very different than being forced to move because of a health impairment or not being able to pay your mortgage. Feeling satisfied that you "don't feel your age" feels very different than when all of a sudden you have surgery and feel 20 years older.

Getting older is not a choice. How we choose to FEEL about getting older is a choice. How we choose to DEAL with getting older is a choice. What we choose to believe about aging impacts every aspect of our lives. How our spouse feels and deals with aging impacts our own choices, too.

For many of us, dealing with the changes of aging, in our bodies, minds and spirits, brings up a range of negative feelings.

We may resist the idea that we are getting older and pretend we are still young and do not have to face limitations. We may invest in expensive surgeries or procedures or supplements that advertisers pledge will keep us looking and feeling young. Some of the anti-aging products and services are seductive and play into the illusions of control. Some take advantage of our fears and make us feel more vulnerable so we're more likely to buy the product or sign the agreement. For some of us it brings up questions of "How much can I control? How much is just my DNA and my genetics?" We want the illusion of control. It feels more comfortable to try to control even if deep down we understand that certain changes are inevitable and beyond our influence. Maybe aging gracefully is about acceptance and choosing to save our energies for what can bring actual results.

Coming to terms with the effects of aging is an ongoing task for all of us. Layers of questions about retirement and its impact on your marriage add more elements of stress and uncertainty. Understand the distinction between the changes and the transitions which follow them. I find this distinction to be helpful as I understand my marriage as being in a state of flux, changing as we respond and adjust to the events of our lives. We are always in a phase of transition, some more intense than others. Change is the event, transition is our adjustment to the event.

However, changing and being in a state of flux can be uncomfortable or disturbing or unsettling. We can feel on shaky ground, fearful, annoyed, more emotional than usual, sad, grieving, discombobulated, even depressed. You pick the words which describe your situation. I have noticed that I get cranky more often lately if I'm confronted even by minor changes. When the towels are moved at the health club or the grocery store switches a favorite item to a different aisle without telling me (or even asking me!), I may be more irritable. I find I want to lash out when I don't get a human voice when I place a call and get a series of automated responses. I know I'll break my cell phone if I throw it, but it feels good to groan or yell in frustration. My husband yells from the kitchen, "Are you OK, honey?"

"Oh yeah, just another change," I yell back.

While we are going through this transition, working through the discomfort and reorientation, adjusting to getting older or retirement or whatever change we are experiencing, try these strategies:

- Speak openly with your partner. You are in this together, even if you might be at different stages.
- Stay mindful of your reactions to change and stay psychologically flexible.
- Give yourself affirmations about your strengths and your abilities to cope.
- Remind yourself that this too will pass and soon you will have a new normal; nothing stays the same forever.
- Reach out to friends and family and ask for help.
- Increase your stress-relieving activities like walking in the woods or sitting by the fountain to hear moving water. Attend a live music performance. Visit an art gallery or sculpture exhibit. Play with your grandchild.
- Consider taking a class, solo or with your spouse, to learn a new skill.
- Declutter and let go of what you don't need anymore. Pass it on.
- Give yourself more comfort right now; treat yourself with TLC.

Look into getting professional guidance, engaging a therapist or coach who specializes in transitions with older folks.

We like to have the company of others as we face aging. A group of like-minded folks — sharing stories, laughing at our foibles or supporting us during the more serious challenges — makes everything easier to handle. We felt like that when we saw the movie *The Book Club,* with a great cast of actors, ranging in age from 63 to 80, taking on the issues of getting older, retirement, sex, ED, marriage, dating, adult children, friendship. We laughed and also felt touched. We also wondered how they could drink that much wine and still be coherent. Luckily no one drove drunk. That would have stopped our laughter hard. We appreciated that Hollywood was willing to invest dollars in a movie about our age group. We'd like to see more of the same.

Bill O' Hanlon, author of more than 30 books, has this memorable way of helping us look at the energies involved in making changes in our lives. He asks us to look at the Four Energies: Do we feel Bliss? Blessed? Pissed? Or Dissed? He suggests that by looking at each of these feelings and the thoughts around them we can intuit what is best for our next step. I offer this framework as you examine what is going on in your marriage, your work and your retirement.

The Second Half

Later in her life, Angeles Arrien, a cultural anthropologist, wrote an inspiring book called *The Second Half of Life: Opening the Eight Gates of Wisdom.* I recommend spending time with this book. Working with the material has been a very helpful guide for me as I keep deepening my relationship with myself and my husband and the process of aging. Arrien writes, "We are all born with a great dream for our lives, a dream that may have been derailed along the way by family and career choices. In the second half of life, after your roots have gone deeply into the world, it is time to resurrect this dream ... and encounter the thresholds we must cross to fulfill the final stage of our destiny."

Earlier in her career, she wrote *The Four-Fold Way.* She studied indigenous people and explored the question of what wisdom they have for us in our Western culture. Over the many years of doing workshops and therapy, I have shared a handout which summarizes her work. It serves as a helpful lens through which we can explore the changes happening to us during this transition into retirement and as we age. It offers guidelines for positive living and healthy relationships.

The Four-Fold Way, by Angeles Arrien

1. SHOW UP (The Way of the Warrior)
2. PAY ATTENTION (The Way of the Healer)
3. TELL THE TRUTH (The Way of the Visionary)
4. STAY OPEN, BUT NOT ATTACHED TO THE OUTCOME (The Way of the Teacher)

I want to examine each point with more explanation and apply it to the process of growing older.

SHOW UP and be present to all life offers. Be a good role model by walking your talk. It means to bring oneself fully to the present moment. Too often we are only partially here. Some part of us is still focused on what just happened or what may happen. By dividing our attention, we are not wholly aware of the NOW. We can correct this by bringing awareness to our consciousness. What am I aware of right now this minute?

Being with babies and young children presents this opportunity. When I am with my grandchildren I choose to practice this exercise of being in the moment. I choose to focus on being with them fully. I let go of the thoughts I might have about what just happened in the kitchen before I started playing with them or what we might be doing later in the day. I bring my awareness to what and where they are. Sometimes it's hard to do. When I can do it successfully I find that I have more fun and actually experience a relief of stress as well as experience the magic of the bond which occurs when we touch each other's lives at such a profound yet simple level.

In the process of aging, SHOW UP means to be aware of ALL that is going on, including what I might be choosing to deny. Does that sound like a contradiction? How can I be aware of what I am denying? This can be remedied by occasionally asking myself, what am I not telling myself the truth about? What am I choosing not to look at? What am I not letting myself feel? It's a good inner check-in. Be gentle with yourself.

PAY ATTENTION to what has heart and meaning for us and what resonates within our spirit. This is especially important as we are going through changes that come with retirement and letting go of a career. As we shift into what is next, notice what gives you a sense of meaning. What vibrates at a higher level in your life? When do you feel bored or have lower energy? What makes you feel fully alive and on fire? (in a good way, not a hot flash way). What feeds your soul? We talk more about self-development in Chapter 11 in the section on Being Your Best Self.

TELL THE TRUTH without blame or judgment. Say what you mean and mean what you say or, from an empowered place, choose to keep "noble silence." Some of us grew up in households where it was not safe to speak our truth. We might get in trouble or cause trouble for someone else. We might have continued this by marrying someone with whom we didn't feel safe to be honest with or as an adult we might have struggled with knowing how to speak up for ourselves. Growing older gives us another opportunity to learn this skill. Others expecting us to be older and wiser may give us permission to speak more freely. This doesn't mean we get to blurt out insults and be rude. It means we embrace the idea that we have some wisdom to share with kindness and respect.

In keeping a healthy relationship with our partners, it is essential to find ways to speak our truths to each other, both to share and to listen. When we are tempted to go underground to avoid the discomfort of saying what is in our hearts, it comes out anyway in convoluted passive-aggressive ways. For example, instead of realizing I'm upset about something Tom did or said, and then finding a way to tell him, I might withdraw and distance myself or get irritable. It is truly more loving to deal with it directly, even if it is uncomfortable.

"Noble silence" is a subcategory of TELL THE TRUTH. It refers to times when speaking our truth out loud is not in our best interests or in our loved one's best interests. In these cases, with discernment, it is best to hold "noble silence." We tell ourselves the truth but we reserve privacy. There are many times in close relationships when we practice "noble silence," when we choose if and when to speak our truth out loud. My husband and I practice this sometimes when we are out with another couple and we don't want to divulge a secret or when we are talking with our adult children and we choose not to go into a vulnerable subject at that time, maybe later. It's not about lying or being deceitful. "Noble silence" is about maintaining appropriate boundaries. In the Buddhist tradition, noble silence is about times of being in silence, not speaking, allowing the quiet to bring up deeper truths.

STAY OPEN, BUT NOT ATTACHED TO THE OUTCOME. Deeply care, from an objective place. Break old patterns. Practice discernment. Trust that in the right time the unknown will become known and live through the process into wisdom. For those of us who like to know in order to feel more in control it is a hard practice to be patient and wait out times when we don't know or we only have part of the necessary information to make the right decision. If we get too attached to the outcome, we become rigid and inflexible and then more emotionally challenged and stressed. At these times, it's good to use our comfort skills and ride it out until we get to a better place.

An example is when we need to wait out test results in a health diagnosis. We get ourselves worked up as we imagine the worst scenario: if this happens, then that will happen. Holding on to each other, we take a deep breath and remind ourselves, "We will know when we know and then we'll deal with it then."

~~~~Reflection II~~~~

Sit with these "truths" for a moment and reflect on their meaning to you and your partner.

- *How do you show up for each other? How do you show up for yourself? How good are you at staying in the moment rather than rethinking the past or projecting into the future? How do you stay in the present?*
- *What do you pay attention to? Are you good at catching each other "being bad" or are you good at appreciating the positives, kind actions and words and efforts? What resonates in your spirit? What excites you about your own interests? What*

excites you about your partner? Your marriage?
- *What are you telling the truth about? What are you holding back about? What gets in your way from being more authentic? How do you hold "noble silence?"*
- *How controlling are you, especially of things out of our control? How hard is surrendering to the mysteries of life? How do you use discernment in your thoughts, words and deeds?*

~~~~Reflection III: Grounding in Strength~~~~

When we are examining ourselves or our relationship we can sometimes get overwhelmed with what is wrong with us, and we can get lost in a sense of hopelessness or feel discouraged. It takes courage to grow. So a technique you can use to counteract this effect is to ground yourself in reminding yourself who you are, your strengths, your goodness and your worth.

"To Everything There Is A Season … "

I find this familiar passage from the Old Testament of the Bible helpful as a guide during this time in my aging process:

"To everything there is a season and a time to every purpose under Heaven; A time to be born, a time to die; a time to plant and a time to pluck up that which is planted; a time to kill, and a time to heal; a time to break down and a time to build up; a time to weep and a time to laugh; a time to mourn and a time to dance; a time to cast away stones and a time to gather stones together; a time to embrace and a time to refrain from embracing; a time to get and a time to lose; a time to keep and a time to cast away; a time to rend and a time to sew; a time to keep silence and a time to speak; a time to love and a time to hate, a time of war and a time of peace." (Ecclesiastes 3:1-8)

Perseverance

Gray tufts poke out from all around her ball cap. Working
her spindly arms, she leans into the mower. It moves slowly,
like a small ship before relentless waves. On the porch,
far from the struggle, he leans over his walker, his mouth
wide open, one arm raised high and waving to catch
her eye. Caught in the roar of her mission,
she mows on. How do we persist against
the perpetual waves of time?

Barbara Sherman Heyl
June 13, 2018

04 - *The Wise Married Elders Speak*

In writing this book I decided to interview couples who are in long-term marriages and have some distance from the events of retirement. I asked them to reflect on what worked for them and what would have been helpful to know as they experienced these transitions. Some couples, even married for 50-plus years, still do not consider themselves retired. Some are still working. In addition, the thoughts of those who had been married for decades and had lost their spouses are included and are particularly touching.

Some of the couples eased into retirement, planning years ahead. Others were forced into retirement because of a health crisis or changes at work. Some of the couples felt their marriages continued to be strong before and after the transition, whereas others had to do a major overhaul after facing the challenges. All of them were willing to share and said they enjoyed being interviewed. One couple expressed what others reported to me: "We kept talking about things you asked us for days afterwards and laughed at some of the memories. We felt even closer to each other."

I also asked about the process of aging and its effects on marriage. I compiled some of their suggestions into this list. Some of the other suggestions appear throughout the rest of the book. I consider this list a summary of their wisdom, the jewels or gems or nuggets, offered to us, the readers, as we navigate our own path through aging, retirement and marriage.

On Aging

- Our attitudes about aging impact every aspect of our lives — mind, body, spirit. The more positive we are, the less pain we feel, the more happiness we report, the more lively our lives.
- Don't sweat the small stuff. Truly. But let go of the feelings of resentment.

- Be gentle with yourself and your loved one.
- Understand that changes bring loss even if we choose the loss.
- Improve your listening skills.
- Aging often involves more focus on our aches and pains. Pay attention to the way you talk about yourself and monitor how much you complain. Consider putting limits on how much and when you complain; for example, only 10 minutes a day or only two times during a dinner party.
- Keep improving your ability to be flexible in your mind, body and spirit.
- Monitor how often you resist change or get grumpy when something new is introduced.
- Look for ways to lighten up and laugh more.
- Use gratitude to improve your perspective.
- Keep exercising the flexibility muscle.
- Commit to regular exercise, moving your body, getting the blood flowing, building strength and increasing your fitness.
- Commit to discovering your optimal nutrition program and keep meals fun and healthful.
- Monitor your use of alcohol, pain medication and other substances to avoid unhealthy dependence or addiction.
- Consider writing your memoir for your own enjoyment and to pass on as a legacy.

On Aging As a Couple

- Get to know your spouse in new ways.
- Change up your stories by creating new memories and adventures.
- Rediscover what is precious about each other.
- Say "I love you" often and with meaning.
- Tune in to your own and your partner's feelings without judgment.

- Learn healthy conflict resolution and how to fight fairly.
- Minor irritants can add up to major resentments. Discuss them and come up with a solution.
- Be clear about boundaries in caring for grandchildren and aging parents. Protect your couple relationship.
- Cherish friendships and include some young folks in your inner circle.
- Snuggle, touch, caress, kiss more often.
- Be naked nightly, be skin-to-skin to release the good health-enhancing (and chronic pain-reducing) hormones.
- Do not procrastinate in preparing your will and advance directives. Tomorrow might be too late.

On Retirement

- Understand how the changes with retirement and aging are presenting challenges and creatively come up with ways to deal with the changes.
- Retirement may involve leaving a job you love and people you care about. Grieving the loss is good and part of a healthy process of letting go and finding a new sense of self.
- Resist making commitments right away, maybe for several months (or years).
- Allow unstructured and unplanned time to explore and discover after years of being tied to a job and a schedule.
- Retire "to" something as well as "from" something. Select something you can look forward to in small and big ways, like a daily walk or trying new recipes or visiting every national park.
- Ease into retirement if you have a choice by going from full-time to part-time to fully retired.
- Plan a getaway — even if it is a short one — to celebrate the event.
- Avoid setting an alarm clock if you can. Allow your body

to find its natural rhythm after what may be years of sleep deprivation.

- Set aside time to tune in and ask about what is important.
- Improve the quality of your relationship by bringing intention to spending time together.

~~~~Reflection~~~~

Look through this list of suggestions from the Wise Married Elders and select five you want to explore in more detail. Talk with your partner about your list and his/her list. Design a way to assist each other to "try it out" in your life right now. Give it a few months. Reflect on outcome and select five more. Or add some of your own.

Selected Wise Married Elder Profiles

I decided to profile some of of the Wise Married Elder couples to give more detail and to show the contrast. I had a wonderful time doing the interviews and learned so much from each couple; in fact, it was hard to condense their stories into a few paragraphs. They each could have had their own chapter.

Mabel and Bud

This couple had to work hard to get their marriage back on track after retirement. Mabel, 77, and Bud, 78, raised eight children, living paycheck to paycheck. He retired from being a foreman at the steel office furniture factory, working his way up from starting on the assembly line right after high school graduation. They were high school sweethearts and married the next year. Their huge extended family celebrated their 59th anniversary with a big picnic, barbecue, potato salad and mouth-watering homemade pies. After an injury caused an early retirement for Bud, Mabel went to work at the deli at the local grocery store. Money has always been tight. His chronic pain and too much beer and her worries about money and some of the struggles of their kids and grandkids led them to neglect their marriage. They both became increasingly negative, angry, depressed, blaming and feeling unloved. Bud threatened divorce. Mabel suspected he was interested in another woman.

They found their way to marriage therapy through a referral from their daughter who had rescued her own marriage with hard work and a willing husband 10 years before. Once in my office, hearing the other tell their stories, they were reminded of the deep commitment they had for each other and how much they still cared. They had just lost their way. They came weekly for a few months and rediscovered how much they enjoyed laughing, being together and being with their families. Bud cut back his drinking and got some physical therapy for his pain. Mabel responded well to a support group for grandparents which seemed to reduce her worrying and made her feel more hopeful. They also rejoined the bowling league, Bud on Tuesdays and Mabel on Thursdays. Their advice to younger retirees is to get help before it is too late and learn to stretch the Social Security checks by finding the half-price deals.

Cathy and Denis

The interview with Cathy, 73, and Denis, 78, was a lot of fun. They've been married 44 years. This couple loves to laugh, and their delight being in the presence of each other is contagious. They are dedicated to each other and their family. Denis is now the patriarch of a large Irish extended family who have gathered at a resort every five years for decades. The generations renew their connections, get caught up on their lives and share the stories of their families. Cathy dons the costume of Grandmother with her Sunday hat and the wire-rimmed glasses and her rosary and purse and tells the story of their family. Denis is the keeper of the stories and puts together a picture album for everyone.

Their own family is tightly knit and closely connected. When Denis and Cathy are in town they see their 6 grandchildren frequently and are involved in their activities. They visit the one son who lives several states away on their way to and from their second home in Arizona, where they live parts of the year. The whole family gathered at a beach house to celebrate their 40th. The portraits are a treasure. Cathy, a former nun, has a special calling to work with children and has special gifts in intuitive energy healing. She retired after decades of teaching. Denis took a buyout with Sears, where he worked as an executive, to start a marketing company. A few years later, because of some personnel changes, he knew it was time to retire. He worked in real estate for a few years and now does volunteer work with Kiwanis. Maintaining physical, emotional and spiritual health is a priority. Cathy has been a lifelong morning meditator, keeping her balanced and connected to the Divine. When the grandchildren visit, they know to either join her sitting quietly or wait till Grandma comes to join them at breakfast after a meditation session.

They identified one of their couple strengths as communication. They trust each other to tell each other directly if they disagree or have difficulties with what is being said or done. "When we were first married, I'd keep things inside," Cathy said. "Denis would say something and I'd be in tears, surprising us both." Cathy shared that she learned from Denis how to be more aware of her thoughts and feelings and to speak up. She learned that they could work it out together. Now, as they are older, this deep trust allows them to cherish both the conversation as well as sitting in comfortable silence enjoying watching the river flow by or the geese fly home.

As a family they have always been campers, first with a small pop-up and after retirement, moving up to a good size RV which they traveled in to national parks. When they downsized to their current home, they sold the RV. Like some of the other WME, traveling helped with the transition into retirement.

As they have throughout their marriage, they put a premium on couple time. They try to keep Friday night free for date night. They know that sometime during the day or in the evening they will reconnect and tune in to each other and make love. They may have sex other times also but they keep this ritual sacred. As Denis explained, "It is too easy to let other events get in the way or get too busy with other things and then soon you realize it's been weeks since we've been together. Now with date night, we make it happen more easily." Cathy added that earlier *when they were raising the children they made date night happen because they truly just missed each other. "We'd put the kids to bed and have our own dinner and then sometimes make love. Once a year we'd go for an escape weekend. The first time we did this when the children were so young and we were so busy, we looked at each other at breakfast and said, 'Well, Hello, I know you.' Now in retirement we can be freer and more expressive, too," she said with a twinkle. Denis understood.*

Leonard and Ira

This next couple are the oldest and the longest together of the WME, although they only recently were allowed to be officially married. Leonard and Ira are the epitome of stability, routine and predictability. They are well-suited to each other and a devoted couple. Their transition into retirement, spending time together, traveling and pursuing their interests has been smooth. They were pleased to be asked to be interviewed for this book because they want their story to be told. They know they do not fit the stereotype of gay men and want others to know there are many couples just like them, living under the radar.

Leonard 80, and Ira, 78, met in college, both studying music. They noticed an attraction for each other and soon became lovers. There were only a few places they could feel safe to be "out" in the late 1950s. Because of harsh rejection from both their families and the culture, they have continued to be very private and have a tight circle of friends where they are completely themselves. After graduation, Leonard was hired as a musician in a professional orchestra and continued there until he retired at age 70. He misses playing the beautiful orchestrations but does not miss the flare-ups of rheumatoid arthritis. Ira did not pursue a music major, choosing to get his degree in accounting. He stayed with the same firm, moving into management, and retired at age 68. Both men retired within the same month.

About 20 years ago, Leonard contacted me for counseling when he made another attempt to reconcile with his mother before she passed away. Psychotherapy helped him with his grief and helped to strengthen them as a couple. Leonard was raised in a strict Baptist family and Ira's parents were Jewish. He stopped attending Synagogue shortly after his Bar Mitzvah when he started struggling with his sexual orientation and felt lost for awhile. He has since reconnected with his Jewish religious training, many of the teachings giving him guidance and comfort. Leonard told me about a sign he appreciated at a Gay Pride Parade, "Jesus loves everybody," and wondered how his mother would have responded. The two men continue to come in for periodic couple tune-ups.

Already joined in a civil union, they started planning their wedding ceremony even before same-sex marriage became legal. It was held at an Episcopal Cathedral with exquisite stained glass windows. The music, of course, was beautiful. So was the poetry. After more than 60 years together, they are now married. When I asked about their legacy as a couple, they spoke of being proud of their community involvement, starting one of the first community gardens in their area more than 35 year ago. Younger folks have taken over the leadership now, and they are confident the project will continue to thrive.

I want to express my gratitude to Leonard and Ira, for courageously sharing their story, and to Mimi and Nancy, who are profiled in Chapters 13 and 15, for allowing me to include their interviews as WME. I am of the generation who have witnessed many of our friends and some of my clients come out of the closet and live freely. Hopefully our children and certainly our grandchildren are already making our world more inclusive and welcoming of all people.

Jean and George

Sitting at their dining room table overlooking the mountains and surrounded in the beauty of the wood and art of their home make us both feel immediately peaceful. We looked forward to interviewing this amazing couple. Jean, 74, and George, 73, have been married 50 years. They moved to Santa Fe, N.M., from the Washington, D.C., area, where Jean did consulting, teaching and training and George worked on the staff of Senator Tom Harkin for 13 years as agricultural advisor. When I asked the question what is your legacy? What do you want to be known for? George said he would like his epitaph to be: "He tried to be kind." Jean's eyes teared up as she heard his response and echoed his sentiment. She added, "I want to be known as a networker, as a connector of people and services."

These two are dedicated to being of service and also being in community. Early in their marriage, living in Iowa, they started a weekly group supper club with several couples and also a monthly Saturday work day. When their two children were born and others in the group started having children, the supper club and the work days continued and were ever more valuable, sharing the load. Jean also started support groups as part of her women's advocacy work, and they started a group for couples just to gather and speak about whatever issues people wanted to share. When they moved to the Washington, D.C. area they continued these traditions. Jean was very active in the Transition Network, a group for women age 50-plus in D.C. and then instrumental in starting a chapter of The Transition Network when she moved to Santa Fe. When George retired from his congressional job, he started rehabbing houses. Jean continued in the company she founded doing training and consulting. She knew when it was time to retire as she eased into working fewer hours even after they moved to Santa Fe.

Community service is also important to this couple. Their way of handling the empty nest of their two children leaving for college was to become foster parents for children needing emergency placement. Over the years, more than 150 infants to teens in the D.C area spent a few days to a few weeks in their welcoming home experiencing a good meal, structure, a clean bed and people who care. In Santa Fe, George cooks one meal a week at the homeless shelter. He, with Jean's help, has been rebuilding the house they purchased and then gutted from the ground up. The skills he learned growing up on the farm have equipped him well as he does all the plumbing, electrical and carpentry work. Jean, a pianist and singer, is an accompanist for a "Clown Choir" that performs at nursing homes and she is in two other area choruses, one of which will be singing at Carnegie Hall this fall.

One of their challenges as a couple has been George's hearing loss. Even with his hearing aids and a cochlear implant, it is still hard for

George to enjoy some of the activities they used to do together. Concerts, music, movies, going out to restaurants present difficulties. They have busy schedules with all the activities, including helping their daughter and son-in-law with care of their grandson. George still runs the hills around their home three miles a day.

One of their strengths as a couple is their commitment to their ritual of lunch and a nap every day. They protect the 12-2:00 time as their couple time. They meet in the kitchen for a lunch that George has lovingly prepared and then retreat to their bedroom for rest or a nap. No matter what else is going on that day, they know they will be together during this special time.

This couple values being intentional, making contributions, supporting each other's interests, and being excellent communicators. When I asked if there was anything else she wanted to share to pass on to other couples, Jean said, "At times in my life, I have benefitted from therapy. It has helped me tremendously. I'm seeing someone now who is helping me be more gentle with myself and more forgiving of others and myself. I feel the difference." George nodded and said he agreed.

As a psychotherapist I appreciated that plug and was struck by how many of the Wise Married Elders made similar suggestions or spoke of ways therapy helped them at times of challenge or difficulty. I'm not sure what the statistics are on how many people in healthy, happy marriages have benefitted from therapy, both as individuals and as couples. What I do know is the value of professional intervention to help us see each other more clearly and come up with creative solutions to make life easier and hopefully more enjoyable.

Nancy and Don

As we drove up the hill to their house we were immediately struck by the beauty of the sculptures in the front and back of their home in the Driftless Area in southwest Wisconsin. It was as captivating as any of the sculpture gardens we have seen around the country. In different hues of marble and limestone, the forms were mostly of couples. Later we toured Don's studio and saw even more outstanding pieces. I was moved to tears by one of a woman pastor praying with an inmate in prison, his shackles carved into the green-brown variegated marble. Inside their home, more sculptures catch my eye, especially one Don did of a woman storyteller surrounded by children, inspired by an event with Nancy when they traveled to South Africa. It is exquisite in orange alabaster and may weigh 600 pounds. My husband and I both agree these sculptures need public viewing. Don became a sculptor in his 50s, being given the gift of a workshop by his wife who knew of his interest. He went away for a week to Colorado and immersed himself in the art.

The interview with this couple was like being plugged into a super generator. They literally vibrate with energy. The ideas just pour forth, almost sparking as they meet the air. They are super innovators. They create ideas and make things happen wherever they go. In their 52 years of marriage they have had several careers: teaching, counseling, pastoring, working as a school librarian, doing research, writing, founding and growing three publishing companies, mentoring, and starting innovative programs. Now in retirement, having closed the publishing companies, Don sculpts and they both continue innovating. Don set up a program working with returning veterans with PTSD. For their 50th wedding anniversary, instead of a big party or a cruise, they commissioned the local theater company to produce an original play focusing on PTSD. At age 75, they are still very active in their community groups, including singing in a touring gospel choir.

Nancy explained that they have retired three times, almost, depending on the definition of retirement. The first was when they moved from Duluth, Minn., to New Mexico. Nancy knew that in order for Don to slow down and be able to create his art, he would need to disengage from all the community activities he was involved in, an impossible task, unless they actually moved out of the area. Moving to be closer to their two sons in New Mexico and building an exquisite home and studio in the hills outside of Albuquerque became the focus and afforded a new beginning. After 10 years they both arrived at the conclusion it was time to return to the Midwest, and they again started over in a new community. Being the highly creative types they are, both are willing to reinvent themselves to respond to what is present in the moment.

In this moment, Nancy is dealing with concerns about memory loss *and cognitive impairment. Her first symptom was heightened anxiety, a condition unusual for her, currently moderated with medication and meditation. Don is also aware of getting older, feeling the limitations, adjusting to the changes.*

This intense couple has a strong marriage built on faith and immense respect for each other. They are excellent communicators. They have a willingness to keep discussing an issue until they have heard each other clearly, resolved disagreements and come to a resolution. It helps that they both have doctorates in the field. However, it is their commitment to one another, to ongoing dialogue and problem solving, which has built this foundation over the years. They are astute and articulate observers of their experiences. In talking about the process of retirement and aging, Nancy commented on the inevitable multi-level losses and the need to build resilience. "As we are aging and feeling more invisible, our sense of agency is eroding," she mused. "We can no longer influence outcomes, processes, systems, etc. as we once did. It's one of the many losses and limitations we encounter and grieve." Nevertheless, this remarkable couple leaves a big footprint, a lasting legacy, wherever they have lived and will continue as they step into the next chapter of life.

Other WME couples stories are interspersed throughout the book. For example, Mike, a retired OB-GYN physician and Carol, a retired nurse, exemplify how to do long-range planning for retirement starting 10 years out. Their story is profiled in Chapter 18 on Retirement Choices. So is Jeanette and Ken's story, in which his stroke sidelined her retirement date and their desire to travel around the world. Chuck and Jeanie are the road traveling gurus, profiled in Lifestyle Chapter 15. Pat and Lorraine share some of their communication lessons in Chapter 8 on conflict resolution. Pat and Ken comment on boundaries in grandparenting in Chapter 16. I am grateful for all the wisdom shared and the opportunity to pass it on in this book. We learn from each other's stories.

Tom's Note:

Once you pass 70, you might wonder just how many people are more "elder" than you. But at any age, people have some wisdom to pass on, directly or through the stories they tell. Well into her 80s, my mom would relate the story of when a woman took umbrage at her brother, my Uncle Bob, because he was holding a door open for her. (Some women took that as some degree of sexist put-down.) "I'm not holding the door for you because you are a lady," Bob said. "I'm holding it for you because I am a gentleman." Courtesy, whether gentlemanly or otherwise, is never out of place.

For My Age

An Affirmation

While I once claimed, "I have a lifetime of excess energy."
I admit now, "I have only enough energy left—for my age."

While I once could acknowledge, "I am blessed with robust health."
Now I must say, "I am as healthy as can be expected—for my age."

While I once affirmed, "Physically, I am immensely strong."
I now only assert, "I am still strong enough—for my age."

While I could once say, "I have great stamina."
Now I can only say, "I have stamina adequate—for my age."

While I once recognized, "I am unquenchably creative and curious."
I now realize, "I am only as creative and curious as possible—for my age."

While I once could claim, "I have more determination than anyone I know."
Now I admit, "I seldom push to the end whatever the cost, as appropriate—for my age."

While I once acknowledged, "I have an amazingly sharp, and alert mind."
I now recognize, "My mind works intermittently on its own timing, as expected—for my age"

At my age many years ago, I proudly believed,
With my excess energy, robust health, physical strength, great stam-
ina, creativity and curiosity, gritty determination and sharp, alert
mind, I could handle any over the top stress
despite the cost"
That is no longer the case.
Now, I dare to affirm,
"With the inevitable limits of age,
I am becoming increasingly centered and at peace with myself."

All in all, not a bad tradeoff—for my age.

By Don Tubesing 3-6-2018

05 - Can Your Marriage Survive Retirement?

"I'm not sure my marriage will survive retirement," jokes a wife complaining about the challenges now that her husband is home all day. The other wives present in the group may nod in agreement and share their stories. In another gathering, husbands may be saying the same thing.

However, sometimes the question is asked in all seriousness when the thought of spending more time together in retirement is felt as a dread and a threat. Instead of the excitement or anticipation one would expect, the opposite is experienced. This might compel a spouse to finally deal with the years of dysfunction which have led to marital unhappiness. In cases where physical and mental abuse are happening, the threat of retirement becomes the impetus to seek a divorce attorney rather than another course of failed marriage counseling.

In Elizabeth's case, she and her husband had tried three therapists and years of individual and couple counseling. Although small changes would result, making life somewhat tolerable, his verbal abuse and threats of physical abuse stemming from his narcissistic personality disorder became intolerable. Their marriage had survived this long only because he traveled frequently for his work and put in long hours when he was in town. When she tried to imagine life with him retired, she felt physically ill. She knew it was time to face facts. She needed to end the marriage. Her sons and their wives gave their blessings. She got names from friends and made an appointment with a divorce attorney. The attorney's first recommendation was to transfer a reasonable amount of funds (from joint accounts) to her own account. Bob was shocked to receive the divorce papers. Years later, he is still bitter and doesn't understand why his wife left him "right when the fun could begin."

Dr. John Gottman, a leading researcher and marriage therapist, reports that the most reliable predictor of a poor prognosis for a marriage — or the best predictor of divorce — is the degree of contempt, disrespect and sarcasm spouses have for each other. In my many years doing therapy, I agree. If in the first session it is obvious to me that the spouses do not even like each other, much less have respect and compassion, I find a way to reflect this observation and ask for an honest appraisal before we continue with sessions. Sometimes the request for marriage counseling gets redefined. What is actually needed is guidance in facing the truth and then an agreement to use divorce counseling to bring peace to all concerned.

If you are in a marriage suffering with the effects of these serious red flags: "gas-lighting", narcissism and alcoholism or other addictions, seek professional help before you continue to try to improve your marriage. It has been my experience that these issues get exponentially worse in the transition to retirement or during stressful times. Too often I witness the struggling spouse relentlessly trying to find the right solution or figure out how to change themselves to make their spouse happier while often sacrificing their own well-being. If you are the only one trying and your spouse is not taking any responsibility for the problems, it truly is not possible to make it better. If these red flags are present it is like coming up to a stoplight. Red means stop. Give yourself the green light. Seek help and get stronger.

Gaslighting, named after the 1944 movie, is a method of emotional abuse where a person systematically brainwashes and manipulates another person in order to feel power over them and make them doubt their perceptions, memory and reality, causing them to "feel crazy." If you suspect this is going on in your marriage, ask to see a therapist individually and explain your concerns and come up with strategies to keep your sanity and self-esteem. Sometimes these strategies succeed and the partner stops using gaslighting, since it is no longer effective, and more healthy communication turns the marriage around. In more serious cases, it may be necessary to separate and eventually divorce in order to feel emotionally healthy.

Narcissism is a personality disorder where the person acts superior and entitled, has a constant need for praise, demands to be the center of attention, is often perfectionistic and gives the illusion of always being in control. The narcissist is unable to feel empathy for others and treats his or her loved ones as extensions of self, not as separate beings. Their public persona is often very attractive and charming, the "life of the party," whereas their private self may be cold, aloof, blaming and abusive. In the beginning it is exciting to be married to the narcissist because you feel special and "chosen." The marriage works as long as you never disagree or express your own opinions and always do it his/her way. If you ask the narcissist to go to marriage therapy to help you feel happier, he or she will point out all the logical reasons why you are to blame for the problems and insist that he/she is not responsible. Sometimes it takes a few go-arounds with a few therapists before the patterns are obvious and you get the correct diagnosis. Unfortunately, unless the narcissist accepts his/her diagnosis and agrees to intensive therapy, the marriage will not improve. It is not a positive prognosis.

Alcoholism is a disorder in which the person's dependence on alcohol, or any other substance, is primary. (It is important to make a distinction between drinking too much and actually being addicted.) For the addict, all other needs, including the needs of loved ones, are secondary. It's all about the next drink or the next fix or the next opportunity to get high. It is essential to address the serious addiction before the relationship will improve. Attend Al-Anon or get other support to help you understand your role in enabling the addictive behavior and get back a sense of your own self. Sort out what you need to do to feel happier. All attempts to change the addicted partner will be useless. He or she has to be willing to take responsibility for the addiction and commit to getting help. After a period of sobriety, the focus can shift to improving the marriage.

If you are dealing with these serious disorders, get support. Do not try to do this alone. Pay attention to your own health and make a commitment to improving your own life.

Sam surprised his whole family and circle of friends by deciding to leave his wife of 38 years after she refused, again, to get help for their marriage. As far as she was concerned there was no problem. She was always right, and as long as Sam did it her way, all was good. He spent years, especially as the children were younger, not rocking the boat, not wanting to deal with her long periods of coldness or her righteous indig- nation if he stood up to her. Finally a health crisis with his blood pres- sure and heart disease woke him up to his rage. He confronted his own fears, found his voice with his wife, and decided to end the marriage when she was unwilling to even hear his concerns. He was gratified to hear from his friends and family their celebration of his liberation from a marriage that was more like a prison.

Retirement As the Wake-up Call

Anticipating retirement can be empowering. It may give us cour- age to face what we have been trying to deny. Then we need to learn the skills of listening to our deeper self, owning the truths, and learning to let go of what isn't working for us anymore. When a person is struggling with the decision to end the mar- riage, I recommend reading *The Journey,* a poem by Mary Oliver. It begins: "One day / you finally knew / what you had to do / and began / though the voices around you / kept shouting ... " The poem ends with this: " ... determined to do / the only thing you could do / determined to save / the only life you could save."

Letting the words and the images of the poem go deep into the questions of whether to go or to stay will often bring up strong feelings — sometimes intense pain — and then a sense of hope. Deciding to end your marriage is huge and difficult and sad. You may experience waves of overwhelming grief. You've shared so many years together and have so many family memo- ries, maybe including some really good times. Be brave and gen- tle as you work through the questions, hoping you will see clearly what is best for you, and maybe for both of you, at this time in your life as a couple.

Sometimes needing to let go is not about abuse or dysfunc- tion. Sometimes it is about finally embracing the real self. Here is an example:

Educators Charles and Pam had a great marriage, two kids, a great old house and fun circle of friends. Happy, good communicators, they had worked on their marriage over the years and it showed. Everything looked good, but Charles was living a lie. He was disowning a part of him that wouldn't go away no matter how much he practiced denial. Finally his inner truth was stronger. He owned his lifelong attraction to men. He came out to himself. And then to his wife and — after good counseling — to his children. Their divorce was like their marriage: loving and respectful. Years later, they are both in loving relationships and meet frequently at family events.

One of the reasons Charles decided to embrace his sexual orientation was the growing inner turmoil he was feeling as he got older and closer to retirement. He thought of the elders in his family. They lived a long time, well into their 90s and one past 100. He wanted to give himself the inner peace of living his truth. He knew what he needed to do and then set out to do the hard work of loving himself and his wife and children through it: "To thine own self be true."

Jane Fonda, in *My Life So Far*, writes about coming to terms with the end of her relationship with Ted Turner:

"The very thing I feared the most — that I would gain my voice and lose my man — was actually happening. It wasn't how I thought the story would end. You see what you need to see in another person, and when your needs change you try to see different things. The problem comes when what you need and what you see isn't seen or needed by your partner. It doesn't mean your partner is bad; it just means that she or he wants something else in life." She goes on: *"It was only after we separated that I discovered that while Ted was telling me he would try to do things differently, he had turned to his old adage: 'Hope for the best, but prepare for the worst.' He had spent our last year together looking for my replacement. That was why he was graying before my eyes: It was killing him to be dishonest with me. The day we parted, three days before the Millennium, he flew to Atlanta to drop me off. As I drove from the airport to (daughter) Vanessa's home in a rental car, my replacement was waiting in the hangar to board his plane. My seat was still warm."*

Serious Accident Brings Change

In the days after Matthew's serious car accident, he had several what he called "epiphanies." He was not happy in his marriage. He didn't want to keep running the company and he didn't know who he was if he wasn't working, making money and achieving goals. He also felt scared. He almost died and was now given a second chance.

His wife, Carla, also had some epiphanies, watching her husband hooked up to all the tubes, not sure if he would survive and what shape he would be in after recovering from all his injuries. She had also been unhappy for a long time. She wanted emotional intimacy with a man who was not paying attention to her or her children and was almost excessively focused on his work. She knew that if he survived and if they decided to stay together they would need to do things differently. She was willing to take some time and sort it out, but she was not willing to just resume the distant and unsatisfying life they had before. Now that the children were adults and making their own lives, she wanted more for herself and for their marriage.

Both of them were evaluating their 33 years of marriage and what they wanted moving forward. Taking an early retirement as he recovers and facing the truth of their unhappiness may bring this couple to create a new and improved marriage. Or not. Time and more epiphanies will tell.

As you read these stories and reflect on your own marriage, take a deep breath. Sit with the question, "Do I need to leave my marriage?" Ask yourself whether the following statements are true. Notice how you feel. Keep breathing and allow the truth to surface. It might be helpful to write your responses. Reach out to a close friend. Remember you are not alone.

Do I Need to Leave My Marriage?

1. You realize your number one stressor is your spouse.
2. You can't imagine being happy with him or her as you age.
3. You realize you feel happier alone than with him/her.
4. After being apart for a time, you dread the reunion.

5. You don't feel much connection or worse, you feel used by him/her.
6. You feel verbally, emotionally or physically abused and battered.
7. Your friends or adult children or relatives show concern and ask why you stay with him/her.
8. You fantasize about leaving.
9. You feel you are a failure for not being able to make your marriage work.
10. You feel depressed and/or suicidal.
11. You don't like who you have become and you notice you are developing bad habits like abusing alcohol or over-eating or other ways to cope with the stress.
12. You fight frequently — or you have stopped caring even to fight.
13. You feel trapped. You worry that if he/she gets seriously ill your hope of someday leaving will no longer be possible.
14. You have tried to fix the marriage with professional help which has been unsuccessful — or he/she refuses help.
15. You or both of you frequently threaten to divorce.
16. Imagining yourself free of the marriage brings relief and a rush of hopeful energy.

We can't be where we aren't. We can only be where we are. That's the starting point. Listen to what is in your heart. Listen to your thoughts about what is in your heart. Listen to your body signals. Listen to what your partner is telling you with words. Pay even more attention to his or her actions.

Then check in with yourself. How are you feeling in response? How are you reacting in response? Tell yourself your truth. Let yourself sit with this in silence without judgment. Your spirit knows. Now do the hard work. Have the difficult conversations. Go into the unknown, through the disruption. Go all the way through to the place of inner peace. Give each other a blessing. Forgive yourself. Forgive him/her. Allow yourself to fully let go and move forward. Forgiveness is not about whether the other person deserves to be forgiven. Forgiveness is because you deserve peace.

When the marriage ends, what is needed to help the children and loved ones deal with the disruption and the changes? It helps to make a commitment to tell your own truth but not disparage the former spouse. Be as positive as possible when speaking of the other. Remember that your adult child is also the son or daughter of this person you are divorcing. You can set the tone for the whole extended family.

There are many powerful examples of blended families who find a way to put aside their differences from the past. For the sake of the children and grandchildren, they come together for celebrations and family events like welcoming a new baby or weddings or funerals. They greet each other with respect and even affection.

After the dust settles and the divorce is final, continue to do your own work to recover a happier, healthier sense of self. Build your self-esteem. Remind yourself that you are worthy of love, and create the life you want now.

Enhancing Togetherness

06 - *Communication: One Talks, One Listens*

If you've read this far in the book, you might be wondering how you and your partner are going to do all this talking I'm recommending. Maybe you haven't really talked since before the kids left for college. Or maybe you stopped really speaking from your heart because of a lot of buildup of hurt and disappointment. Or maybe talking just makes you too uncomfortable, so it's easier to just chat about the business of life and not go any deeper.

Most self-help books about marriage include sections on communication and conflict resolution. This is because it is essential for enriching your relationship and improving emotional intimacy as well as physical intimacy. However, I've worked with couples who get along great and don't talk much or deeply. Each to their own. If your sense about your marriage is that you need more and wish your partner knew you better, dig in and try these ideas. You may already be nurturing your relationship in these ways and can feel validated that you are on the healthy marriage track.

Find Ways to Reconnect

Examining patterns in retirement that help sustain and nurture the health of your relationship involves good communication and ways to keep connected. When you have been separated, for hours or days, take a moment to reconnect. It might be in the kitchen chopping vegetables for dinner, or a foot rub while watching your favorite TV drama. Or in the hot tub. You might already be doing this every day. Now add more intention and awareness. Weave the fibers of your relationship together again. Repair any leakages or breaks or tears. Bring appreciation up to to your heart and into your eyes and convey it to your partner with words or touch or tenderness. The message: "You are important to me. You are not alone. I am here. You are loved. We're together no matter what."

Try agreeing to a daily full body hug, facing each other, first looking into each other's eyes then embracing for a full minute. You don't have to speak. Just embrace, gaze, take in each other's essence and breathe deeply. Ahhhhhhh! When I have couples do this in the office, they are sometimes surprised by how long a full minute is. It's not as easy as it sounds. But the benefits are profound.

A kiss and hug also activate the "happy hormones" and gives us a healthy kickstart with our brain chemistry. The neurotransmitter dopamine, which is linked to feelings of craving and desire, increases, as does oxytocin, known as the love hormone, which creates a sense of closeness and attachment. In a positive manner, adrenaline boosts our heart rate. Blood vessels dilate, cheeks flush, pulse quickens and then we take a deep breath and relax. Hugs also release nitric acid, which is the spark of life between our cells and needs to be rejuvenated every few seconds for our organs to hum along in harmony. Some couples enjoy reconnecting in a ritual at bedtime, sharing about their day, the ups and the downs, what delighted and what saddened, what made them proud and what gave them pause, ending with a hug and kiss. Maybe more ...

In Dr. Christiane Northrup's delightful book *The Secret Pleasures of Menopause,* she speaks of the many ways women and men can increase their creation of nitric oxide by having more pleasure, both sensual and sexual, and even thinking happy thoughts. She calls nitric oxide the Wow! molecule, and explains that it continually resets our ability to connect body, mind, heart and spirit. We increase its production by good self-care by getting plenty of sleep, doing exercise, eating life-giving foods, letting go of resentment, and opening up to affirmation and love.

Our lives can seem to be a lifelong balancing act to feed and nurture ourselves, our passions, our interests and our couple relationship. I'm always grateful, even if I'm not immediately responsive, when Tom reminds me when we are getting out of touch, or when he lets me know he is feeling neglected or needing quality time together. I count on him to help me with this delicate balancing act. Sometimes the best thing I can do is to take a breath, go inside and be still. Tune myself up, reconnect with Tom and re-emerge more centered and focused.

Communication builds emotional intimacy. Talking about the bills or what to have for supper or when you fed the dog are necessary in the business of living. However, communication that builds intimacy is when we share from our hearts, when we speak about what really matters to us. We want to be known. We want to be understood. Even if your spouse is not your best friend, you want him/her to know you and you want to know him/her. This takes good listening skills.

I like to remind my clients when we are talking about communication of a wordplay about the word intimacy: into me see. And in not making assumptions with the word play on assume: When I assume I make an ass of u and me. Both of these help me to remember to communicate more clearly.

Couples in healthy marriages know each other pretty well, appreciate each other and also have skills for problem solving and conflict resolution when needed. Moving into retirement presents opportunities to tune up communication skills and get even better at listening and sharing.

Pointers for Good Listening Skills

We all know when we're not being listened to. We start to talk and we notice our partner is not looking at us and still reading the paper or typing on the computer or checking cell phone messages or watching TV. Or we get interrupted or he changes the subject as if he hadn't heard what we said or ignored us or didn't respond. We also don't feel heard when the other person interjects her thoughts before letting us finish our own, or starts responding defensively before we explain ourselves. When we truly listen to each other, it is a precious gift. Healthy couples invest quality time listening and sharing.

It is important to use "I-language" instead of "you-language." In the first, you are describing the situation and how you react. For instance, "When that happens, I feel this." You are giving information and asking for understanding. When "you-language" is used, it sounds more like an attack and may trigger a fight. For instance, "You aren't listening to me. You are so rude. Can't you even look me in the eye?"

As soon as I slip into "you-language," I am doing my partner a disservice. I am telling him what he thinks and feels, which is a projection of what I think he is thinking and feeling — which may be right or wrong. Many fights start because the couple have not listened carefully to each other and might not even know what's actually being said.

Even though it is difficult and might sound stilted at first, it is more effective to learn how to use "I-language." It gets easier with practice and starts to feel natural. It's good discipline. It forces me to be more clear about what I am feeling and also what I am asking for from my partner (or child or parent or the store clerk or anyone you are wanting to be clear with).

Some of you are highly skilled at using these listening techniques and may feel validated by reading this review. For others, the ideas presented here may be new and almost seem like a foreign language. Even if you end up laughing through your practice sessions, please give them a try and see if with repetition it helps you understand each other better.

Try this tool when expressing what you feel and what you want from your partner:

"When you _____(briefly describe the situation), I FEEL _____(sad, hurt, afraid, or impatient, or another emotion) BECAUSE_____ (explain the psychological need you have that leads to feeling the way you do)."

EXAMPLE: "When you don't look at me and keep staring at the TV when I come in from work, I FEEL ignored and hurt BECAUSE I've been missing you and want to reconnect."

The more precisely you describe what you want from your partner, the more likely she/he will be able to give it to you and the less likely you will trigger his/her "blame detector" or defensiveness. It works for reinforcing positive behaviors also.

EXAMPLE: WHEN you stop typing at the computer and look at me when I'm speaking, I FEEL respected and listened to BECAUSE you paid attention when I asked. Thank you.

Reflective Listening

Another powerful tool is called reflective listening. What this means is acting as if you are a mirror and reflecting back to her what you are hearing her say. You can use exactly her own words or you can paraphrase. Do not add any of your own thoughts or feelings. Reflect only what she has said, using a tentative tone of voice. Then ask, "Did I hear you correctly? Do you want to say more?" It is OK to ask questions for clarity, for instance, "Are you talking about today or what happened yesterday?" Keep using reflective listening until your partner agrees that you understand and she feels heard. Then you can ask, "Are you ready for me to respond?" When she agrees, then you switch and she acts as a mirror and reflects back to you what she is hearing you say.

EXAMPLE: Dana: "I was so upset with you last night, I couldn't go to sleep. I felt so undermined when I got home and saw Tony with his iPad after I had taken it away and told you he could not have it till the next day."

Jack: "Let me see if I understand. You saw Tony with his iPad and thought I had given it back to him after you had taken it away and you got really angry with me, so angry that it was hard for you to get to sleep. Is that right?"

Dana: "Yes, you heard me right. Why did you undermine me like that?"

Jack: "You are feeling I undermined your punishment of Tony because he had his iPad after you took it away."

Dana: "Yes."

Jack: "Do I understand? Is there anything more you want to say?"

Dana: "Yes, I feel like this often with the grandkids. I feel like you do not support my discipline. I think you want to be the good guy and *make me the bad guy."*

So the discussion continues until Dana feels heard and Jack gets his chance to respond. Then they can move to problem-solving and resolve this conflict.

The shorter the time that passes between incident and dialogue, the better the chances of success. Try to share with each other within 24 hours of the event. When time passes our memories get fuzzier, and we've also had more time to simmer and stew and build resentment.

Reflective listening is also useful when you notice you are stuck repeating yourselves and not making progress in understanding each other. If one partner switches into reflective listening, especially using a neutral tone of voice, and keeps mirroring or repeating back what he/she hears for a few minutes, usually the other partner starts to feel validated and the couple gets unstuck. Real progress is made. Communication is successful.

This skill is very effective when you are in disagreement or if the subject at hand is controversial or filled with emotion. When we have a lot at stake and are feeling vulnerable, it is harder to listen to the other viewpoint. For example, what if in the previous dialogue, Jack had responded defensively as soon as Dana said her opening statement?

Dana: "I was so upset with you last night. I felt so undermined when I got home and saw Tony with his iPad after I had taken it away and told you he could not have it till the next day."

Jack: "What are you griping about now? I didn't agree with you about taking his iPad away. He finished his homework and asked for it. I didn't see any problem giving it to him."

Dana: "Problem? You didn't see a problem? What did I ask you to do? Why don't you ever listen to me? I can't count on you to do anything I ask."

(Around they go whipping themselves into an argument and feeling more resentful and less understood with each comment until Jack remembers what he learned at that couples workshop and he switches into reflective listening.)

Jack: "Dana, I am sorry. I want to know what is bothering you. Tell me again what happened when you saw Tony with the iPad."

Dana: "Before I left for the meeting, I told you I had taken his iPad away because he had refused to take out the garbage after I asked him 3 times. I asked you to back me up and help him understand there are consequences if he ignores me. I expect him to do as I ask and do his chores."

Jack: "So, when you saw him with the iPad, it looked to you like I didn't do what you asked me to do, is that correct?"

Dana: "Yes, and there are other times I feel undermined by you with the grandkids."

Jack: "Please tell me more about what you mean when you say I undermine you with the grandkids."

(So the communication continues back and forth for several more minutes with Jack listening and Dana sharing and Jack reflecting what he is hearing.)

Jack: "Dana, do you believe I understand what was upsetting you? Is there anything you want to add?"

Dana: "No, I think I've said it all. I really appreciate how carefully you listened. Thank you. I'm ready to hear what you need to say now."

(Now Jack has a chance to express what his reasoning was and what he wants Dana to understand about handling the grandkids.)

You may think this is way too stilted and that people don't really talk like this — using reflective listening and I-statements. And I agree. When you are first learning these skills it feels artificial and not natural. Maybe even humorous. However, many of my clients say that when they learn the techniques and experience both listening better and being listened to, they feel closer to their partners. They also feel more trusting that their partner will care enough about their thoughts and feelings to really listen. I will repeat what I stated earlier. It is a precious gift we give each other. It works really well with just about anyone.

Let me use another example. I'll use the same couple.

Jack: "Honey, I'd like to talk with you about something that is bothering me."

Dana: (Pausing the TV show they were watching), "What's up, babe?"

Jack: "It seems to me that we are doing a lot of couch sitting and watching NCIS every night. I like these shows, but I feel kind of bored sometimes and I miss you. Plus, it seems that the neighborhood watch group is taking a lot of your time and you go to a lot of meetings. Were you even home one night last week?"

Dana: "So you're saying you miss me and you're kind of bored watching TV. And you've noticed I am gone to meetings a lot."

Jack: "Yes, Do you miss me too? Could we plan a date soon? Try that new place that opened over on Prairie?"

Dana: "Actually I do miss you and I know I've been really busy with this project. It will be over soon. I think the date is a great idea. We don't have the grandkids next week. Hey, I don't have a meeting tonight, how about we turn off TV and walk around the block? We can catch up on 'NCIS' later."

In this example, Jack felt Dana listened to his concerns, shared her own and both felt validated. They agreed on an action plan for a date and then took an immediate action with a walk around the block. This exchange made them feel closer to each other. They might have even held hands on that walk.

The Male Brain vs. the Female Brain

There are gender differences in how the brains of women and men are wired. Some researchers suggest that women are able to multi-task, handle several topics, listen better face-to-face and value connection more than men. Men are more single-task focused, tend to listen better when facing in the same direction, side by side, and are not as plugged into their emotions. Men want to feel respected. Women want to feel loved. Remember the best seller, written by John Gray, *Men are from Mars, Women are from Venus?*

Gray writes, "When a man can listen to a woman's feelings without getting angry and frustrated, he gives her a wonderful gift. He makes it safe for her to express herself.

"The more she is able to express herself, the more she feels heard and understood, and the more she is able to give a man the loving trust, acceptance, appreciation, admiration, approval and encouragement that he needs. Men are motivated when they feel needed, while women are motivated when they feel cherished."

My sense in working with hundreds of couples over several decades is that there may be some differences, and that some of the generalizations fit some of the time. However, each of us is unique. Research can inform us and help us ask the right questions to better understand ourselves and our partners. But we still need to learn how each of us is wired and what we need from each other to get our needs met. I have had the pleasure to work with many men in my therapy practice who are amazing listeners and know their feelings very well. Their emotional IQ is very high. I've also encountered some women who do not fit the stereotype and do not listen very well and who do not know their own feelings, as well as the reverse. What matters is the specific dynamic of each couple. What do you know about your spouse? And yourself? Are you interested in getting better at listening to each other so you can feel closer? Of course, we know the most important question is who has control of the TV remote.

Building Emotional Intimacy

One of the ways to improve communication and keep building emotional intimacy is to have regular weekly couple check-ins where you set aside special time to reflect on how you are doing, expressing appreciation as well as grievances. It's also a good time to identify patterns or issues you may want to address for more lengthy discussion. I suggest you follow the check-ins with a planned outing or dinner date or a nice comfy snuggle. The next chapter outlines how to use this tool to enhance your couple connection.

In addition to improving communication and having regular check-in times, there are other ways to build emotional intimacy with your partner. If you're noticing you feel distant or detached, begin by asking yourself what's been getting in the way of closeness. Is it stored anger or resentment? Is it hurt? Is it your own issue, such as depression or dissatisfaction? Is it a too-busy schedule? Or too much focus on others? Or balance of work vs. retirement?

When you're ready to start sharing, ask your partner for some uninterrupted time and ask that he just listen without comment as you try to express your deeper thoughts. Reassure him that this is not a bitch session or time to put him down or criticize. It is time for you to explore and express.

Allow yourself to be vulnerable. Brene Brown, author of *The Gifts of Imperfection* and *Rising Strong,* in her groundbreaking research on shame and resilience, defines vulnerability as uncertainty, risk and emotional exposure. "Vulnerability is the core of all emotions and feelings," she writes. "To feel is to be vulnerable. To believe vulnerability is weakness is to believe that feeling is weakness. ... Vulnerability is the birthplace of love, belonging, joy, courage, empathy, accountability and authenticity. ... Vulnerability sounds like truth and feels like courage."

Building emotional intimacy involves getting more comfortable with yourself and choosing to accept and embrace all of who your partner is, even if you sometimes don't like him or her at the moment. In the bigger picture, holding on to the trust that comes from loving each other for so many years and knowing each other so well invites that deeper vulnerability and sharing.

It also involves an awareness of where your primary focus is in the work/family/others balancing act. When our children were younger, Tom and I co-parented by having opposite work schedules. As they got older we also deliberately designed our house to be the "magnet house," the place our children's friends wanted to hang out. The toys, the Xbox, the pool table in the rec room, the piano, music, relaxed furniture, the trampoline and fire pit in the back yard, the homemade cookies and pizza. And the ever-present parent, supervising. With this child-centered household we also had to make sure we made time to focus on each other. For several years that meant hiring a babysitter every other Saturday for a date. We made rules that we could not talk about the kids or bills or home improvement projects on our date. Sometimes a movie followed dinner or a walk along the river. Those dates helped keep us sane. And our children benefitted by seeing happier parents.

Now as an older couple with one of us retired and the other working, we still need to build in time to stay connected and practice good couple check-in. Sometimes we need it more urgently, like the following story illustrates:

Bad Weather And Great Sex

We were on the road when a blizzard set in. The storm turned into a delightful date both of us greatly needed and didn't know it. We had been getting kind of crabby and short with each other, a sure sign that we needed some reconnection time. We were headed down to help our son care for our toddler grandson during a week that his wife had been called away for a business trip. We willingly rescheduled so we could help. As we headed south in wind-driven snow, the weather got worse. We passed cars and trucks in the ditch. We saw spinouts and patches of black ice. Traction became skittish. We decided to get off the highway. By cell phone, we got a good deal on a hotel room for the night. We ended up having a lovely evening, walking in the snow to a restaurant a block away, catching a good movie, and returning to our comfy room for delightful hotel sex. We got to our son's the next morning, refreshed, reconnected and a lot less crabby. With some special smiles, even. It's a good reminder to reconnect more often at home.

Higher Self Vs. Lower Self

We sometimes talk of the "higher self" vs. the "lower self." Higher self or best self is about relating from an integrated place of mind, body, spirit. A place of authenticity, a place of realness. It is about knowing yourself and choosing to relate from a place of higher vibration of love. This does not necessarily mean "nice." Love is not always nice. Sometimes love is also expressing anger or hurt or resentment or grief. Love is about speaking truth and being honest.

Lower self is the opposite, when mind, body and spirit are not integrated. It is often emotion-driven and is not about ownership of feelings but about blame or projection or deflecting responsibility. It is sometimes used in relationships to threaten, hurt, bully, or to assert excessive power. It is power "over" as opposed to power "with." Lower self is felt as a lower vibration, feeling heavier, denser — often the way resentment, jealousy, fear or anger feel.

So when I speak of honoring your partner by coming from your higher self, I am speaking about this place of authenticity grounded in honest love. Too often we treat others outside our family with our best selves or higher selves. We treat our colleagues, friends, other family members, even the clerk at the grocery store with more respect and compassion than we do our own partner. Sometimes, we let it all hang out at home and relate from a depleted self, a lower self, a reactive self, a place which is not about love. If you have fallen into this pattern, examine the factors and make a decision to shift into a higher place in your interactions.

This quotation from *Notes From Universe Calendar* speaks to this: "If you can fall in love with one thing about him or her, them, it, or yourself, just once a day, and speak it aloud, you'll be surprised by how quickly it will transform your entire life."

Love Languages

Learn your partner's "love language." Gary Chapman, author of *The Five Love Languages,* suggests that we each have a primary love language, a way in which we receive affection. These are: words of affirmation, acts of service, receiving gifts, quality time and physical touch. The one that makes you feel most appreciated and cared for is your primary love language. It is important to know your own as well as your partner's primary and second-ary love languages to make sure you are communicating clearly.

For Tim, his primary language was acts of service and his second-ary was physical touch. His wife, Jessica, really missed the boat. She just thought he enjoyed doing laundry and cooking and didn't understand he was saying "I love you" each time he cooked a meal or brought up a finished load of laundry from the basement. She hardly ever said thank you. Instead she got irritated because he rarely said nice words to her about how she decorated the house or how the centerpiece looked. He rarely complimented her on a new outfit. She felt neglected and he felt under-appreciated because they did not understand each other's love language.

~~~~Reflection I~~~~

Rate from 1-5 how important these languages are to you and then to your spouse: 1 is most important; 5 is least important

	You	Your Spouse
Affirmations:		
Acts of Service:		
Receiving Gifts:		
Quality Time:		
Physical Touch:		

Reserve some time to discuss your answers. Listen with open heart. Pay attention to when you feel defensive. Be gentle with yourself and your loved one.

Giving Criticism

Sometimes we have to say hard stuff to each other. Or we need to express an irritation or thought which may be perceived as criticism. It's important to speak our truth with respect and find a way to help our partner be able to receive it with respect. It is better to not say it outright. It is better to give some clues that it is coming. An example: "Hey honey, I'm giving you a heads-up.

I'm feeling bent out of shape about what you said about my driving. Can we talk?"

Set the stage. Ask for a moment or for her listening ear. Then say it. If you can, it's also really better to say something positive first and then what you are experiencing as negative. Please do this carefully. This is not to be manipulative or "managing" your spouse. It is just good communication practice. We are more likely to listen if we've been complimented first or someone has stated our value to them. An example: "Hey honey, I had a really good time with you last night. However, I need to tell you something that happened when we were out that really bugged me. Is this a good time?"

An example from our life, while writing this book:

Tom was on his way to the gym for his workout, then to the grocery store. I was waiting on hold on the phone. As he was leaving he shared a thought he had while editing the book yesterday.

Tom: " You know, we should really practice what we preach in the book more often."

Sally: "What do you mean?" (noticing I was bracing for what he'd say next.)

Tom: "You know, like having a more regular couple check-in and naked nightly."

Sally: (with irritation) "Well, you've been sick for a week and we've been super busy."

Tom: (car keys in hand, rushing out the door) "I want to get going."

Ten minutes later I got a text:

Tom: "I'm sorry for introducing so many items on the crowded agenda of the last hour. I don't like to part with so much unsettled. I'll try to do a better job when I return."

Sally: "Do not worry. We have a 46-plus-year track record. I was feeling criticized. I wanted to feel encouraged. Yet I want to hear your thoughts. I guess I would listen better if you'd said something we do well before you said what we're not doing. I'll do better, too."

Tom: "Old pattern of mine that I need to break. You shouldn't need to remind me."

Sally: "Me too. Thanks, babe. Have a great workout."
I can show you the text. That's actually how we talk.

Making Love All Day

Retirement offers more hours in the day to treat each other more kindly and with respect. To say thank you more often. To allow disagreements with calm discussion and to share moments of happiness out loud. To express ourselves freely and spontaneously without fear of judgment or needing to be defensive. These are all habits of happy, healthy, stable couples. It is how we treat each other and how carefully we listen to each other each and every day that predicts long-term happiness.

A memory I cherish from my childhood was watching my father, even on his limited minister's salary, bring my mother fresh flowers, either purchased or from a church member's garden. I remember enjoying this simple kind exchange of appreciation. Tom has a similar memory of his parents. We have continued this in our marriage. It feels good to be around couples who obviously delight in each other. They are likely to be the ones who practice little ways of showing kindness and tenderness which build intimacy. Some possibilities:

- Make his favorite meal.
- Get out some special photos.
- Re-create a first date.
- Rent a favorite movie.
- Bake her favorite cake (don't skimp on the frosting).
- Choose music to fit the mood.
- Clear the clutter, either around the house or in your mind.
- Listen to requests. Show that you heard them.
- Say yes whenever possible.
- Send a text, "I miss you already. I'm sending you a hug."
- Tender, nonsexual touching at unexpected times.
- Tell your partner how attractive they are to you.

- Do daily texts to let each other know how important you are to each other.
- Do for him or her what you would like done for you.

The transition at retirement allows for a recommitment to get to know each other better and deepen the emotional intimacy you share. Harville Hendrix, a prominent marriage therapist and author of *Getting the Love You Want,* says, "Make love all the time — and sometimes have sex." He goes on to explain that "many couples confuse physical closeness with emotional closeness. Sex makes you feel connected, but if you're not emotionally intimate, the connection is short-lived." Sometimes it is just simply choosing to treat each other with more kindness.

~~~~Reflection II~~~~

Take a moment, close your eyes and remember a time with your partner when you felt really appreciated by him or her. Bring the feeling up into your heart and deepen it. Now imagine sending appreciation back to him/her and notice the bond between you strengthening.

Tom's Note:

Sally describes certain activities in a relationship as walking a tight-rope. That's true, but it's not a circus tightrope when one false step can send the performer plummeting earthward. The marriage tightrope is wide enough to be walked securely, and the safety net is broad and welcoming — if the couple trust each other's ability to communicate and willingness to change.

People advise not to sweat the small stuff — and that it's all small stuff. I would add the caveat that just what is not small stuff is the partner's call. What stops "little things" from being "big things" is the willingness to hear just what irritates — or pleases — one's partner.

When I retired, I forgot to retire some habits of my four decades as a newspaper editor. Editors are quick to look for mistakes and flaws. That's part of our job, and many of us earn the designation of curmudgeon. However, newsroom editors often fall short in praising writers for the best qualities of their work. I'm afraid many reporters were left to look in the mirror for reinforcement. My point is, when you retire, bring the best of your skills to improving your marriage. Skip the rest of them.

In retirement there can be the illusion of having many more free hours — and the illusion that since you spend more time together you are communicating better and about the important stuff. That is often not the case. It is amazing how much time we can fill chatting about the business of life while being seemingly oblivious to the undercurrent of our emotional lives. Therefore, I strongly recommend committing to a weekly Couple Check-In to enrich, nurture and sustain your relationship.

Set aside an hour. Uninterrupted. It's best if it can be done at the same time on the same day each week so you learn to depend on this time to recalibrate. Just as you clean your house, it is important to "clean" the relationship of residual tension or built-up resentment, dusting and polishing the treasures of who you are together.

Reserve the time and be intentional. Otherwise you wait till tomorrow, and we know what happens then. This is a time to take a breath, focus in on each other and make an assessment: How is it going lately? Anything brewing we need to discuss? Anything we need to problem-solve? Irritations we need to clear or complications we need to talk through? It is also a time to share appreciation and reinforce your importance to each other. This is a time to share. Not a "bitch" session.

Couple Check-In does not take the place of speaking your truth in the moment. It is always best to speak about an issue or problem as close as possible to the time when it happens. Building up resentment without an outlet turns into toxicity; it is never good and always comes out smelling bad.

If you are in conflict or have a disagreement about something, it is still a good idea to ask for a time to talk about it and practice good listening and fair fight skills. Don't wait for the Weekly Check-In for this problem-solving. Do it within 24 hours if you can. If you need some pointers about fair fighting or you want to be more effective at conflict resolution, turn to Chapter 8, "Conflict Resolution: Can We Both Be Right?"

Couples who practice regular Couple Check-Ins report increased emotional and sexual intimacy. They feel closer and more trusting. They notice fewer quarrels and less tension because they know they can count on the Check-In to air the problems and feel connected.

Weekly Couple Check-In

1. Agree to meet at a specific time and place. Be comfortable.
2. Set a timer for 30 to 60 minutes
3. Take a moment to ground and center yourself, light a candle and/or share a prayer or a silent moment or read a poem or meditation, establishing this as a sacred time set apart from regular talking time.
4. Begin with sharing words of appreciation for something your partner did or said in the last week that you appreciate. Just receive the words with a thank you. This is not time to discuss in more detail.
5. Next share something that your partner did or said that was a problem or resulted in resentment. Avoid being judgmental, blaming or shaming. Use "I" language. "I feel_____, when you do or say _____. I need you to _____. Or I would feel_____ if you would _____." Example: I feel hurt and neglected when you come in from being gone for several hours and you don't greet me. I would really love it if you would find me, give me a hug and say hello. It makes me feel I am important to you."
6. Listen carefully to each other. Reflect back what you are hearing as if you are a mirror. Ask questions to clarify. If you are the one sharing, let your partner know when you feel he/she has understood you. Then have a respectful dialogue. Avoid being defensive. Remember: This is not about being right or wrong. This is about understanding each other and being there for your partner.

7. Suggest solutions for the problems discussed if appropriate.
8. Take turns.
9. If you run out of time, agree to an extension or set another time to resume the Couple Check-In.
10. End with a statement to each other about something your partner did or said during this ritual you really appreciated. For example, "Honey, I really appreciated how carefully you listened when I was sharing about my upset with you last week. I was babbling and you helped me get clear. Thank you."
11. Celebrate doing this ritual by giving each other a hug, and then go out on a date or share a glass of bubbly or a fine meal or make love. Somehow honor your commitment to yourselves and your relationship.
12. Repeat next week at the agreed time and place.

~~~~Reflection~~~~

Commit to trying the Weekly Couple Check-In a few times and discuss how it is working for you. Tweak it to fit your circumstances better. Remember to celebrate afterwards even if you didn't complete all the steps. Keep it fun even though it takes work. Keep it about improving your marriage one sentence at a time, one hug at a time, one weekly check-in at a time.

Tom's Note:

The need for appreciation does not end when one partner retires and the other keeps working. The "retired" partner should be thankful for the abundance created by the continued income. The "working" partner should look for tasks that the "retired" person has assumed, even if quite small. Getting the car washed and the gas tank filled. Having supper prepared and the kitchen cleaned, the mail sorted, the laundry started — whatever. Take note and say thanks. The evening is bound to go better.

08 - Conflict Resolution: Can We Both Be Right?

Their house overlooked the Pacific, the sound of the waves creating a lovely soundtrack. "This is Heaven!" I exclaimed as I introduced myself and thanked the couple for agreeing to be interviewed. I felt an intense rush of joy fill my body from head to toe, imagining myself living with this spectacular view every day.

Unfortunately, for this couple, the view of the ocean was not enough. I quickly learned as the interview progressed that this couple was not happy. The wife stared off in stony silence as the husband, oblivious to her obvious pain, extolled the joys of retirement, primarily his freedom to do what he pleased when he pleased.

His wife, on the other hand, hated his retirement: the disruption to her day, the giving up of hours of solitude and unstructured time. Now he was home so much more and commenting or critiquing her every move. "Why do you do the laundry this way? This way would be more efficient. You load the dishwasher backwards. You should do it this way." Coming home from time with buddies at the health club, he sails in and says, "Is this all you got done today? What are we having for lunch?"

The husband, who had been a software engineer, enjoyed talking with me about the fun of retirement and and got livelier the more he told his story. In contrast, the wife shrank even more into her chair where we sat around the kitchen table. The muscles in her face tightened. She looked so despondent. This increased as I asked about deciding where to live during retirement. She said she wanted to be closer to her adult children and the grandchildren. He said he was happy where they were. He felt attached to his activities and friends and didn't want to move. Visiting the kids was enough for him.

He also wanted to travel more. She looked even more hopeless as she said, "How can I travel when I can't eat out anywhere?" Her gluten intolerance and other food allergies, as well as her high-maintenance health regimen, made traveling almost impossible or certainly difficult. Yet he wasn't open to traveling without her, nor did she want to visit the grandkids without him.

Over their 40-plus years of marriage, they had not found a way to meet each other's needs. Conflict was avoided. Her style was to mute herself, suppress her voice and needs and let him have the power while heaping resentment on him in the form of withdrawal of affection and intimacy, plus growing negativity. His response was to pull away further and decide, "No matter what I do, I can't please her." They had given up on each other. They had few couple friends. No wonder their children did not choose to visit more often. They were not clued in to each other, and hadn't been for many years, if ever. It appeared they were not going to change, nor were things going to improve. Unless they worked intensively to get more happiness, things would worsen as age took more of a toll.

Working It Out and Making It Work

Ann and Kevin were like the previous couple earlier in their marriage. When they first came for counseling, Ann, a stay-at-home mom, had stopped being candid and had surrendered all the power of family decision-making to Kevin, a labor lawyer. They were struggling with some issues related to parenting.

As they worked together in counseling, the patterns of a more traditional marriage started to shift. Kevin started enjoying the positives of sharing the authority and responsibility, while Ann gained confidence and found her voice. As they developed skills of good listening and conflict resolution, their happiness and satisfaction level increased measurably. Their enjoyment of each other showed in more laughter and lightness. They sat closer together on the couch during counseling sessions. They reported they had resumed more regular lovemaking. Their smiles told me their intimacy was also a more satisfying intimacy, both emotionally and sexually.

From OK to Really Good

So how do you move your marriage from dysfunctional or mediocre to happy and fun? It starts with a commitment to communicate — the good, the bad and the ugly — in nonthreatening, loving ways. The purpose is to understand and be there for each other, not to bully or intimidate or win the debate. The purpose is to move closer, to stop feeling like he or she is the enemy. The purpose is to choose to be on the same team.

And to feel hope again. I often hear husbands say to me, "I've given up on trying to please her. Nothing I do is good enough." And I hear wives say, "I'm afraid to tell him how I feel. He'll just get mad at me and pull away." Getting locked into stubborn positions which rule out the idea that change can happen is understandable but not helpful. Renewal is possible. It begins with honesty and mutual vulnerability. It begins with courage and a belief that your loved one, despite the most recent behavior patterns, does truly want to please you, just as you want to please him or her.

Be Right, Or Be Happy?

Harriet Lerner begins her very good book *The Dance of Connection* with a story: "Two little kids are playing together in a sandbox in the park with their pails and shovels. Suddenly a huge fight breaks out, and one of them runs away, screaming, 'I hate you! I hate you!' In no time at all they're back in the sandbox, playing together as if nothing happened. Two adults observe the interaction from a nearby bench. 'Did you see that?' one comments in admiration. 'How do children do that? They were enemies five minutes ago.'

"'It's simple,' the other replies. 'They choose happiness over righteousness.'"

In my waiting room I have a handout entitled "Do you want to be right or do you want to be married?"

There's also the Native American story of the two wolves. It goes like this:

One evening an old Cherokee told his grandson about a battle that goes on inside people. He said, "My son, the battle is between two 'wolves' inside us all.

"One is the shadow: it is anger, envy, jealousy, sorrow, regret, greed, arrogance, self-pity, guilt, resentment, inferiority, lies, false pride, and superiority.

"The other is light: it is joy, peace, love, hope, serenity, humility, kindness, benevolence, empathy, generosity, truth, compassion and faith."

The grandson thought about it for a minute and then asked his grandfather: "Which wolf wins?"

The old Cherokee simply replied, "The one you feed."

So in each interaction with our partner, we have a choice. We choose how we move through this stage of life. Are we going to choose to move toward more happiness and intimacy with our spouse, or are we going to choose to pull away, withdraw, reject or shut down?

This isn't a win/lose contest. This is a partnership where both of you win by meeting each other's needs as best you can and trusting in times you can't. When you're in conflict or disagreement, ask yourself, "How important is this really?" If it seriously impacts your relationship, then address it directly, following good listening guidelines.

I discovered a gem of a book written by Peter Davidson, called *Marital Advice to my Grandson, Joel.* It is especially for newlyweds, but his words about conflict fit for us older marrieds, too. "If there are conflicts, a lose-lose situation is, 'I don't care what happens to me as long as I destroy him or her." A win-lose resolution is, 'Not only do I want to win, but I want my spouse to lose.' The goal should be a win-win, where both people come out feeling good."

77 Years Of Love — Typical Of Their Generation

"Love is patient. Love is kind. It does not envy, it does not boast, it is not proud, it is not rude, it is not self-seeking, it is not easily angered, it keeps no records of wrongs. Love does not delight in evil but rejoices with the truth. It always protects, always trusts, always hopes, always perseveres. Love never fails ... " (I Corinthians 13:4-8)

My mother read this passage from the New Testament at our wedding in 1972. We also read it at Mom's memorial service.

My mom died at age 89 after a decade-long struggle with Alzheimer's. As the disease progressed and her recall dimmed and her speech deteriorated, her spirit shone more brightly. She became our guru for being in the moment. She epitomized unconditional love.

My dad passed at age 93. I am so grateful for the model of love my parents gave us in their 67 years married, 77 years together. They met when they were 12 and 14 at a church youth group Halloween Fall Festival Party, bobbing for apples (really, honestly!) at the height of the Depression. They loved each other deeply, and extended that love to their five children and spouses and grandchildren and great-grandchildren. However, typical of their generation, they also never figured out how to deal with anger and resentment in a healthy way.

Healthy Conflict

Every married couple has disagreements. The key is knowing how to handle the conflict. Avoiding conflict, "walking on eggshells," being afraid of rocking the boat, or keeping peace at any price will hurt your marriage. So also will the temptation to jump down your partner's throat at the slightest infraction. Developing ways to handle your own and your partner's irritations and disagreements is essential if you want to cope with the process of aging. It's hard enough to grow old. We need each other's support.

Conflict is good. It means you are paying attention to your own desires which might not match up with your partner's desires. That's OK. You are different people. You also can't read each other's minds, even though it would make things easier if both could. Feeling angry is also OK. Acting in anger is not. Anger is just a message, like any other feelings. It tells us something is not right or that we feel disrespected or threatened, or our boundaries have been violated. Learning to listen to our feelings helps us clarify our needs.

Often couples get stuck in fighting as a way to manage conflict, rather than listening and problem solving. If we engage when we're angry, we aren't thinking clearly and we just want our partner to shut up, sit down and do it our way. It is remarkable how many couples say, "I don't want to fight about this, but I don't know what else to do. I feel helpless. I just want it to change."

Guidelines For Managing Conflict

1. Set aside a time to talk when you are both calm. Do not try to discuss when either of you is angry. Agree to a cooling-off period, and then negotiate.
2. Practice good listening skills.
3. Do not interrupt. Be aware of your own and your partner's body language.
4. Avoid pushing each other's buttons or triggers. If this happens, stop. Resume later.
5. Talk in a calm, respectful voice. Do not use sarcasm, name-calling or purposefully hurtful language.
6. Do not bring up old hurts and resentments from the past. Stay current in your discussion of the conflict.
7. Get to the bottom line. What's most important?
8. Remember you are both wise in years and experience. Remember that a fair disagreement can enhance your understanding.
9. Don't fight each other. Fight for the marriage.

Put These Pointers Into Practice

These pointers sound easy until you put them into practice. Sometimes we are blind to our destructive patterns which make it so difficult to really listen.

One pattern is blaming the other person for your unhappiness. You are in charge of what you think and feel. Asking your partner to do or say something differently which may help you feel better is OK along as you remember who is in charge of you.

Unintentionally, we can give away our power to be happy to the other with logic that says, "If you do this_____, then I will be happy. If you stop doing this_____, then I'll stop doing_____. If only you would_____ then I could _____." If only you would say you're sorry, then I could forgive you. If only you would tell me the truth, then I could move on. If only you would stop yelling, then I could tell you what I need. If only we could have sex, then I would treat you nicer."

The remedy is to commit to what YOU are going to do differently so that you feel good about how you are loving your spouse. And in turn, hopefully your spouse will do the same and you will both get what you desire.

Another destructive pattern is to make our partner responsible for our healing. From our childhoods, we all carry baggage — unfinished business, places of hurt and betrayal — which we then are tempted to project onto our most intimate partners, holding them to the task of healing us. Too late. Impossible task. The only person who can heal me is me. The task is to figure out how to give myself now what I needed then, not to ask another person to give it to me. His words of affirmation and touches of affection can make it easier for me to love myself, to finally see myself as worthy and lovable and to heal the shame we all carry. If we surround ourselves with people who treat us well and as the lovable people we are, it is easier to give it to ourselves. However, the bottom line is that we need to give it to ourselves. That's easier said than done.

Feeling Shame

We all carry places of shame or things about ourselves which make us feel unworthy of love. One source of shame for me is accepting that I am not "Suzy Homemaker," nor did Tom marry me thinking I was. I admire people who work full-time and also keep a beautiful house. I am not that person. If I have free time my go-to is to sit and read or watch a movie, not clean. Tom and I sometimes laugh that we both need the traditional "wife." We are two toddlers waiting for mom to come home and clean up. I laugh but it is also a source of shame. It can also be a trigger if Tom makes a comment about the condition of the house, and I may hear it as a slam at me when he was just making an observation.

There is an African saying, "There can be no enemy from the outside if there is not an enemy within." If I hear criticism about myself which echoes what I already feel about myself, I may feel ashamed or be hard on myself. In contrast, if someone speaks an untruth or says something I don't feel about myself, I can just brush it off or not have any reaction.

When I notice a strong reaction in myself, it is a clue that it might be a part of myself that needs healing or a place where I am being too self-critical. In other words, I need to clean up my own act. In Alcoholics Anonymous talk, I need to clean up my side of the block. Take my own inventory, not the other person's. The Serenity Prayer fits here: "God grant me the serenity to accept the things I cannot change, the courage to change the things I can — and the wisdom to know the difference." Amen. So we make our relationships better by making ourselves better.

Right Or Wrong?

As we have asked, "Do you want to be right, or do you want to be married?" We often get very invested in proving our partner wrong or proving ourselves right. It is not necessarily important to agree. It is important to understand the what and why of each other's positions. If I'm trying to convince you how right I am, it could be tempting to turn into a bully. If I speak my thoughts and feelings and listen with equal passion to your thoughts and feelings, I have a chance to understand our disagreement. Elevate the discussion to a place where you can both be right even though you disagree. The visionary poet Rumi speaks of this place: "Out beyond ideas of wrong-doing and right-doing, there is a field. I'll meet you there."

Fight Fairly

Fight fairly. It is never OK to call your partner a name or make hurtful personal remarks. It is not OK to attack, no matter how vulnerable or frightened you feel. You are responsible for your own actions and words, including your defense mechanisms. If your defense default is to attack with words ("You're a bitch." "You are loser." "You are so stupid." "I can't believe how slow you are.") dial it back. Be silent. Take a breath. Do not give yourself permission to be mean. It is not acceptable. EVER. If you need to just let it out, say it to the car dashboard or the trees or in your journal. If you do cross the line, ask for forgiveness. No one is perfect. We are all works in progress.

Know your patterns of default when you are under stress or feeling threatened. Examples include the avoider-pursuer; controlling mother-naughty boy; critical father-shut down daughter; angry spouse-cold shoulder. Know your style of conflict management.

Examine Expectations

Are you a pessimist or an optimist? Do you have unrealistic expectations which then cause dissatisfaction when you're disappointed? Or does your spouse call you a "downer" because you're always ready to point out the negative? It's OK to have different styles. Opposites often attract to balance each other out. However, this could be a source of conflict if the couple doesn't have a way to talk about it or an understanding or even an appreciation of what each brings to the relationship. Before you start a project or go on an excursion, it is a good idea to have a discussion about your expectations. What do you see happening? What's the best case scenario? What might interfere? How do you agree to handle disagreements?

Check out a well-written and funny take on this on a blog called "Reset Your Expectation, Improve Your Life" by Kevin Moriarity on his website "The Voice of Doom and Gloom." While Moriarity is making a bigger point about American advertising and attitudes, I'm including this reference as an excellent illustration of how expectations can cause unnecessary conflict for a couple.

Your Brain on Emotional Overdrive

Research shows what happens in the brain during conflict. When we are angry or hurt or have a strong emotional reaction, or we have "flipped our lid," so to speak, we are responding from our amygdala or the emotional center of the brain. The prefrontal cortex, or the cognitive, thinking part of our brain, is on hold. So it is hard to think. We are all feeling. In order to use our "whole brain" we need to comfort ourselves, feel calm, and then we can be both reasonable and have controlled feelings. This is a simplified explanation of how our brain responds. However, it is wise to keep in mind when either or both of you are too angry or hurt to be reasonable. Wait for a cool-down period.

If your discussion is getting too heated and it's starting to feel like it's going to self-destruct or do damage, ask for a time-out. Allow your partner to do the same. Time will allow you to cool down or reflect or get your bearings again. Then make sure you follow through. Open the subject back up for discussion at an agreed-upon time so your partner can trust that you will work toward a resolution. If you ask for a time-out and don't get back to the problem at hand, the issue doesn't go away. It just gets heaped up on the garbage pile of hurts, resentments, betrayals and unresolved issues. Fix it. Then start afresh.

Having a heated discussion followed by silence or a separation without a resolution can stir up feelings of fear or anxiety. We can be quick to imagine the worst scenario.

After one of the couple's many arguments, specifically about her husband's declining memory and his unwillingness to seek treatment, the wife drew him close and asked why he looked so dejected. He responded, "I feel so distant from you. We're growing apart. I'm afraid you're going to leave me." From a tender, compassionate place, the wife was able to respond, "Honey, I'm sorry if I made you feel that way.

You've got me. I love you. I'm here for the long haul. Even if you lose your memory and forget who I am."

We all need reassurances from our partners. That's part of the marital bond. Talking things through to a resolution also involves offering yourself and your partner authentic forgiveness. Let go of the past. It's gone. Stop worrying about the future. It's not here yet. Stay in the preciousness of the present moment. Be here now. Fully. Thank you. I am sorry. I forgive you. Please forgive me. I love you. Use these phrases frequently — but only when you mean them.

Wisdom In Action

One of the wives of the Wise Married Elders described a pattern she and her husband played out often when he had to leave town for an extended work project. It stirred up abandonment issues. He would get angry about something and pick a fight, sometimes on the way to the airport. In the past, she would take the bait and they would end up fighting and then part angry. On some unconscious level that made it easier for him to be gone from her.

She learned instead to redirect his comments, using reflective listening and loving support. She would say, "This is probably not a good time to talk about something of such importance. I'd like to wait until we're both rested and not under the stress of getting to the airport on time. How about if we talk about this again after you've arrived? It's like trying to talk when we're both hungry and dinner isn't ready yet. Do you want to call me later from the hotel?" This worked to help turn a destructive pattern into a healthy one.

Learning To Let The Other Talk

Pat and Lorraine were eager to be interviewed for the book and share about their relationship. Professionally, they retired after operating a business together, and had relocated to an area with great bike trails. Each had been married once before.

Pat: "It took a lot of years for me to let down my guard after we got married. It was the therapy process that let me do that. I'm a strong personality and very much of a control freak. In the first part of my marriage Lorraine did the same thing my first wife did and didn't speak up when she was upset with me or if I had offended her. And then she would hit me with it. What I learned in therapy was that I was not allowing Lorraine to feel safe enough to talk with me. I had to learn ... not to interrupt her, not challenge what she was saying, and to really hear what she was saying. I had to learn to encourage her to talk with me, not challenge her, not be defensive, not get angry or storm out. I'm still working on this, but if I had a problem I expected her to be a mind-reader. It took time to be able to let her know what I want."

Lorraine: *"I came from a family where you did not talk about problems. ... My first marriage probably failed for many reasons, one being because I did not have the confidence, for fear of my husband getting upset, to speak up about what I needed or what was making me unhappy. When Pat and I met, my inability continued. I didn't have many good tools to clearly communicate with someone I really cared about. Therapy allowed me to realize I must, and could, take the risk of honestly speaking my mind. This has improved immensely. We're still working on it."*

This couple exemplifies the positive changes that come with commitment to listen better and have a willingness to change longstanding patterns.

In the syndicated comic strip Mr. Boffo, a couple is asked, "You guys never argue. What's your secret?" The husband replies, "Twenty-five hundred taboo subjects." This makes a great joke but is a setup for a troublesome marriage.

Some researchers have concluded that most of success in marriage is two-thirds acceptance of who the other is and one-third problem-solving of differences. How does that ratio fit for your marriage?

Practice "And What Else?"

Jonathan Robinson, in his book *Communication Miracles,* suggests using a method called, "And What Else?" This method is especially good when you are in conflict or you sense building tension. Ask your partner to speak about what she/he is feeling and wanting. Promise you will not interrupt. Occasionally ask, "And what else?" or "Tell me more." Let your partner speak till she/he is finished.

Do not respond or even ask clarifying questions. Wait at least one hour before you respond. You may ask for your partner to exchange the "and what else" and allow you to speak without interruption. Again, wait at least one hour. Then calmly have a discussion. If you don't have time, find a time soon and agree to continue the dialogue.

A variation on this exercise is to ask three prompts, repeating each for five minutes after each response. So for five minutes the listener says, "What I fear is ..." "What I want is ...", "What I hope is ..." This method can bring clarity to an issue in which full awareness is just below the conscious level, which often happens if we don't feel safe or have strong fear or anxiety.

Contempt vs. Kindness

Dr. John Gottman, a researcher and marriage therapist, in his excellent book *The Seven Principles for Making Marriage Work,* identifies what he calls The Four Apocalypse Horsemen: criticism, contempt, defensiveness and stonewalling. When couples treat each other with these behaviors it can cause serious difficulties. When I meet with a couple who are contemptuous of each other and use a lot of sarcasm, I do not have high hopes for their marriage. Most likely they have come to counseling to place blame on the other and get permission to exit.

Contempt is the number one factor that tears couples apart. Dr. Julie Gottman, wife of John Gottman and fellow researcher and family therapist, says, "We observe they are scanning the partner for what the partner is doing wrong and criticizing versus respecting and expressing appreciation. People who are focused on criticizing their partners miss a whopping 50 percent of the positive things their partners are doing, and they see negativity when it's not there. For instance, people who give their partners the cold shoulder — deliberately ignoring the partner or responding minimally — damage the relationship by making their partner feel worthless and invisible ... "

The Gottmans cite research showing that contempt and criticism not only kill the love in a relationship, but also reduce the partners' ability to fight off viruses and cancer. Meanness affects the immune system and physical health of those involved.

However, John Gottman also points out that if couples are committed to what he calls "relationship repair" and use the 5:1 ratio of 5 positive statements for any 1 negative statement, the relationship can improve and even thrive. Showing kindness and generosity is the most important predictor of satisfaction and stability in marriage. "The more someone receives or witnesses kindness," he writes, "the more they will be kind themselves, which leads to spirals of love and generosity in a relationship."

Showing kindness is like strengthening a muscle: the more we exercise it, the stronger it gets. Good relationships require sustained hard work. But the rewards feel so good.

One of the first homework assignments I give to couples who come in feeling very discouraged about their relationship is to commit to one week without criticism and give only compliments and appreciation statements. It's very hard to do. Just trying it brings increased awareness of the destructive patterns and each person's role in repeating them. Often they come back reporting how good it feels to stop the negative talk and just be kind. One husband said, "I noticed that because I was working on being kind, I just felt better about myself. The more kind I was, the more kindness I received, not just at home but at work, too — even at the grocery store."

If you are concerned that your marriage is too dysfunctional, please seek professional help. If you want to retool and improve how you relate, check out the books listed in Notes & Resources. If you find yourself in a stuck place and it feels pretty chronic, like it's all too familiar, this is a good time to ask for help. We can't see our own blind spots. If you're brave, ask your partner for some feedback. What does he /she see as your stuck places? Take the feedback as part of your assessment. If that proves not enough, seek professional help.

Don't settle for less when it can be so much better. And don't try to tough it out alone. Having the right assistance can make the journey to a healthy and satisfying marriage so much easier.

Taking The Risk

An example from my own life involves a period of intensive personal growth in conjunction with advanced training in my field. Over a period of three years, I was flying to the East Coast for weekend or week-long training while Tom stayed back managing the children and the household and working his job. When I returned Tom might not ask how it went. I might not share. We would both just jump into work and the kids' school schedules and laundry and the demands of daily life. Meanwhile I was transforming myself. I was changing and I wasn't clueing my husband in on the changes — nor did he seem to want to know or even notice.

I watched several of my colleagues, as well as clients, lose their marriages at this time. "We just grew apart." "We wanted different things." "I don't feel he/she knows me anymore." I watched other couples in similar situations drift apart, accusing the other of not caring or showing interest anymore or losing attraction for each other. I made a decision that changed my relationship and refocused my commitment to stay married.

After returning from a life-changing, powerful seminar, I asked Tom for some time later in the evening. I told him I needed to let him know what was happening to me. I took the risk and began to share. Even if Tom wasn't interested or didn't approve or was threatened, I knew I needed to give him a chance to listen and try to understand. Our marriage depended on it. Fortunately, he rose to the occasion. He listened, asked questions, pushed back a bit, and we weathered the storm.

We continue to do this. We commit to share about experiences at our cutting edges of personal growth. In our own styles, me as the psychotherapist and he as the journalist. It was also at that time that Tom came up with the "woo-woo scale," used to assess just how "out there" my experiences are (for example, if he rates something a woo-and-a-half, it's pressing the limits of his understanding). It is very amusing. He likes to tease me, and we both reap the benefit of reconnecting and deepening our trust. In turn, I ask Tom about the stories he reads, the music he hears, the news he reviews — even his golf.

Good Enough

There is the concept of the "good enough" parent. It comes from the work of Donald Winnicott, a British psychiatrist. It is a wonderfully forgiving idea that none of us are perfect parents and despite our mistakes our children will do OK if we give them love, guidance, connection, structure, "show up" and stay present for them. I remember vividly a conversation with one of my older colleagues who was also a mentor to me when I first worked in the field and was struggling with balancing the demands of work with the demands of being a first-time mom and feeling like a failure at both. She assured me, after listening through my tears, that I was being a "good enough" mom to my little one. I felt like she understood my struggles without sugarcoating them, and that her advice gave me genuine relief. Over the years of counseling parents, I've shared this concept when applicable and hoped they could experience the same comfort.

So, I'm wondering if we can extend that idea to each other as husband and wife. Even though we are not perfect spouses and we do not have a perfect relationship, we can be "good enough" partners. Accept. Forgive. Breathe and smile.

I saw this post on Facebook recently: "If a woman is upset, hold her and tell her she's beautiful. If she starts to growl, retreat to a safe distance and throw chocolate at her." (This quotation is from www.grumpyoldgits.) Although I cringe at some of the humor on the website because of how stereotypically women and men are portrayed, it is good sometimes to laugh, even if it is not politically correct.

To conclude this chapter on conflict resolution, I want to share this handout from marriage gurus Harville Hendrix, author of *Making Marriage Simple,* and his wife, LaKelly Hunt, also a therapist and author. In examining the question of why couples fight, and in their work with thousands of couples, they have come up with this list of the habits which make relationships miserable. Think of this as a summary of the recommendations we have given in this chapter — but in the negative.

TEN MOST COMMON BAD HABITS

1. **Be as critical as you can.** Even "constructive" criticism can make your partner defensive and reduce the feeling of safety in a relationship. Being harsh and judgmental when angry can trigger a "flight or fight response."

2. **Insist your partner be exactly the same as you.** "Absolute compatibility" is an express route to a dull relationship. If you insist your partner have the same feelings and perceptions as you do, it can lead to despair and misery.

3. **Flee from intimacy.** If you habitually avoid being physically or emotionally close with your partner through escaping into work, hobbies, television or other activities, you risk creating a divide between you and your partner that may become impossible to breach.

4. **Play the blame game.** Using "you" language when upset will make your partner put up defenses. When your goal is to communicate in a way that fosters intimacy, use statements that begin with "I feel" instead.

5. **Bargain.** Hendrix and Hunt say that both "giving conditionally and receiving cautiously" erode relationships. They warn against doing something for a partner only when you want something in exchange.

6. **Be casual about romance.** No relationship can be spontaneously joyful forever. Once the initial excitement of a

new romance wears off, some couples think their relationship is over and give up trying. They risk missing out on experiencing a deeper kind of love.

7. **Focus on the negative.** If you constantly think and talk about your partner's flaws, it can amplify your discontent. Hendrix points out that a paradox of most forms of couples therapy is that you spend your sessions complaining about your partner — something that can actually be detrimental to your relationship.

8. **Refuse to listen.** Thinking you are right all the time and engaging in a one-way monologue is a great way to end up in a relationship ... of one, LaKelly Hunt and Hendrix warn.

9. **Hide your needs.** If you don't express what you need and want to your partner, you'll constantly feel deprived and frustrated. Hendrix and LaKelly Hunt say it's crucial to share "the things that truly touch your heart."

10. **Expect a fairytale romance.** Fairy tales are just that, and eventually we all have to come down to earth. Demanding the fantasy go on forever prevents your partner from ever being their authentic self and fosters resentment and distance.

Hendrix and Hunt know from firsthand experience how hard it is to sustain a genuinely loving commitment. Several years ago, after working together and raising five kids, they found themselves on the brink of divorce. Using their own methods, they worked their way back to what they say is a renewed love that feels as genuine as it did 30 years ago.

~~~~Reflection~~~~

Review the list above and pick out one of your bad habits. Identify one of your spouse's bad habits. Set aside a time to discuss this with each other and come up with a plan to change the bad habits into a healthy ones. Check back in a few weeks and evaluate how you are doing.

Tom's Note

*Politics can be a source of conflict, even when you or your partner are in basic agreement. The obstacle can lie in differing appetites for political discussion. We read about politics in newspapers, magazines and books. We hear about it on the car radio. We watch newscasts on several networks, all of which offer analysis when we might be just seeking facts. Sometimes I have simply had enough of all of it. I need to just shut it off for a few (or more) hours, even if I need to leave Sal alone while she fills her minimum daily requirement. The conflict arises when I want to move on and do something else **together**. I just need to step away and return when she is ready.*

Tom's Note II

Once an argument begins, tensions can escalate quickly. If either partner finds the tension too great, there needs to be an exit word that suspends all talk for awhile in the hope that cooler heads can prevail. Perhaps, "I need a reset" can initiate a 10-minute break (in different rooms, if need be). It's more effective than just walking out.

09 - Naked Nightly and Afternoon Delight

One regret, dear world,
That I am determined not to have
When I am lying on my deathbed
Is that
I did not kiss you enough.

— *Hafiz, a 14th-century Sufi mystic poet*

Sex is good. Making love is good. Having the time to feel close and emotionally connected leads to desiring to be close and sexually connected. When sex feels good you want more of it. When sex feels good you think about it more and make more time for it and when you do it you say to each other, "This feels so good, why don't we do this more often?"

For some couples, however, sex is not good. Sex hurts. Or the biological equipment doesn't work. Or it's not as much fun. Or chronic pain or illness gets in the way. Or we don't feel loved so we aren't interested. Or we have an idea that sex is just for the young.

What if sex has stopped for a long time? Maybe you don't remember the last time you had sex. Maybe you've taken it off the table altogether. You don't even fantasize anymore. Or ask or initiate. Maybe you've made peace with having a sexless marriage. If that's the case and you've **both** decided it's OK, I recommend leaving it alone. However, for most couples I work with and have interviewed, there is **not** an agreement that it's OK not to have sex, and one spouse is suffering. I think it is important to have the conversation about sex, even if it's uncomfortable. Make your own statement about where you are. Then listen to your partner and evaluate what to do next. Be gentle. Be kind.

Retirement allows for the time and space to create the romantic life you want without the distractions of children and work schedules. The bottom line is: If you have stopped having sex, find a way to start again, even if it is just cuddling. If you're still having sex but are bored or it is the same old same old, change it up. Explore. Be creative. Light the fire! Get your juicy self going! Enjoy!

We've divided the discussion about sex into two chapters. In this one we focus on the effects of aging and ideas to encourage those of you who are already enjoying an active sex life and may be wanting to turn up the heat. In the next chapter we focus on couples who have stopped having sex or are facing challenges like chronic pain or resuming sex after infidelity. Both chapters might have ideas applicable to your situation.

How Often and How Satisfying?

In an AARP survey of 8,000 people 50 years or older, "31 percent of couples have sex several times a week; 28 percent have sex a couple of times a month; and 8 percent have sex once a month. However, 33 percent of respondents said they rarely or never have sex. But even among couples who report being 'extremely happy,' an astonishing one-fourth rarely or never get it on."

In another AARP study done in 2014, 71 percent of the 1,816 people surveyed said sex is still important in their lives. However, only slightly more than half (54 percent) are satisfied with their sex life and 67 percent admit that their sexual desire has receded in the past 20 years. When asked the question, "Do you ever have sex out of obligation when you don't really feel like it," 13 percent of people in a relationship for a year or less say yes, compared with 50 percent of people in a relationship for 21 years or more.

If you want to know how you compare, consider taking an online survey at www.davidschnarch.com. Go to "Other Offerings" listed at top, pull down the menu and click on "Sex in Relationships Survey." This will give you a score and show how you compare. Just answering the questions might give you some ideas. For instance, what happens to your excitement /arousal when you keep your eyes open while she is touching you or while you're inside her?

Differences in Perception

In the movie *Annie Hall,* on a split screen, you see a therapist working with a couple in separate sessions. He asks the man about frequency of sex and he responds, "Oh never, never, not enough, maybe three times a week." In her own therapy session, the woman's response is, "We have sex all the time, maybe three times a week." They agreed on the frequency but were far apart about the satisfaction level.

Why this difference in perception? After years of working with clients, I believe the answer is both complex and profoundly simple. We all just want to be loved. To both feel loved by our partner and to be loving in return. And yet we make it so difficult. We are not raised in a culture where it is easy to talk about sex. We feel embarrassed or are afraid of rejection or do not want to hurt our loved one. Sometimes due to religious or parental training we feel bad or dirty or naughty if we talk or even think about sex. For some, abuse and trauma or negative body image issues have affected us. Even as we get older, we sometimes haven't updated our ideas and let ourselves fully embrace our sexy sides.

Rejuvenating their sex life was one of the goals of the transition into retirement for some of the couples I interviewed, in addition to many of my older married clients. I often hear husbands speak of their desire to be closer to their wives in all ways, and to enhance their emotional as well as sexual intimacy. It is not a surprise that this feeling is expressed more often by the husbands.

For too many couples, the wives have long since lost interest in actual sex for many reasons. However, they still desire and actually crave being held and cuddled, sometimes without a word being said. When I counsel couples separately, it is sad when I hear the husband tell me that he misses his wife, misses holding her and having sex — and then the wife tells me she also misses her husband and being held. Too often the wife has stopped responding to his overtures because he would too quickly move straight to intercourse. No foreplay. No whispered sweet nothings in her ear, no emotional connection.

I also work with wives who are still interested in sex and miss making love but are suffering because their husbands are no longer interested and may not even cuddle, hug or kiss anymore. These women tell me they don't speak up in groups of women because they feel out of sync or fear they will be made fun of by their "sisters." This adds to their feelings of isolation. They feel reassured when I let them know they are not alone.

Although there are exceptions, there is support for the generalization that men view sex as a way to emotionally connect whereas women want to emotionally connect and then maybe have sex. Men want to do "it" to feel closer. Women want to do "it" after they feel closer. The saying that men are microwaves and women are slow-cookers also adds to the mix. How does each define foreplay?

Therein lies the proverbial problem, one which I believe can be addressed with communication and compromise, especially when done respectfully and even playfully. Try offering your husband some connection time while you rub his head or scratch his back while you talk about what is in your heart and ask him to listen and then ask him to share for a few minutes and then move to the bedroom for some sexual romping. Win-win. And you might each have a happy glow.

Many couples who have been married for decades, are comfortable with each other and trust each other in and out of the bedroom report that the sex is OK, but they wish for more satisfaction or excitement, or it's gotten boring and predictable. They'd rather watch evening TV or call a friend. Some of that is about our bodies growing older. Some of that is about taking each other for granted. Sometimes we get too comfortable. The brain craves novelty. Bringing awareness to these feelings in a loving way may begin a rebooting to being sexy with each other.

Sensate Focus

I often recommend using sensate focus as a step toward a more complete connection emotionally, physically and sexually. In the first steps, the couple agrees to touch and be touched but not to have sex. No genital play. No sexual stimulation play. With or without lotion or massage oil. This might follow a check-in to connect emotionally and then just holding each other, followed by taking turns touching parts of the body just focusing on how good it feels. Taking the prospect of having sex off the table allows the wife to let go of the tension of what might happen next or what her husband's agenda is, and just relax into the pleasure of being held and gently touched. As they have more "practice" sessions, and she rebuilds her trust in him, resuming sex play is a natural progression, mutually pleasurable. Some couples tell me that doing this exercise several times over several weeks deepened their intimacy and increased their pleasure in and out of bed.

In the movie *Hope Springs,* the wife, played by Meryl Streep, expresses her vulnerability at feeling so rejected by her husband, played by Tommy Lee Jones, who had moved out of the bedroom years ago because of a back injury. "When it's off, it's off," he says. The therapist, played by Steve Carell, prescribes "sensate focus" as homework. The movie shows us this couple awkwardly approaching each other after many years of sleeping separately and not having sex and barely touching. I often recommend this movie as homework for couples. Who knows what might happen?

How Aging Affects Sex

As we get older:
- It takes us longer to get turned on.
- When we're turned on, it takes us longer to reach orgasm.
- Taking longer can be uncomfortable. For example, ar-

thritic joints can limit movement. We might get fatigued. Our digestive systems may be upset.

- Blood flow can be reduced, diminishing the sensitivity of vaginal, clitoral and penile tissue.

Many of us don't respond like we used to. However, a number of older women report that they feel more sexually responsive than when they were younger. And some men agree.

Hormonal changes can cause intercourse to be painful for women. Reduced estrogen can cause the vagina to become drier and the walls stiffer. The vagina may also shorten and become more narrow. It is called vaginal atrophy. The natural lubrication of the body decreases, requiring use of a lubricant to increase comfort in having sex. Water-based compounds or gels containing silicone are popular. Please stop intercourse if it is painful. Do not associate pain and discomfort with making love. Find solutions. The good news is that vaginal atrophy can be treated with using lubricants and having more sex.

Some of the changes women experience in our older years may be a continuation of what happened before and during menopause: hormonal fluctuations, hot flashes, fuzzy brain, insomnia, loss of desire for sex, mood swings, depression, weight gain, lack of energy. Many women have few or none of the symptoms. Every menopause is unique. The good news is that the symptoms often pass and the body adjusts. The postmenopausal woman may emerge supercharged and ready to go in every area, including her sexual being. She might be much more prepared to speak her truth and claim her wisdom.

As men get older, the penis loses some sensation. It may take longer to get an erection and it may not be as firm or large as it used to be. It may not last as long. The erection may subside more quickly following an orgasm. It may also take longer to get another erection in the same lovemaking session. Sexual fantasies are no longer enough to bring erections. Men need more stimulation, fondling, stroking. Minor distractions like the phone ringing can cause a loss of firmness. Worry can exacerbate the problem, since anxiety causes the arteries that carry the blood into the penis to constrict, making erections less likely.

"Here's my advice to older men with balky erections," says sex therapist Dr. Marty Klein. "Relax, breathe deeply, ask for the kind of touch that excites you — and instead of mourning what you've lost, focus on the pleasure you can still enjoy."

Some men experience ED or erectile dysfunction — the inability to have and keep an erection. Many factors can contribute to ED. If ED happens only occasionally, try again soon and don't let it become a worry. However, if it starts to happen more often, seek medical advice.

Many medical conditions can impact sexual desire and responsiveness. The list includes diabetes, high blood pressure, multiple sclerosis, heart disease, chronic pain, arthritis, hormonal imbalances, thyroid conditions, cancer and surgery. Medications used to treat some conditions can cause vaginal dryness. Others can reduce arousal, erections or ejaculations. Check with your pharmacist or doctor to see if there is a different drug without such side effects.

Too much alcohol can cause erection problems in men and delay orgasm in women. The second or third cocktail or glass of wine may interfere. Maybe one drink helps get you in the mood and more gets in the way. You find out what works.

Consider using supplements, like Maca, amino acids, and organic testosterone boosters or female hormone balancers. Research carefully.

Can Sex Still Be Satisfying?

ED can affect the partner relationship. Sometimes wives will tell me they feel responsible. "He isn't turned on by me. He doesn't find me attractive or sexy anymore. It's my fault." Or the husband will feel embarrassed and pull away and hide that he's afraid he's losing his mojo. Or he becomes obsessed with his erections. The sooner the couple can start to talk about what is happening, the better.

Even if prostate cancer or diabetes or blood-pressure medication or antidepressants take away a man's ability to have an erection and full penetration intercourse, it is still possible to have a satisfying sex life. Creatively. Lovingly. It may involve mutual fondling and pleasuring, side by side, or oral sex or use of a vibrator or other sex toys, erotica and sexy talk. It's called "outercourse," doing everything but intercourse. It's about feeling passionate; maybe playful. It's about feeling good and responding to each other.

Even true ED need not limit sexual pleasure.

"Men don't need erections to have orgasms," says Dr. Ken Haslam, a retired anesthesiologist who teaches workshops on sex and aging, "I'm 76, and I've had wonderful orgasms without erections, thanks to manual stimulation or oral sex."

Focus on what feels good and where the husband wants to be touched and how the penis, scrotum and perineal area can be stimulated without getting an erection. Remember to explore other erogenous zones. Some men love to have their partners kiss their scalp, ear lobes, neck, nipples, back, down the spine. Even a sensuous foot rub can be a turn-on. For women, too.

And remember, husbands: even if your libido is lowered, check in with your wife. She may still be cooking and wanting some fun. Too often when the husband experiences ED or even lowered libido, sex stops. So does kissing and hugging, without a recognition that it may still be important to the wife. Keep talking about it. Show consideration for each other's needs.

It may be a surprise for some couples at this age to experience new orgasmic sensations because of the changes. Maybe it is not possible to have penile penetration of the vagina, so more attention is given to stimulating her clitoris with fingers or mouth or a vibrator. Remember that even though penetration may be exciting and feel good, the clitoris is the main focus for women. The clitoris has a much higher concentration of nerve endings than the vagina. Breast stimulation can add to the arousal. Some women tell me they have had better orgasms and more sexual satisfaction than ever before.

After Jack's surgery for prostate cancer, he lost the ability to have erections. Not willing to give up this important part of their relationship, he and Judy increased getting aroused through prolonged foreplay and fondling. They found that oral sex and mutual masturbation or self-pleasuring was very satisfying. They both missed the feelings of penetration during intercourse, so they incorporated the use of a dildo and vibrator into their lovemaking.

Use of Porn and Addiction to Porn

I have encountered several couples whose sex life was negatively affected by the husband's addiction to pornography. The easy access afforded by the Internet has caused this problem to sky-rocket. The image on the screen becomes more of a turn-on than the partner asking for closeness. The fantasy, quick arousal and orgasm becomes more of a reward than the human interaction. The reward system of the brain can get wired to crave this "fix" and an addictive pattern gets going. If this is happening in your relationship, seek professional help. If you're not sure if the behavior is at addiction level and your partner is open to discussing how this is affecting all aspects of your marriage, please do not argue or deny it is a problem. Talk about it.

The use of erotica is not the same as pornography. Erotica is sensual and sexual material prepared for respectful mutual pleasure in contrast to pornography, which is exploitative. Some couples find erotic videos and stories enhance an already healthy sex life.

Sleeping Separately

Some couples enjoy the closeness of a double bed. Others, needing to spread out, opt for larger mattresses. There's no right or wrong. That includes choosing to sleep separately, in different rooms. Sometimes it's the snoring or an injury or the need for a deep peaceful sleep. Whatever the reason, find time to cuddle. Maybe you start out together in bed, and then one moves down the hallway to fall asleep. Or maybe you have afternoon delight in one bed or the other. As we found out in *Hope Springs,* it was not just his back injury that started this couple sleeping apart.

Negative Self-Talk

For too many women it's hard to feel sexy when we feel old. Men too. In the privacy of the therapy room we talk about how hard it is to feel attractive if we have gained weight or are not as fit as we once were or have surgery scars or in general don't feel attractive. The face in the mirror is wrinkled and old looking, the skin is sagging and the breasts are no longer perky. You've read this far in the book, so you know my first recommendation, after self- examination, is to share these feelings with each other. Use affirmations. Practice acceptance. Focus on giving your body gratitude for the ways in which it lets you move or gives you pleasure. Be gentle. Be kind. Touch and kiss. We are who we are right now in mind, body and spirit. Even with the chin hairs. (Do they grow overnight?)

Dr. Northrup reports, "The number one predictor of a strong libido at menopause (and beyond) is having a new sexual partner — even for women who previously had less-than-wonderful sex lives. This doesn't mean you should throw out your partner. It means you yourself can become the new partner. As long as your head and heart are willing, your body will find a way."

Benefits of Sex As We Get Older

So we older folks have changes in hormonal levels, drier vaginas, lack of lubrication, ED, arthritic knees and shoulders and hips and thumbs and toes, weaker muscles, chronic pain, breast or prostate cancer surgery, other surgery scars, heart disease, diabetes, neuropathy, intestinal cramps, constipation or diarrhea, incontinence, urinary pads, weaker muscles, medication side effects and other changes in our bodies — and we're still thinking about sex. Amazing!

What we do know is the more sex we have, the more everything works better. For the guys and the gals. The best treatment for vaginal changes is to have more sex. Sexual activity helps keep delicate tissues moist and supple, helping the body to create more lubrication, which can reduce the risks of pain. And having orgasms, even just touching skin to skin, increases the feel-good hormones. Nitric oxide gets the neurotransmitters vibrating and the cells singing. We feel years younger.

Sensual and sexual touching lowers stress levels, reduces tension, relieves depression, eases pain, contributes to better sleep, strengthens the immune system, contributes to a healthier cardiovascular system and increases longevity. We are likely to live longer and be happier.

Joint Replacement Surgery

At our age, it is safe to say that many of us have already had joint replacement surgery. In the next chapter there is a discussion about chronic pain and sex. In this chapter I want to highlight some of the good news about sex, aging and surgery. A controlled study done by a group of orthopedic surgeons found that the sex lives of their patients improved dramatically after joint replacement surgery, specifically hip and knee.

Their findings are impressive: 42% of post-op patients reported improvement in libido, 36% reported increased intercourse duration, 41% reported increased intercourse frequency, 55% had improved sexual self- image and 84% had improvement in general well-being and 90% of patients had improved overall sexual function. Check out the safe positions for sex after joint replacement surgery. Google "safe sex positions after joint replacement" or go to peerwell.com for a discussion and guide or check with your physician or health provider.

Keep the Juices Flowing

One of my clients returned from a luscious week at the Miraval Spa in Arizona. At age 57 she decided to attend the afternoon seminar on sex and aging presented by a nurse practitioner. She quoted the presenter saying, "As you age, keep your juices flowing. Have at least one orgasm a week and put something in your vagina at least once a month: a penis, a vibrator, a dildo or a cucumber, whatever. Just take care of your vagina." My client, a single woman, giggled and said, "I guess I better get busy learning how to pleasure myself or get a partner."

In the wonderful and funny Netflix series called *Grace and Frankie,* with Lily Tomlin, Jane Fonda, Martin Sheen and Sam Waterston, the women get the brainstorm to design a vibrator for the older female user that is easier on the arthritic wrist. It becomes wildly popular. You can imagine the comedy. It is reported that vibrator sales have jumped and women over 60 account for the largest increase. Sometimes for solo use; sometimes for use with their partners.

Remember vibrators are also to enhance men's pleasure and can be helpful for ED. Joan Price has a very readable explanation of how to select a vibrator on *Senior Planet* website, Senior Guide to Vibrators. Also check out a website called *A Woman's Touch Sexuality Resource Center,* designed by a physician and a sex educator.

It's also OK sometimes to just have sex because your partner wants to even if you're not in the mood. Because women as we get older do not feel turned on as often and it takes us longer to get aroused, if we wait to have sex when we crave it, it might not happen. Desire might not precede arousal. You might find out that once lovemaking starts, and you are physically stimulated, arousal begins. It might take having sex to start feeling turned on. And then your body may catch up and get going. So women who think they need to be in the mood to have sex, might in fact need to have sex to be in the mood!

It's good to pick the right time to suggest sex, maybe when you are both rested, and not too hungry. It's also OK to let your partner off the hook if he or she is not in the mood. And it's OK to see what happens.

Sometimes the stress of living and having a lot on our minds gets in the way of being able to slow down and be in the moment in order to get aroused and enjoy lovemaking. Allow yourself to relax, get out of your head and into the whole body experience. If you find your mind somewhere else like doing the grocery list or redecorating the bedroom or going over the last conversation you had with your adult son, that's probably a sign you are not into the experience. Bring your attention to the sensation of the moment, where you are being touched or where you are touching. Take a deep breath, smile and take in the pleasure.

A brisk walk, a well-spiced meal, a comedy followed by dancing in your living room to your favorite love song may all serve to get the juices flowing. Foreplay can be all day.

An older male client laughingly told me about hearing a popular psychologist joke, saying, "I am 74 and I have sex almost every day. Almost on Monday, almost on Tuesday, almost on Wednesday ... "

Kegels

A word about doing Kegel pelvic floor exercises: it's good for both women and men. This unobtrusive exercise helps strengthen the muscles that support the bladder, bowels and the perineum. By strengthening these muscles, you can reduce or prevent urinary leakage problems. It also increase sexual satisfaction as it tones and strengthens the muscles of the vagina and the muscles that support erections. It also increases the blood flow, which contributes to arousal.

To do a Kegel, pretend you are trying to stop your urine flow. Squeeze the muscles. Just the pelvic floor muscles, not your belly or thighs. Hold the squeeze for 3 seconds. Relax for 3 seconds then hold again for 3. Repeat 10-15 squeezes per session, 3 or more times a day. Each week add another second until you can squeeze each time for 10 seconds. This is a private exercise, and you can do it anytime anywhere. To remind yourself to do it, pair the Kegel with brushing teeth or watching the news or sitting down to read the newspaper or when you are on the phone. Soon it becomes automatic.

Desire To Be Desired

Unlike Ado Annie in *Oklahoma,* who sings, "I'm just a girl who cain't say no," too often wives are the girls who CAN say no. Work on receiving the idea he desires you. Ado Annie has no trouble doing that: "What if he says you're like peaches and cream and he's gotta have cream or die? What you gonna do when he talks like that? Spit in 'is eye?"

Desire to be desired. Desire to desire. Instead of rejecting his desire, embrace the idea of being desired. And in turn, allow yourself to desire him or her. Think your way into a new way of acting. Feel your way into a new way of thinking.

Husbands tell me how much it means to them when we wives initiate making love — even just a quickie. It lets them know we desire them. Lorraine found this out when her husband Pat asked her to initiate sex more. From their interview:

Lorraine: "I thought that the man was to be the aggressor in love-making and then I joined in wholeheartedly."

Pat: "When I initiate our lovemaking, it's always wonderful. But what I'm not getting from that is whether she finds me desirable. It's always in the back of my mind, "I know that you're enjoying it, but were you really interested?"

L: "It's the most important part of the day, when we go to bed together. We spoon, we touch ... It's battery-charging."

P: "Our sex life has slowed down, but the intimacy in our marriage has grown stronger."

L: "We realize our sex life will wane, but ..."

P: "The bonding, the snuggling, the holding hands in movies become more important."

P: "We talked about playing more physically, so you (L) would be more willing to initiate sexually. We started making out like crazy." (They say the snuggling does not often result in "climax or anything," but they then spoon and go to sleep.)

L: *"Touch. Just touch, touch, touch. Hold hands. Do the things that young kids do."*

P: *"I just marvel at how much closer we've gotten over the years."*

Sexting — Old Folks Style

From my own experiences:

One night I almost missed an invitation. I had my phone on airplane mode while I was at the office seeing clients. I usually turn the phone on as I'm closing up, listening to voicemail and checking texts. This night I waited until I got to the car, connected to Bluetooth and immediately returned a phone call to a client. Then I called my sister. I was still talking to her when I arrived home and came into the house. Dinner smelled wonderful. I was hungry. Lunch was a long time ago and only soup. Then I noticed the text Tom had sent to my phone an hour earlier: "Wine is open. Beef simmering slowly. Simmering ... hmmmmm. PBear." I smiled and laughed and gave Tom a hug. "I love your invitation. Has the time passed?" "I'm too hungry now," Tom replied. "And we know what happens if we're both too hungry. Later?" "Sounds real good to me," I said, giving him an extra squeeze. I like knowing he fantasizes. I do, too. I feel a tingle and do a Kegel. Squeeze tight.

Resources

Some good resources to get you going with some new ideas include *Naked At Our Age* by Joan Price and *"The Secret Pleasures of Menopause* by Christiane Northrup, M.D. Reading the stories of others our age may help rev up your engine. Check out *Seasons of the Heart: Men and Women Talk About Love, Sex, and Romance after 60* by Zenith Henkin Gross, or *Love Sex Again* by Lauren Streicher, MD. Check out the *Senior Planet: Aging with Attitudes* website.

Steps to Enhance Romance

We've covered a lot of ground in this chapter. There is a lot to say about sex, aging and romance. So quick summary for you if you feel sex is OK and you want to bring more passion and heat it up:

- Make a date to have sex; light a candle, use a favorite scent, put on favorite music, begin slowly touching each other and build the excitement.
- Mix it up; touch body parts in different order; switch out fast and quick, soft and tender. Use a feather all over. Oral sex?
- Introduce more playfulness. Spontaneous is good. Planned is OK, too.
- Change locations. Not just the bedroom. How about the family room? The kitchen? The car? (Really?) A hotel?
- Experiment with different positions. See *The Joy of Sex.*
- Introduce sex toys or erotic literature or videos. Talk about it first. Pick them out together. (See *Naked At Our Age* website.)
- Touch more in general: hold hands, cuddle on the couch, kiss, fondle, do daily foot rubs, head massages. Dance.
- Skin on skin, naked gets the juices going and the oxytocin bonding hormone flowing.
- Speak about having sex with each other more often. Share fantasies.
- Let her know you're thinking about her. Send him a sexy text. Share special memories of sexual or sensual times together.
- Say "I love you" more often with your eyes and your touches.

~~~~Reflection~~~~

Make a date to make love. Light a candle. Put on your favorite music. Scent the bedroom with a favorite fragrance. Look into his or her eyes with a soft gaze. Start with caressing and kissing, a back rub or a foot rub. Let the clothes come off. Skin to skin. Take your time. Focus on touch. Feel the pleasure. Let yourself be in the moment. Bring your attention to where your fingertips are and where your partner's hands are on your body. Be only there. Breathe. Ahhhhhh ...

Healthy Sex Life For A Healthier You

There might be women who read this chapter and feel attacked or judged because they simply do not want to have sex. They feel that they birthed the children and have had it with "giving" their man sex. They just want to be left alone.

As a marriage therapist I struggle with this. I do not want any woman or man to feel their feelings are not supported or that how they feel is right or wrong. However, I believe that a healthy sex life is vital to a healthy marriage. Research supports this premise. So do my 40 years of experience doing therapy with couples. So do my 46 years in a committed vital marriage. Most of the couples I interviewed for the Wise Married Elder Council counted an active, healthy sex life among their strengths.

But not all of them. And we all know couples who appear happy and healthy who are not sexually active. My bottom line as a therapist is that I believe it is still important to talk about sex. It is crucial to make a mindful decision about your intimacy, sexual as well as emotional. If you are agreeing to a sexless marriage, and it is OK with both of you, then it is not a problem — nor am I in a position to judge. Couples who come to me asking for marriage therapy can be assured that I will ask about their sex life, and recommend a discussion.

Even though we baby boomers are supposed to be from the '60s "sexual revolution," we also have inherited many of the taboos from previous generations. There is still way too much shame associated with feeling sexy and being sexual. If you're nodding your head and you resonate with what I'm saying, I invite you and your partner to explore this together.

And yet there is no simple prescription for every marriage. One size does NOT fit all. You need to figure out what works best for you both. If you like the idea of "naked nightly," or "afternoon delight" keeps the home fires burning bright, you are among the couples growing older who are not letting age stop them from having the sex life they desire. Even if that's just cuddling. As one wife said to me, " Sex is good — real good. But sometimes it's the cuddling that's the best."

Tom's Note:

The lyric by Alan and Marilyn Bergman at the beginning of this book talks about the necessity of being the best of lovers, yet the best of friends. The two are inseparable. The late Leo Buscaglia would caution, "Don't just make love to a body. Make love to a person." It takes invitation, preparation and consideration. The payoff for both husband and wife can be immeasurable.

10 - When Sex Has Stopped

I listened to a wife, 62, married for 44 years, tell me that she and her husband had not had sex since they conceived their daughter, now 26 years old. They loved each other, had a happy and fulfilled life in every other way. I asked what her husband might say about the lack of sex. She shrugged and said that they hadn't talked about it for years and he had stopped touching her or even hugging or kissing years ago. "Would you be open to renewing that part of your relationship?" I asked. She again shrugged and said, "Why bother? It was so boring when we did it. I don't miss sex." "What if your husband does?" "Oh, I think he's just content to keep himself busy with all his volunteer work. I'm certainly not going to bring it up. Besides, all my girlfriends complain about their husbands begging for sex. I'm glad my husband doesn't even approach me anymore."

In this case, unless one of the spouses is motivated to pursue the subject, they will probably continue in this pattern and be OK. However, if the husband is like many who speak with me in my office, he is **not** OK about not having sex and has just given up, deciding to drop the pursuit after so many times of his wife's rejection. That's painful.

There are many reasons why sex has stopped or may have never been very good or enjoyable. Inadequate understanding of how sex can be pleasurable for both the man and the woman and an overemphasis on penetration and the male orgasm can result in boring, unsatisfying lovemaking. Childhood abuse, or trauma related to unplanned pregnancy, may set the stage for difficulties, sometimes causing a lifetime of shame, low self-esteem and chronic low-grade depression. Body image issues related to weight gain or surgery or chronic pain may cause a spouse to feel embarrassed or disinterested. A husband may not even know why his wife is so shut down. Or a wife may not understand why her husband seems so turned off. It takes energy and courage to start the conversation. And compassion.

Even though it is so difficult to get the conversation going, there is no way to get through this impasse without talking. Start out gently. Ask to talk at a good time. Try saying something like:

- "Honey, I love you. Somehow we have stopped making love. I'm not sure why. Are you not enjoying sex anymore? Or have I hurt you somehow and you are angry?"
- "Honey, I love you. I need to talk. I am not happy that we are not having sex anymore, and it seems when I bring it up you clam up. I think we need help. Would you be willing to see a therapist together? Ted gave me a name of someone who helped them out when they were having this problem."

Reassure. Ask. Then listen. Share your feelings. Make a plan. Follow up.

Seeing a trained therapist can help support the heavy lifting of creating a safe place to talk and learn the skills to deal with what is happening — in addition to helping you cope if the solution involves needing to accept a sexless marriage and pleasuring yourself. Trust that your love and commitment to each other will guide you to a better place, even if that is finding other ways to express your love.

Len and Annie's story illustrates this issue. Even though they are 10 to 15 years away from retirement, they were courageously working hard in marriage therapy, hoping to deal with issues now to help ensure more marital satisfaction later as they got older.

They started the session updating me about the summer which ended in dropping their son off at college for his freshman year and their daughter for her senior year. The wife was missing them and feeling teary, caught in that place of knowing they needed to leave to grow up and knowing their special bond was already changing. Bittersweet. Her husband had been tender and understanding. Now, halfway through the 90-minute session, Len began to speak of his "hunger" for her, for just couple time and especially for his craving to be touched. "I'm pitiful when the highlight of my week is when the physical therapist rubs my shoulder for 10 minutes," he said. "I feel like such a loser." He began to tear up as he spoke of his feelings of rejection. "I'm not even talking about sex. I just want to be touched. When you turn away, I feel so re-jected."

I watched Annie's face harden as she braced to defend herself and yet also feel compassion for her husband. She responded in a resigned voice, "I would touch you if you didn't pressure me for sex. We hug, and you right away grab me and touch my boobs."

We talked some more about how she was feeling. I suggested the standard protocol of taking sex off the table for the time being, and put-ting the wife in charge of all touch. When, how, if, where. I asked if she would be open to touching her husband (rubbing his bald head or mas-saging his back, shoulders or feet) if he agreed to not pressure to take it further. She agreed and added, "But no pouting, either, when you don't get it. I hate the pouting." He agreed and reached out across the couch for her hand. She took it and felt his squeeze. I waited in the silence to see who would speak next. A barrier had been crossed.

I know this couple had been struggling for years with finding time for their marriage relationship. Very kid-centered, they had busy lives with school activities and community groups as well as her job at a not-for-profit agency and his as a company executive. Their son leaving for college opened an opportunity to transition into more time for them-selves as well as their marriage. An obstacle has been their opposite schedules. He is an early riser, to get in his workout and get to work by 7 a.m. He's in bed by 9 p.m. Annie enjoys late-night TV before she turns in before midnight and is still sleeping when he leaves in the morning. Without children at home, their schedules might sync up better.

As the session continued I noticed Annie quietly crying as her hus-band held her hand. I asked what was going on, if she was willing to share what the tears were about. She started in a quiet voice, turning toward Len. "You know, not having sex is not all about you. It is about me. I am so mad at myself for gaining all this weight. When you married me I was thin. I've always been thin until all the fertility treatments, and then I've not been able to lose and now with all the arthritis, I hurt eve-rywhere. I'm always in pain. I hate my body. I'm just a head." She placed her hands at her neck as if to separate the two parts of herself. "I don't want to deal with my body."

Len listened, moved closer and put his arm around her. "Honey, I *know how much pain you're in and I feel badly for you. I want to help you feel better. Remember when we did have sex, you seemed to enjoy it and I enjoyed making you feel good. I've told you, I don't care if you weigh 100 pounds or 300 pounds, I love you. I want to feel closer. I can satisfy myself. I want to satisfy you." They were starting to find their way back to intimacy, emotionally and physically.*

Even though this couple are years from retirement, the work they are doing now is ensuring a more satisfying life later.

When another husband asked for guidance with his wife's refusal to have sex anymore, we spoke about what he should do. After hearing the ways in which they had discussed sex before and hearing how often his wife turned him away or got annoyed at his references to sex, I suggested that he stop asking and stop joking and have an honest conversation. I also suggested that he ask his wife if she would be open to just cuddling if he stopped expecting intercourse. In the meantime, he could use masturbation as a way to reduce his own sexual frustration and feel the pleasure as well as reap the health benefits.

It is important to get a complete physical. Talk with your doctor. Explain what is happening to your body and consider any physical explanations for the lack of sexual desire. Also be honest with yourself about self-care. Are you getting enough sleep? Exercise? Eating nutritious foods? How much alcohol are you using? Are you depressed or emotionally drained? Stressed? Are you escaping rather than facing life head-on?

If this is a chronic issue, assess whether this is the time to explore how to heal from the abuse or trauma from years ago or other issues getting in the way. Seek professional help and commit to believing you can feel better. And it is still your choice whether to resume an active sex life.

Steps to Rekindle Romance

If you have stopped having sex, consider the following:
- Agree to discuss what went wrong in the past and why sex stopped. Be open, not defensive. Listen with a loving

ear. Ask what she/he needs to feel safe. Apologize. Ask for forgiveness. Ask for a new start.

- Plan "touching sessions" with the agreement that it will be only touch in "safe zones" — like massaging the back, hands, feet or head — with the no expectation of sex, fondling or kissing, even if you get aroused. This is often called "sensate focus." Concentrate on the pleasure.
- Remember it is often not about the sex. It is about vulnerability, building trust and sharing emotional intimacy, which can lead to sexual intimacy.
- Take it slowly and lovingly.
- Stop if there is any pain with vaginal penetration. Get a gynecological examination. *Love Sex Again* by Lauren Streicher, MD, is an excellent resource, including recommendations for medications which may help. If all is OK physically, try lubricants, such as Replens. Use brands that decrease the chance of yeast infection. See *A Tired Woman's Guide to Passionate Sex* by Laurie Mintz.

Chronic Pain and Sex

It is an understatement to say that dealing with chronic pain is no fun. Of course being in pain will affect your desire to have sex and your ability to feel aroused as well as your comfort in touching and being touched. Having arthritic pain in your joints can become the primary sensation. You're feeling the pain and nothing else. Your mind is on getting some relief. Sex isn't even in the picture. Understanding brain chemistry helps here. The pleasure center of our brains can only feel one way at a time. Arousal and pain cannot coexist. Usually. A story from our life:

I was really enjoying our lovemaking. It had been too long. I had had a flare-up of my knee pain and an unfortunate hamstring muscle injury when I used a resistance weight machine at the health club incorrectly, (Darn, I am stubborn sometimes!) which was taking too long to heal. So while the pain was acute, I was not interested in sex. We were both missing our snuggle close time. Now the pain had subsided and we were having some morning delight. Just as I climaxed, my arthritic toes curled. I was making pleasure sounds just as I was saying "ouch." I told Tom, "It is the weirdest feeling to have the ecstasy of an orgasm while feeling the crunch of my arthritic toes curl. Luckily it doesn't really hurt. It just makes me chuckle." And I am reminded that I am no longer 22 or 42 or even 62.

Surgery — whether for joint replacement, cancer, hysterectomy, prostate resection or heart conditions — can affect our sex life. It's a challenge to feel sexy for quite some time after these medical procedures. Be patient with each other. Hold hands. Share. Stay close. Then when you are ready to resume active sex, take it slowly and gently. No rush. You have the rest of your life. See the section on joint replacement surgery in the previous chapter entitled Naked Nightly and Afternoon Delight.

Please do not let any of the above limitations stop you from having the physical and sexual intimacy you desire. All of these challenges can be accommodated creatively and lovingly.

If Sex Has Stopped Because Of Infidelity

When infidelity has caused a rift it might be necessary to go back and work through the stages of forgiveness for both husband and wife. (See chapter on Spirituality.) Healing involves uncovering the wound, understanding how big or serious it is and then discovering the steps to recover trust.

Part of the process is examining your own role in the marital dysfunction that preceded the affair. Sometimes a pattern of pulling away and treating each other like you're always mad at each other, or being cool and aloof, sets up a disconnection that seems hard to undo. The couple stops seeing each other as partners, on the same side of the team. They become adversaries, at odds with each other.

In my work with clients, I share the warning: Be careful not to forgive too soon. Allow the violation and the betrayal to be fully felt. Allow the wound to be known body and soul. Keep the betrayer on the hook to allow him or her to feel the consequences of their actions.

Dr. Janis Abrahms Spring, author of the books *After the Affair* and *How Can I Forgive You? The Courage to Forgive, The Freedom Not To*, speaks of four types of forgiveness: cheap forgiveness, refusing to forgive, acceptance and genuine forgiveness.

Cheap forgiveness is when the hurt one "for gives" the person who hurt them too soon. "Oh, it's all right. No problem. I'm OK." Cheap forgiveness can happen if we are afraid to really feel the hurt for fear that it will threaten the relationship. It can happen if we avoid conflict or if we are passive-aggressive, where we say we forgive but get back at the person by emotionally distancing, giving the cold shoulder and forgoing any chance of healing and rebuilding the closeness. Cheap forgiveness is also offered by the "self-sacrificer," who identifies as the victim who does all for others and never gets her own needs met. Not fun to be around.

In my practice, sometimes wives (or husbands) who discover an affair go through the hurt and anger stage very quickly and move to the make-up stage, complete with benefits. This may be an attempt to bypass the real hurt and also to avoid looking at the dysfunction in the relationship which includes their part in not meeting the other's needs. They enter therapy wanting to patch things up and start over. Until they go back and look at what happened, the quick fix doesn't last. They may do some surface marital work and feel better, maybe happier than they've been for a long time.

However, a year or two later, they are back questioning if the marriage can survive. Maybe then they start to do the real work of building relationship skills like communication, conflict resolution, increasing intimacy (emotional as well as sexual) and learning truly who they are individually and then as a couple. They learn how to meet each other's needs as well as their own. This is genuine forgiveness.

For many couples, the best of their years together is reason enough to explore reconstruction of the marriage. The hard work pays off, and both benefit from a renewal of love and commitment. So do children and grandchildren and other loved ones. It is such a joy to be around a couple who have found each other again and have a renewed appreciation for each other at a deeper level. The opposite is also true. It is an energy drag to be around couples who have stopped caring. After your hard work of renewal, this is a good time to plan a celebration or even a recommitment of wedding vows ceremony — or at least a mighty fine anniversary party.

~~~~Reflection~~~~

If your marriage has suffered infidelity, take a moment to reflect on where you are in the healing process and how this affects your sexual experience of each other. Discuss. Express appreciation for ways each of you contributed to your healing. Identify other ways you could continue to deepen your intimacy and trust.

If you have not experienced infidelity, think about a friend or other couple you know who have been through this. Discuss the experience of watching them and what you learned about yourself. Identify strengths in your own marriage which help keep you "affair-proof."

A healing chant I use for myself and for others is a blessing by Melanie DeMore. Check this out on YouTube, *Sending You Light,* as sung at "The Mother's House."

I am sending you Light
To heal you
To hold you
I am sending you Light
To hold you in Love.

Being Your Best Self

11 - *Personal Development: Rediscovering Yourself and Each Other*

The questions come quickly: "Who am I if I'm not working? Who am I if I'm not a professional or have a career or a job? What is my value if I'm not producing or bringing in money? What is my self-worth? Am I just being and not doing? Is it OK to just be and not do? What am I missing in my life? What do I want to do less of? What do I want to do more of? What parts of myself have I neglected because of work and other busyness?"

Often work life has been about achieving and accomplishing. Sometimes people are resistant to planning retirement for fear that they will be "put out to pasture," which may feel like giving up or being put on the sidelines. Instead, retirement can be a time of setting new priorities, deciding what is most important in your remaining years and planning how you and your spouse want to make the best of them. It is about quality, not quantity. It is about building upon the rich life experiences you bring to this time and living with more choice and freedom.

Retirement offers the opportunity to remake yourself. A reboot. Getting to know your spouse better starts with making sure you know yourself better. Affirm your strengths and understand your cutting edges. Check out Strength Finder or The Enneagram or other inventories. Discover where you need to grow. Assess whether you are thriving or just surviving.

Check a park district brochure, community college catalog, lifelong learning institute, or retreat center bulletin. Check local newspaper listings of events, plays, lectures, live music. Review lists of volunteer opportunities. Mark all of them from most to least interesting, and go back and see if there is a pattern. Talk with your friends and your spouse about the process. Make a commitment to try something new soon. At our age it is tempting to just coast. Or to stagnate and then deteriorate. We need to keep awake to possibilities.

As you deepen your relationship with your partner, also deepen your relationship with yourself on all levels: spiritually, psychologically, emotionally, physically, sexually.

Reboot Your Perceptions

It is important to update the information stored on your "hard drive" about yourself and also about your spouse. Rejuvenate. Renew. Rediscover what attracted you in the first place and reclaim mutually pleasing memories.

How would you describe your spouse? What is their personality? How would they describe you? Now ask yourself the same questions. You get the idea. Take the time and attention to really know each other. On an intuitive level you might already be adapting your response to your spouse's personality without even being aware. On another level, ask yourself how each of you has changed over the years and how the changes affected your marriage.

If you notice there is a change in personality of your spouse or he or she suddenly does things out of the ordinary, take note of it and talk about it. It could indicate a change in health, depression or a medication side effect. Or it might be an emerging self needing to develop, now that there is the time and freedom in retirement.

Do we attract opposites or someone like ourselves? You can probably think of examples of both or some variations of both. This idea is important only in terms of understanding your own style and how that interfaces with your partner. Is one of you a pessimist and the other an optimist? If so, it's good to talk about your expectations before you start a project or go on an excursion. How do you butt up against each other? When she's angry is it better to give her space or ask her directly? When you're angry, what do you need? How do you complement each other? How do his strengths balance yours? How do your gifts enhance the marriage?

If one of you is an introvert and the other an extrovert, there is a built-in difference that is important to understand and accommodate. Neither is right or wrong, although in our biased culture, extroverts are seen more as "winners" and introverts as "shy." Susan Cain, in her excellent book *Quiet: The Power of Introverts in a World That Can't Stop Talking,* writes, "At least one-third of the people we know are introverts. They are the ones who prefer listening to speaking, reading to partying; who innovate and create but dislike self-promotion; who favor working on their own over brainstorming in teams. ... There's zero correlation between being the best talker and having the best ideas."

The introvert often has strong social skills and enjoys gatherings but may feel overstimulated, drained and want to go home before the extrovert is ready to leave. The extrovert gets energized by other people and can't get enough, whereas the introvert gets filled up quickly and needs to be alone to regroup.

I often recommend a couple complete the Myers-Briggs Inventory and then discuss their differences in thinking, feeling, problem-solving and how their brains work. It's helpful when the wife understands that as an extrovert, she speaks her process out loud and may meander all over until she arrives at a decision, whereas her introvert husband keeps his thoughts private until he has considered all the angles and then still might not share his conclusions. For the extrovert, it doesn't feel real until it is said out loud to someone. In contrast, the introvert has a very rich, satisfying inner life. Each has value. As Cain says, "We have two ears and one mouth, and we should use them proportionally."

The Yes/No Pattern

It was so helpful when I understood a pattern Tom and I have in our marriage. I'm too ready to jump on an opportunity and say yes and then be overcommitted. The opposite is true of my husband. My default setting is YES! His is NO! I went through a time in our marriage where this pattern really discouraged me. I even wondered if we were a good match. But then I looked at our pattern more closely. I realized that although Tom often said no initially, he would say "yes" or "maybe" or "I'll consider it," if I gave him time to think about it or adjust to the change in plans.

I wondered if this pattern started even before his first breath, after his Mom's labor was induced (on a Friday the 13th, no less). I'm not sure this little baby was ready yet to come out into the world. I pictured him trying to put on the brakes in utero, "No, no. I'm not ready yet! Stop the train, I want to get off!" Whereas I was born a week early more than ready to greet the world, showing my lifelong pattern of impatience. "Now or yesterday, and more, please." (Tom's woo-woo scale is engaged fully here.)

Tom's initial resistance fits well with my over-exuberance. He balances me and tempers me and has saved me from some potential disasters. Now when I propose an idea, I wait for the no, then reintroduce the idea later with more discussion and lots of reassurance of choice. Over the years he knows I rarely push anything unless I really feel strongly and, if I do, he respects me. We balance each other well.

How Have Events in Your Life Shaped You?

It is interesting to realize we are every age we've ever been. We carry from each age the emotional and physical memories, scripts and messages. The more impactful the event, the deeper the impression. As we explore how life has shaped us into the people we are now, we can do a review of our lifeline. This involves going back over the major events in your life. Start with your childhood. Think about your age and your circumstances, where you were living, who you were with, what happened and how events affected you. Review memories from puberty, high school, early adulthood, your 30s, 40s, 50s, 60s and on. Reflect on the events of your life as a child, teenager, adult, and your married life. Write in a journal or talk — or both. A worksheet, a chart for a life timeline review, is available for download on the website. For purposes of illustration, let me share an example from my review:

As a child, we moved frequently because of my dad's job. I moved six times before I left for college. I had to get really good at being the new kid on the block and making friends at school. On the downside, I didn't know how to develop lasting friendships. On the upside, I learned how to make friends quickly. The family message was to carry on and deal with the changes without letting the emotions get us down. Unless you can do something about it, don't feel it. So it was not acceptable to feel my grief and loss and anger at having to move and give up friends and activities and start all over. I stuffed it down and put on a happy face. "Be a good sport, Sally," my parents would say. "It will be a new adventure." As an adult, I had to learn how to be real with my emotions and to learn what anger and sadness really felt like. To own it, feel it — and then let it go.

Another example: I grew up not feeling attractive. I was pudgy, had glasses, acne and, for a while, two silver-capped front teeth. But I was really smart. And a good listener. And I could sing and act so I had many opportunities to perform. And I was also fortunate because I had a bubbly personality, so I dated a lot from age 14 on. When I met Tom I was ripe for someone who was also affirming and sexy and smart and patient.

One of the events from Tom's life which helped shape him was being drafted into the Army out of graduate school, putting his life and dreams on hold for three years. (Gratefully, all his service was stateside during the Vietnam War.) Another event earlier in his life was working with his dad at a church fundraiser car wash. He wanted to go home after he had put in the hours they had signed up for. His dad looked around, saw there was still work to do and not enough volunteers, and said, "You don't leave when your time is up. You leave when the work is done." That moment became a life theme.

~~~~Reflection I~~~~

Do the life timeline review and pick a few events to share with your partner. Discuss the effect of each event on your life, and then go further to talk about its formative effect on your marriage.

~~~~Reflection II~~~~

As you do the life timeline review, think of when — as a child or an adult

— you faced a challenge and felt successful. What strengths did you access? What messages did you carry away about yourself? Now think of a time in your marriage where you both successfully faced a challenge together. How did this strengthen your marital bond? How do you use this foundation now as you face the challenges of retirement and aging? If you want to go deeper, think of a an event that stopped you cold and resulted in sadness or despair. Examine how this changed your life and how you coped. Share this with your partner.

Married-60-years Lifespan

Imagine a timeline of the lifespan of a couple married 60 years. Look at the amount of time spent in childrearing. It will be just a fraction — albeit a large one — of the length of the marriage. Happy couples in long-term marriages have wisely continued to nurture their own needs, as individuals and as a couple, while balancing the needs of their children. When couples are too child-centered they lose some of their own couple connection. They need to intentionally work at re-orienting, especially when the children hit adolescence or "leave the nest." The retirement transition is another opportunity to get it right. Rediscover what brought you together. Fall in love again. Rekindle the spark. Learn anew.

Barbara Bradley Hagerty, author of *Life Reimagined,* interviewed hundreds of people, including neuroscientists, medical doctors, psychologists, academicians and folks in their 40s, 50s and 60s about the process of aging and specifically about midlife. She writes, "Researchers today who have examined people across their life spans, peered inside their brains, uncoiled their hopes and fears, and observed how they deal with love and alienation, trauma and death, good and evil, say that midlife is a time of renewal, not crisis. This is a time when you shift gears — a temporary pause, yes, but not a prolonged stall. In fact, you are moving forward to a new place in life. This moment can be exhilarating rather than terrifying, informed by the experiences of your past and shaped by the promise of your future."

Taking Each Other For Granted

It is normal to pay more attention to the new and take the old for granted. That is one of the reasons why travel can be so invigorating. Seeing new sights and having new experiences can awaken our senses and help us feel more alive. One of the complaints about being in a long-term marriage is that we are at risk of tuning out our spouse. We actually stop seeing him/her. We stop noticing what they are wearing (seen it before, boring), the new haircut, maybe even what they are saying.

When we study the brain, we find that this phenomenon is related to our survival. We get acclimated in situations which are familiar. We notice less. Our brain gets less vigilant, and less aware of differences. The theory is that the brain is being more efficient, which is good for our survival overall. It keeps the brain's resources more tuned in to protecting us in new situations and assessing for danger. However, in long-term relationships it can contribute to being so comfortable that we feel bored with each other and take each other for granted. We might crave stability, while the brain craves novelty and excitement.

A remedy for this is to introduce more excitement into the marriage. Do new experiences. See each other with new eyes. Really look. Listen to each other with new ears. Bring attention to the sensation of exploring as if you are discovering each other for the first time. It takes a shift in perspective.

As you do this for your spouse, do so for yourself. Stretch your own view of yourself by deliberately placing yourself in new situations. Explore what interests you. Examine where you may be getting too comfortable and push yourself.

For example, a few years ago, I needed to travel for a work conference. I realized I had not traveled alone for many years. I had become used to Tom (or colleagues or friends) making the arrangements. As I imagined getting to the airport and fetching the rental car and finding my way to the hotel I started feeling anxious. I almost talked myself out of going. I reminded myself that when I was younger I used to travel alone and take care of these arrangements independently with no problem. I vowed to not allow my discomfort to stop me from taking risks or giving up the independence I value. For as long as I am capable. (I'm giggling as I write this, picturing myself as this funny looking 90-year-old schlepping through the airport wheeling my bags, determined to do it myself!)

Parts of Self

Know thyself. In my practice both with individuals and couples, I use a technique from psychosynthesis called voice dialogue. It's a process of identifying the parts of ourselves, or the "voices." Almost all of us have an "achiever" who motivates us to go to work, the "critic" who corrects us when we are wrong, the "inner child" who holds the hurt, the "playful child" who is ready to explore and have fun, the "artist" who loves to create beauty, and the "nurturer" who comforts and reminds us to be gentle with ourselves. We also have parts of ourselves we might disown or deny, like "the vulnerable child," "the naughty child," "the angry one," "the lazy one" or "the cheat."

It is important to give attention to all our parts, especially the disowned parts which can sometimes take over if not given proper attention. The more we can know all our parts, the more we can understand why we behave as we do. You can think of this as conducting an orchestra. You are the conductor. Your parts are the instruments. Each instrument has its part in the score, its own voice, combining in harmony to make beautiful sound. If a part or instrument is denied or is hushed, that player might protest and play even louder and then cause dissonance.

In their work *Embracing Ourselves,* Hal and Sidra Stone suggest couples spend time getting to know each other's personality parts. It can be fun and enlightening.

It's also important to ask what parts of yourself have been neglected because of work schedules or other demands on your time, like caring for your ailing parents or your grandchildren. For example, maybe you miss working on hobbies or art projects, or demonstrating or volunteering for your activism causes, or playing a musical instrument or singing, photography, trying new recipes in the kitchen or birdwatching or hiking in the forest preserve. Ask yourself what you used to enjoy that might enrich your life now.

My colleague, Dr. Jeanette Zweifel, has written a book called *Will the Real Me Stand Up?* in which she describes using the voice dialogue method in journaling with yourself to better understand how your parts interact. I'll use a personal story to illustrate:

Jeanette helped me during a time in my life when I was exploring a neglected part of myself: the singer/performer. I had really enjoyed doing musicals in high school and during my first year of college, and I had always sung in church choir. Years later I decided to start voice lessons just for fun and as a stress reliever. It was impossible to think about stressful things while focusing on voice technique and learning an aria in Italian. On a whim, I submitted an audition tape for the chorus for a summer opera music festival. Instead of a chorus part, I was offered a major supporting role (Zita in the opera "Gianni Schicchi.") I freaked. I was so excited and yet so scared. I hadn't been on stage for 20-plus years. I started rehearsing in earnest and realized I was paralyzed by fear.

Jeanette used voice dialogue with me to identify where I was stuck. I discovered a little girl part of me who had been traumatized when I sang a solo in church when I was only about 4 years old. That little girl was having no part of this opera deal. I also discovered the business/entrepreneur part that thought it was stupid to take a six-week break from my private practice and lose all that income. The mother part of me was OK because I knew my kids would be well cared for by Tom. After negotiating agreements with the strong voices of these parts, I was able to move forward and had a wonderful time going on tour and hanging out with the real professional musicians. I ended up doing two more tours with the festival and having my daughter, then 9 years old, perform with me in one of the operas ("Susannah").

Another example involves a couple I worked with where the husband, a graphic artist and a mellow Type B, was married to a very driven businesswoman and a Type A.

They often felt out of sync. He had a very well developed "playful child" and was always ready for adventure and outings and didn't care much about the weekly budget. Their three children loved hanging out with Dad, especially when it included stops for ice cream. Mom wanted everyone to finish cleaning their rooms and doing their chores before going out. Mom also wanted to keep on a schedule. As we worked together the husband asked the wife to "chill" and the wife asked the husband to agree to take more responsibility. As they continued improving their marriage, they extended their "parts work" and decided to each develop a more playful creative "sexy part" who had fun flirting and letting each other know when, how and where they wanted to make love. I recently checked in with them. Their children are grown and out of the house. The husband is planning his retirement soon. Their marriage is good, and they reassured me that their "sexy parts" still have a lot of fun.

~~~~Reflection III~~~~

Take a moment and reflect on your parts of self. Whose voice is the loudest these days? Whose voice is neglected? What do you miss about yourself? What are you pleased about? Discuss with your partner.

Retirement allows for more time to fully explore your own personality as well as your partner's. In a long-term marriage it's not always about changing oneself or one's partner. It is more about acceptance and managing from a place of compassion.

When my husband tells a story I have heard a hundred times, if I'm feeling grouchy, I'll not-so-nicely tell him, "Heard that, done that." If I'm being nice and remembering to practice what I preach, I'll dig deeper. I'll ask a question underlying the story. I'll probe and often find a gem —- a story he hasn't shared after all these 46 years. I smile, and again am grateful for this marvelous man with whom I have the privilege to share my life.

Perceptions of Aging and Retiring

We carry into retirement our perceptions of aging and getting older. It is important to examine those belief systems, especially the unconscious ones as they hold power over our feelings about ourselves and the choices we make about if and when to retire, or what retirement and aging looks like.

Examining our beliefs about "being retired" and growing older includes looking at our role models. In my family, my parents lived to be 89 and 93. My dad retired from full-time ministry at 68 and then worked part-time for another 20 years. His creativity kept flowing even when the morphine for his pain in the last years would sometimes dull his mind. My mother kept active with volunteering for a literacy project and at her library and church — and of course being very involved in the lives of her brood. The first signs of her dementia were pulling away from life and moving into social isolation. She started not to care about people and things in the way she used to. Alzheimer's started taking her away. It is the long good-bye.

My husband's mother died at 92 and was very active and vibrant up to the last year, declining after a hard fall. Tom's father died at 60, 18 months after being diagnosed with ALS after years of hard work and long hours with few vacations as manager of an optical shop, making eyeglasses. There had been little talk about his retirement. Tom's mom felt robbed of her many dreams for travel and a more relaxed life with her husband. She still had a son in high school and a daughter beginning college, along with three older adult children. She depended on her faith and her optimistic outlook and lived the next 34 years without her loving spouse. She continued to enrich the lives of her children, grandchildren and great-grandchildren who love her and miss her now.

Look at how long your relatives lived and how well they lived their lives. As they aged, did they stay active and engaged or did they check out and sit staring at the TV, complaining about how life used to be? What did you observe about your parents' marriage after they retired and as they aged? Or if they divorced, how did they live into their older years? If they died earlier, how does that affect your own perceptions of your life span? Maybe one or both of your parents are still alive. You might ask them these same questions and initiate a discussion about what makes a good life as we get older.

We look to our family for role models. We also look to others we encounter. When I see a grouchy old person who seems bitter, judgmental and complaining, I remind myself how I do not want to be. When I see an older woman or man whose face is glowing, eyes sparkly, actively moving and laughing, I notice my enjoyment. I smile and feel inspired. In turn, I realize my demeanor affects others just like theirs did me.

I enjoyed a column by Eric Zorn in The Chicago Tribune, in which he writes about his expectations about aging as he turned 60. His words are echoed in the advice from the Wise Married Elders.

"This aging thing stops right here, right now. I turn 60 this week. I know, I know. By my generally dyspeptic attitude and hectoring tone you thought I was much older already. But nope. Just 60. And by stopping the process I don't mean cosmetically, sartorially or even, necessarily, physically. The body wears down. That's nature's way. I'm not going to become one of those spry seniors who competes in triathlons, takes fistfuls of vitamins, dresses like a 25-year-old and hires plastic surgeons to smooth over the ravages of time. I'll try to keep active, healthy and neat, of course. But mostly I'm talking here about putting a stop to the emotional process of aging — to the hardening and narrowing of thought, the skepticism and technophobia, the world-weariness and complacency that often seem to afflict people as they get older. So I've assembled a list of what I'm calling new-decade resolutions — a set of 14 rules to try to live by so as not to become a certifiable codger."

His 14 rules include limiting discussion of aches and pains, staying curious, listening to the wisdom of those who love you, keeping your mind open, remembering to smile, cultivating hobbies which helps you find new friends, and keep moving. Get good hearing aids when the time comes to stay connected. His final rule: "Don't hide — or hide behind — your age. It's at least partially a state of mind. Even as the years drag you down, don't let them define you. Be grateful for, not resentful of, the number of days you have been granted."

Tom's Note

These detailed personality inventories are a lot of hard work. If it's more work than fun, put them aside for awhile and enjoy what you've learned so far. Sally's book is not "Personal Development for Dummies." She did not write "The CliffsNotes for Life." But it's not just about the work. Enjoy the journey.

12 - Health: Laugh, Move, and Green Smoothies

"Health isn't just the absence of disease. It's being physically and emotionally able to live joyfully and in alignment with your deepest self. You have the ability to build health every day. Just be open to new ideas and to adopting new habits."

— *Christiane Northrup, M.D.*

Retirement affords the time and resources to focus on improving emotional and physical health. From most of the couples we interviewed, the prevailing advice is to move your body. Incorporate regular exercise into your daily routine. Research supports this prescription.

Exercising together as a couple may be the answer. Nita and Kent found it helpful to hire a personal trainer who specializes in working with older bodies. Lynn and Dave found physical therapy, prescribed by their doctors, helped teach them the stretching and resistance exercises to alleviate pain from chronic conditions. Pat and Lorraine live in an active adult community and are avid hikers and cyclists. They enjoy the trails near their home as well as across the country and beyond.

For other couples, exercising at different times and in different ways fits their needs better. Eileen enjoys her gentle yoga and tai chi. Her husband, Lou, counts on his aerobic and cross-training classes to keep up his stamina for his part-time job as a hockey referee. Ken loves his walks around the neighborhood doing his 10,000 steps and Jeanette loves her daily swimming, tai chi and yoga. Terry walks along the beach while Cheri uses the machines at the fitness club to give her a good workout.

Don and Denise, both in their 80s, are retired missionaries from South America. They are inspiring. They come to the health club every day except Sunday. I met them in my arthritis water aerobics class. They are quick to smile, laugh and tell jokes about each other. They have also survived and supported each other through several health crises as well as loving their children and grandchildren through the ups and downs of life.

Sherry has always enjoyed dancing as her form of exercise, stress relief and fun. Now in retirement, after a hip replacement, she and her husband John are competing in ballroom dancing competitions across the country. They make quite the attractive couple in their fancy costumes and big smiles.

For couples who are lifelong athletes, their transition into an active retirement will be a reflection of an active life already well established. My sister and her husband, both internists, bicycle or walk the two miles to their clinic every day and run, hike and cross-country ski on weekends, My other younger sister and her husband are lifelong campers and backpackers and practice daily yoga. Now with replaced knees they are back to walking miles a day and enjoying their active lifestyle. Even as my older brother's Parkinson's has progressed he and his wife will cross country ski, walk or bike on his good days.

Many park districts and senior living facilities (many of which allow non-residents to participate) offer classes in Pilates, chair yoga, weight training, high intensity workouts, stretching bands, ballroom dancing, Zumba or aerobics, as well as access to workout machines and personal training advice. Pools for water aerobics or lap swimming are available. Fees can be reasonable. And there is always walking, at no cost, with excellent benefits.

For home use consider DVDs or online videos for aerobic dancing or yoga. Lee Holden has a DVD, Qi Gong for Seniors, where his exercise partner is his mom. The exercises boost circulation and deep breathing while gently stretching the joints and muscles. Using a FitBit or a pedometer can be reinforcing as you see the numbers of steps tracked, your heart rate and sleep cycles monitored, good information to know.

I've included these stories to illustrate the strong message that comes through from our interviews with the Wise Married Elders. With only a few exceptions, our interviewees are committed to fitness. Some came late to the game after they retired. Others have been doing it their whole lives. It's as natural as the daily habit of brushing their teeth. Research documents the value of exercise, including positive impact on brain health.

However you decide to do it, exercise, fitness and nutrition all contribute to a healthful retirement and aging process. This may be the perfect time to try those recipes you've been saving. There is no greater wealth than health.

As my husband says, "Any kind of movement is good." Tom, a former racquetball player, gets to the gym two or three times a week and walks or works outdoors when weather permits. I had also been a lifelong exerciser until I let chronic pain sidetrack me. It's been more difficult to get back into a routine. I'm hoping that as I move more into part-time work, it will be easier. I know my body tells me when I've been neglectful. I'm inspired when I remind myself we're both in training for our hoped-for trip to Italy, walking up and down those hills.

~~~~Reflection I~~~~

Take a quiet moment. Close your eyes. Take a few deep breaths, exhaling tension and allowing yourself to calm your mind. Now with each breath, be aware of your body. Feel each breath as it comes in and goes out. Bring attention to each part of your body, starting at the top of your head and moving down to your toes. What are you aware of? Imagine your body sending you messages or talking to you. What is your body saying? What does your body need? Our bodies know. Now ask the same questions about your mind and your spirit. Tune into the deeper wisdom. Take another deep breath. Thank your body for working with you. Open your eyes and take a moment to write down this experience.

~~~~Reflection II~~~~

A variation on the above exercise is to give yourself a self-massage, touching all the places you can reach and tuning into what your fingertips are telling you. Even if this sounds a bit far out for you, give it a try. Plus it just feels good. If your partner is willing, do it for each other.

Resistant Partner

What do you do if your spouse is not on board and is resisting joining you in a focus on fitness and eating for good health? Do what you can to ease the way. Express your concerns, then let it go. You can only change yourself. Nagging and hinting are counterproductive and may build up more resistance. Respect your spouse's journey. However, increase attention to yourself. Be in charge of your own health decisions. Do not compromise for the sake of harmony. You have an intuitive and educated sense of what is right for you.

My husband would take a shot of my green juices — grudgingly — but when I started doing smoothies, he put his foot down. However, he willingly buys the organic vegetables I request, and also tends and harvests our garden with me. He teases me good-naturedly, but knows my green smoothies reduce the inflammation and pain of my osteoarthritis and give me what my body needs nutritionally. I know he's pleased that I'm taking care of myself.

I chuckled as our 7-year-old grandson was helping make the salad for our July 4 picnic. He looked in the salad bowl and took out some purple cabbage. As he munched, he commented on all the colors of the red tomatoes and yellow and orange peppers and black olives and green broccoli and told me, "You know, Grandma, you need to eat the rainbow to be healthy." He's got it all figured out.

Tom's advice: Enjoy what you eat. Unless your physician specifically says otherwise, there are no bad foods in small portions. (Do we really want a life without chocolate, ice cream, cookies and popcorn?) If meals are not an occasion for enjoyment, we've lost a major source of pleasure and satisfaction.

Be Your Own Advocate

Embrace your role in being your own best health advocate. Put together a medical team with your primary care physician and any specialists you need. Find professionals who take the time to listen to your concerns and are knowledgeable about research related to the aging body. If you think your team is unwilling to think beyond traditional medicine, ask why. Be inquisitive, be informed, be proactive. If offered medication for symptoms, ask these two questions:

1. Is there a lifestyle change I can make first to avoid taking this medication?
2. What is the underlying cause of the condition the medication is meant to treat?

Often seniors have multiple doctors for different conditions and may not have an internist who is coordinating care. If we lack a connection with our health care providers and do not feel we are part of our own team for wellness, it may be easier just to take the prescription, fill it and be passive about own own health care. As a couple, help each other take active roles.

Since I have struggled my whole life with weight management, it has been important to me to have medical providers who are well-informed and use the health-at-every-size approach. Our health is too important to allow ourselves to be shamed or mistreated in medical settings. Remember, you are the expert on yourself. Help your partner to be the expert on his or her health.

Self-Care

There are so many self-care methods that can help ensure better health, boost our immune system, help prevent illness, and help us feel more vital and energetic. Talk to friends. Read. Put advice through your own truth filter of what is best for you. Check with your doctor.

- Understand that what we eat is more than just fuel. Food is medicine. Some folks are intolerant to gluten or dairy or eggs; others respond better to a vegan plant-based diet or a low-carb, moderate-protein, high-good-fat regimen or feel better with less sugar. Some respond to three square meals a day, some to 5-7 small grazing meals, others to interval fasting. Explore herbs and spices. Find out how to make broccoli taste good. While it can be a challenge when you are following different regimens, find out what works best for you and your partner.

- Drink more water. Don't wait till you're actually thirsty.
- Massage. Invest in regular massage from a licensed massage therapist. The health benefits are numerous plus it feels so good.
- Get to know your partner's body with massage — in this case, non-sexual touching. Start with a hand massage or a foot massage or back rub. Once a month, light a candle, turn off the cell phones, put on some soft soothing music and have your partner lie on the edge of the bed or couch or padded tabletop, or invest in a massage table.
- Check out complementary and alternative health services: chiropractic, acupuncture, nutrition coaching, supplements, EFT (Emotional Freedom Technique), tapping, reflexology, essential oils, facials, homeopathy, yoga, tai chi, chi gong, meditation classes, healing touch, energy medicine, sound baths, drumming, music therapy, dance parties.
- Psychotherapy, depression and anxiety screening and management.
- Physical and occupational therapy, especially for injuries and chronic pain.
- Support groups for caregivers, grief, addiction, weight management, etc.
- Regular physical, dental, hearing and vision exams.
- Add brain stimulation games and exercises to your daily routine, such as Lumosity or Cognifit, crossword puzzles, sudoku, learning a new language or taking piano or dance lessons to help grow those brain dendrites and new neural pathways.
- Websites like drnorthrup.com, or

aarp.org/health/healthy-living and seniorplanet.org.

- Time in nature. Soak in the beauty and health benefits of sunshine, fresh air, trees, water, mountains, deserts, oceans, sunrises and sunsets. Try leisurely paddling a kayak on quiet water.

Hearing Loss and the Brain

It is important to expand on the ideas about getting our hearing tested and using hearing aids as soon as needed. Many of the WME older couples shared stories of getting their hearing tested and being surprised with the results. The hearing aids made life better for the couple, greatly improved communication and cut down on a source of irritation. Jeanette noticed Ken starting to isolate as he began to lose his hearing. It impacted their relationship and how he related to family and friends. His already introverted self became even more withdrawn, changing his personality.

George, who wears hearing aids and has benefitted from cochlear implant surgery, shared what his audiologist taught him: "She educated me about what happens to the brain as one loses hearing. That part of the brain starts to sign off, check out and actually atrophies, causing not only hearing loss but also cognitive decline. Hearing loss is correlated with increase in dementia." In addition to improving communication with friends and loved ones, hearing aids are also good for the brain. The audiologist also suggested using brain stimulation games to keep building brain resilience.

Memory Loss

One of the concerns I hear expressed in the over-65 age group and that I also have about myself and my partner is about the difference between memory loss that is "normal" aging and memory loss that indicates the beginning of dementia. There are some sites you can check out listed in Notes & Resources. Certainly bringing this concern to your primary care physician may be helpful. Notice if you are asking the same question because you can't remember the answer or your partner repeats the same question he asked five minutes ago. I monitor myself noting when I recall new information which means my brain is still recording new information by putting down new neural pathways. In cases of declining memory due to dementia the brain loses its ability to record new information. Sometimes my short term memory loss may be due to inattention. I'm not paying attention so it is not be recorded. As one wife said in speaking about her husband, "He can tell you who played what yesterday in the game and who scored this but he can't remember what I told him about my schedule." Probably not dementia. Maybe lack of attention or selective memory — or hearing loss.

Misplacing an item or forgetting a name or an appointment may be "normal" memory problems. It is more concerning if you notice difficulty sequencing steps to completion of a project, getting easily distracted and having difficulty completing everyday tasks, having difficulty solving problems and showing poor judgment, and an inability to work with numbers or pay the bills, losing location or sense of time, date and place, and having a change in personality, especially a dramatic increase in anxiety. Ask for an evaluation. Information helps decide the next step. In the meantime, pay closer attention to how you pay attention. Commit to brain stimulation programs. Learn a new skill. Stretch and grow.

Emotional And Psychological Health

Since I am a psychotherapist, it is no surprise that I want to bring your specific attention to your emotional and psychological health. I particularly want to encourage you to seek professional services if you are concerned about depression, anxiety or have suicidal thoughts. If you have similar concerns about your partner, deal with them — especially if you notice a sudden change in your partner's personality and energy level, such as lethargy, unusual irritability or explosive anger. Watch for abrupt loss of memory or difficulty forming sentences. These could be signs of a medical condition or medication side effect needing evaluation and treatment. Act promptly. Delay is not likely to help.

Loneliness is being identified more as a health concern in recent years. Even married people can feel lonely. Neuroscientists have identified regions of the brain that respond to loneliness, and a powerful body of research shows that lonely people are more likely to become ill, experience cognitive decline and have shorter lives. In some studies, people who feel lonely are more likely to be depressed, sleep and eat poorly, use more alcohol and exercise less. We know there are health benefits to be socially connected. If you identify with this picture, please reach out. Talk to your partner. Seek help. Join a support group. Call a friend. The recent sharp increase in completed suicides in 50- to 65-year-olds is alarming and calls attention to the need for more awareness, better services and education.

Mid-life and beyond presents an excellent time to heal our emotional wounds. I believe that when we ask to be healed, what needs to be healed in us comes up to the surface, accompanied with ideas from our inner wisdom of what we need. As we get older, our tolerance for being distressed can decrease and our willingness to do what is necessary can increase. I have also found that when we are ready to let go of past hurt, trauma or distress, we can be laser-focused and get to a place of peace quickly. Sharing with our partners increases our bond, and we feel closer because we faced an ordeal together.

Unexpressed emotion or stored hurt can show up in our bodies. If we are feeling distress or chronic pain it is therapeutic to ask, "What am I carrying?" One client noticed that her hip pain got worse when she was dealing with crisis issues related to her adult son. Psychotherapy and physical therapy brought relief.

When I'm aware of feeling burdened or tired, I sometimes ask myself, "What do I need to allow myself to feel? When I sit quietly with that question often what comes up is sadness or anger (or sometimes I just need a nap!). Since I am a slow responder (meaning it takes me awhile to let my feelings catch up with my awareness), I occasionally need to do an emotional "detox," letting go of built-up feelings. And because I'm tuned in to others' feelings I can unknowingly absorb, I also do what I call "fluffing my aura," cleaning it out, shaking it off.

Feelings are just messages. They are meant to tell us something, much as we experience other signals like hunger, heat or cold. We love feeling happy and joyful. Notice and amplify these feelings and combine them with gratitude, breathing in deeply, then letting it go to be ready for the next wave of feelings. In contrast, anger, fear, guilt resentment, grief, anxiety are signals that something is out of balance and needs attention. So we need to get the message, feel the feeling, then stop holding on to bad thoughts. It is in holding on that we create imbalance, distress, dis-ease and illness.

There is so much loss to deal with at our ages. The losses that are inevitable with our aging bodies, the losses that come with retirement and change, and the grief of losing our loved ones. Emotional wellness means getting really good at grieving. Feeling the grief, moving the sadness through and then letting it go so you can feel happiness, joy and other feelings again. We discuss grief in more depth in Chapter 14.

Delores, 72, noticed that she was snapping at her husband more often and would get set off by her granddaughter's temper tantrums. This usually calm woman was feeling very upset. She had found psychotherapy helpful in her early years of marriage. She decided to try it again; she knew she needed some relief. During our first session, after she talked about what brought her to make an appointment, I asked her about her physical health, pain level, stress level, recent events, and what she did for her own self-care. Through her tears she spoke of the sudden death of her brother six weeks before and then described a disturbing interaction she had with her sister at the memorial service. She had spoken with her husband about it, but she was still carrying the hurt and anger. She told me more about the incident and we came up with a plan for releasing the strong emotions which included writing a letter to say good-bye to her brother and one to her sister which she could decide later whether she wanted to put in the mail. We agreed to meet again in two weeks.

Body Acceptance

This is also a very good time in our lives to finally let go of any body shame and self-hatred. Replace the negativity with positive affirming messages, expressing gratitude for your body for working so well, processing your food, carrying you around, giving you strength to pick up and hug your grandchildren, pumping blood and circulating those nutrients to every tiny cell, giving you energy for a full life.

In *Live Large: a book of ideas, affirmations and actions for sane living in a larger body,* author Dr. Cheri Erdman invites us to "live the life you want in the body you already have!" One of her messages of acceptance is to "respect your body and its truths, even if the culture doesn't. Your body has its own shape, size, biology, rhythms, coloring and genetics, and it carries your own unique life experiences. Your body has its own truths, which may be different from the culture's truth." One of my messages over the decades, and especially now as I am older, is to encourage myself and others to pay close attention to what we are telling ourselves about who we are and commit to loving ourselves as we age in our own way in the body we have now, in every state of health. What better time than now? Remind our partner also to be loving, accepting and gentle.

Playfulness And Stress Reduction

Health and wellness includes our mental, emotional and spiritual health. It's about balance and reducing or managing stress. When our first grandson was not quite 2 years old, he spent the weekend with us while his parents did some adventures in Chicago. We had a fabulous time, and I was reminded of the valuable gift of being in the moment by this smiley, good-natured, always-ready-to-play-peek-a-boo, laughing, well-loved child.

He was very busy discovering new toys at our house, stirring his "soup" (made of "wawa," milk, avocado, and blackberries from breakfast. Yum!). Outside, we threw snowballs and watched them explode, taking chunks out of the snowman grandma was building, spotting a "big truck" and getting excited when a dog walked by. Children at play do not work or worry.

Often we are in planning or repairing mode for big chunks of the day, missing the pleasures, spending our precious energy in worrying about what has happened or what we need to do next. Heed the message from folk singer Jim Post: "To worry does nothing but steals from the loving and robs from the pleasure that's there."

Take note of where your concentration is. What are you thinking about? What are you feeling? Take a deep breath, look around. Notice. Be in the moment. Whatever it is. Be there. The present is the only place we can actually be.

Mindfulness meditation may be part of your "growing older tool box." It is a method of quieting the mind, calming the emotions, and bringing attention to the present, using breath and repeated phrases, like "I breathe in, I breathe out." Check out the works of Tara Brach and Pema Chodron. Dan Harris, author of 10% Happier and Meditation for the Fidgety Skeptic has developed a very effective app to give guidance. I also recommend the Calm app. I encourage you to develop the ability to quiet your mind and calm your breath even if you are not interested in learning meditation. It can help all your organs and blood circulation work better, and might enhance your sex life.

In This Moment: Five Steps to Transcend Stress Using Mindfulness and Neuroscience by Kirk Strosahl and Patricia Robinson presents several exercises or practices as well as explanations of what is happening with the brain. One you might try this very moment as you are reading this book is called "Engaging a Half-Knowing Smile." The authors explain: "The technique is simple and straightforward. You smile ever so slightly, just enough to lift the edges of your lips up. If you like, you can think of something mildly funny or someone or something that makes you feel happy. The simple behavior of smiling ever so slightly is enough to activate quiet mind. ... It's especially helpful in moments when you're taking stress so seriously that it's getting the better of you. ... (It's) a nonverbal cue to step back from the situation, look at it from eagle perspective, and love yourself." Ahh! Smile!

Sleep

Give a lot of attention to your sleep cycle. Allow your body to find its natural rhythm again after years of schedules for work and family demands. Several of the couples we interviewed spoke of being surprised by this result in the years following retirement, especially for those who went directly from working full time. Leslie was used to getting up at 5 a.m. and being at work by 7 and putting in a full day. For months after she retired, she didn't set an alarm and would often sleep 9-10 hours. "I felt like I was making up for years of sleep deprivation," she said. Her experience was echoed by several others as was permission to take power naps to recharge and be able to stay alert for evening entertainment.

If you suffer from insomnia, find methods that help. Research correlates good sleep with better health; poor sleep increases susceptibility to health problems. Check with your doctor about long-term use of sleep-aid medication, which might be linked to cognitive impairment. See if you notice if you sleep better on days you have had a good physical workout. Check out supplements like melatonin and amino acids which may aid in restful sleep.

Chronic Pain Management

For most of us, growing older presents the challenge of coming to terms with all the changes with our aging bodies. That might sound like stating the obvious. However, some of us have not accepted that our bodies are changing, and we need change in response. As one of my clients said to me, "We used to tell our bodies what to do, now our bodies tell us what we can and can't do."

We do have more aches and pains as we get older, and it is tempting to tell each other about them. However, it gets boring. When I asked our interviewees, "What is something that annoys you about retired couples?," complaining about health was noted most often. Whining and moaning about the aches and pains is different than genuinely discussing the latest biopsy or ultrasound results and the doctor's recommendations for treatment. It's important to share with your loved ones and select friends as you go through medical challenges. It is also important to strike a balance.

One of our friends set a policy when they have gatherings and dinner parties: Each person is allowed only one health-related story per gathering. And make it brief. (He allows two if you're 80 or older). If a guest forgets and launches into multiple complaints, the hosts very graciously remind them, "You already told your story. Next? What else is happening in your life?" There is so much more that is interesting about each one of us.

Pain is an inevitable part of living; suffering and misery is not. In James Dillard's book *The Chronic Pain Solution,* research is cited which documents that soothing techniques, like massage or even light touch, travel faster than pain along the neural pathways. This fascinating finding suggests hope. If you are suffering from chronic pain, I encourage you not to give up.

Keep exploring methods that might bring relief, such as physical therapy, acupuncture or meditation. Supplements like ginger, turmeric and dark cherry juice, omega 3 fatty acids and amino acids have been shown to reduce inflammation. Increase your greens. Explore use of medical marijuana if that is legal in your state. The research is intriguing. It's plant-based and you don't get stoned. Bottom-line: Do not settle for a pain-filled existence.

Unplug the 24/7 Screen Time

Technology can be bad for our health if we are not mindful of the amount of attention we give to the "screens" in our lives. Too often people feel tied to their phones or tablets, constantly checking texts, voicemail, Facebook, Twitter and other social media. We may feel that we need to respond immediately — like how a ringing phone used to get our attention growing up. Some of us suffer from what is called "telepressure" from our gadget-gazing, a form of addiction. We can feel increased anxiety, feeling on edge, addicted to checking our screens every few minutes to make sure we haven't missed anything. We can also be tempted to take it personally or shame others if they don't respond to us fast enough. Fear of Missing Out (FOMO) is a real disorder, often activated by social media. It is experienced by an alarming number of adults and children, characterized by anxiety related to a belief that others are more interesting and have better lives and can lower our self-esteem. It is our job to monitor, control and limit our exposure.

Individuals and families should intentionally set times to be unplugged. There is a sense that technology is driving us instead of the other way around. Put the focus on interacting face to face and on what's happening around you.

At restaurants, too often my husband and I observe parents and children (grandparents too), focused on their phones and not on conversing with each other. Recently at Yosemite National Park, we took a picture of a row of about 20 people of all ages, sitting on a railing looking at their cell phones, seemingly oblivious to the majesty around them. Even though we retired folks may not feel as much pressure, we are also susceptible to the feeling of urgency to respond and needing to always be available. 24/7. It's good to stay updated as long as we remember to keep balance. What is most important? Responding to this text to set up the golf game or looking your grandson in the eye and saying, "Do you know how much I love hanging out with you?"

More Pleasure

Sometimes we just have to laugh, no other response does the trick. When Tom was about 50, he had to have emergency surgery for a badly infected gall bladder. It was serious. Toward the end of his recovery, we decided to venture out to attend the annual company holiday dinner, a lavish dress-up affair, at a local banquet hall. It was starting to snow again, but the parking lot was cleared, mostly. We very gingerly got out of the car and made our way to the entrance. And then found the only patch of black ice, slipped, and landed on our butts. Luckily we grabbed onto each other as we tried to fall gently (and gracefully?), me concerned about Tom's incision and Tom concerned about my evening gown. Neither of us was hurt. We both felt pretty silly but relieved. We started laughing and then of course, doing snow angels. We looked up and noticed the publisher and his wife walking by, smiling. They offered to help and then invited us to sit with them for dinner. Bonus.

Another funny story involves any time we take the kayaks out to cruise around the lake. Tom can just sit down and easily stand up from his seat. I have more difficulty folding my bigger body down into the kayak and then I have to roll out to get out. Most of the time, if I'm not too embarrassed, I have to laugh as I imagine the sight, a manatee maybe? However, I would not miss the pure delight I have feeling like a dolphin as I paddle through the water, only occasionally splashing Tom.

When we do positive things, including thinking pleasant thoughts and feeling pleasure, our bodies respond by producing more nitric oxide, sometimes called "the God spark" or "life force." Nitric oxide is released in little puffs of gas, mostly from the lining of the blood vessels. It diffuses rapidly right through the cell walls, turning on neurotransmitters which carry the messages from our brain to the nervous system.

Pleasure increases the neurotransmitters of beta-endorphins. This process dulls pain and lifts our mood. It also boosts oxytocin, the bonding hormone which increases our feelings of connection and intimacy and facilitates relaxation. So feeling pleasure from eating good chocolate or a well-spiced dish, giving a loving hug, having an intense feel good work out, or brisk walk, having sex, having an orgasm, seeing a beautiful sunset, laughing, enjoying each other are all health enhancing activities. Yay, nitric oxide!

When I need to pump up my energy I sing this adorable little children's song:

> *"Every little cell in my body is happy*
> *"Every little cell in my body is well (Repeat)*
> *"I'm so glad Every little cell in my body is happy and well."*

> *"Every Little Cell in My Body," by Karl Anthony.*
> *https://you.tube/P_95QiVJN-U)*

I began this chapter with a quotation from Dr. Northrup and will end with one also. From *The Secret Pleasure of Menopause:*

"Whatever doesn't feed our soul and doesn't make us feel vibrantly loved needs to fall by the wayside now. Our lives have no room for such things anymore. Everything we think, say, and do from this point on will either keep us active, engaged in living passionately and joyfully, or it will hasten degeneration and increase our chances of poor health and disease. It's our choice to make."

Christiane Northrup, M.D.

Tom's Note

Healers don't always follow their own advice. As I was editing the section in this chapter on our hyper-attention to "screens," the computer began to beep, repeatedly, as Sal sent no fewer than NINE reminders from her cell phone. That was never a problem with our old Royal upright typewriter that rose up from a special compartment in an antique oak desk. Not that we're sad to see the end of correction fluid and carbon paper ...

13 - Spirituality: Be Here Now, or the Gratitude Dance

*The physical atoms that make up your body
have been completely replaced
in the last nine years.
Yet you remain.
You may feel the effects of age,
but your spirit is always renewed
in each and every moment.
Remember this when you are tired or ill.
Let each breath renew your spirit.*

— *The Sage's Tao*

As you begin to read this chapter, take a moment and go outside, if the weather is OK. Stand and take some deep breaths. Connect with the ground. Have a sense of Mother Earth nourishing you as you breathe up through your feet. Bring down from Father Sky the light and radiance of the sun and moon and stars. Feel your connection with all creation. Get a sense of the vibrations around you. Connect with the Divine, your sense of God.

We are spiritual beings. Not beings being spiritual. Teacher and author Ram Dass and others often quote Pierre Teilhard de Chardin: "We are not human beings having a spiritual experience. We are spiritual beings having a human experience." No matter your belief system, we are always beings of Spirit. Just as we cannot separate from our bodies, thoughts and feelings, we also are not separate from our spirit selves. It's just a matter of our mindfulness of each of these states of being.

In *Soul Stories,* Gary Zukav writes of being committed to each other's spiritual development, desiring the best for yourself and your partner's highest good. In generations past, marriage was more like a business agreement, a partnership to settle the homestead, produce the food and livestock and raise the children. With the Industrial Age it was more about paying the bills and educating the children. And then later, in the 1950s, marriage was about keeping up with the Joneses and acquiring the house, car, backyard pool and private college tuitions. Since the millennium, many of us have become prosperous enough (or evolved enough?) to pay attention to our spiritual selves. It's not so much about what we own or what we do. It is about who we are — our "being-ness."

Wholistic health includes our spiritual self in addition to how we are physically, emotionally, psychologically and sexually. Some of us arrive at our ripe "old" ages and may be very disconnected from a sense of spirituality, a sense of being connected to a power or life force bigger than ourselves, a sense of being part of all creation, living a life of meaning. We may still be attending the church or synagogue, mosque or temple of our religious training from our youth. Or we may have gone through a religious search in our adulthood, studied and claimed a new set of beliefs. Some of us have stopped believing in God (if we ever did) or have doubts and are not sure what it means to be "spiritual" vs. what it means to be "religious." Or we have "spiritual wounds" that disconnect us, and we feel isolated or lost. When others speak of their relationship with God we feel empty or even upset.

Some of us arrive at our older age confidently grounded in our faith, depending on our beliefs and connection with the Divine to guide us through life stages. People of faith, church-goers, and those who report a strong spiritual connection are rated as healthier, have fewer medical problems, less stress and live longer. This is a consistent finding across all age groups and especially stronger as we age.

Ritual and Meditation

One way to bring awareness to our spiritual selves as individuals and as a couple is to use ritual and meditation. Some couples begin their day with a ritual of sharing from a meditation book or reciting a prayer or singing a chant. They connect early in the day and then have a ritual to connect at the end of the day.

Mimi and Nancy sit facing each other on their futon in the living room, legs outstretched. Each takes a turn reading aloud from a favorite daily meditation book. They practice this morning ritual to start their day before they go off to their separate activities. They might not see each other again for several hours as Mimi goes to her part-time job at a bookstore and Nancy does her community organizing volunteer work. They practiced this ritual in their early years together as a couple when Nancy was teaching high school and Mimi was doing elder care. Schedule conflicts and walking the dog intervened, and this morning ritual went by the wayside. Now, in retirement, they have resurrected it and find it helps immensely in sustaining closeness, especially during times when either is stressed-out or needs extra support.

Other couples create similar rituals for the afternoon or evening. Micheal and Mary attend church services weekly and often read the Bible to each other. Cheri and Terry host their Buddhist meditation group at their home weekly and meditate daily, sometimes twice. Jean and George practice a noon break ritual. Even though both of them have busy schedules in retirement, they faithfully preserve the noon-to-2 p.m. time every day for each other. They have a nourishing lunch, prepared by George and then they nap or rest, from 1 to 2.

Gratefuls

Nancy and Jed practiced a ritual they called "Gratefuls." When they stopped for the day, they would put a plate of olives and cheese and crackers together, pour a glass of wine and sit overlooking the Caribbean at their island home. They would sit in silence and then begin to share what happened during the day, often spent separately, and name things and people they felt grateful for. It was a way to reconnect and a quietly joyful, soulful thank you, setting the tone for their evening together. They would follow this when they returned to their Midwest home where they spent 6 months of the year. After Jed's death, Nancy continued the ritual, sometimes alone or with others who may be visiting.

Cathy and Denis, profiled in Chapter 4, also practice a daily ritual as they reconnect at the end of a day or before dinner, sometimes sitting on their deck. Tom and I call it our "reconnoiter time" when either of us asks to go sit on the swing in the back yard or on the couch in the living room. It may not be at the end of the day. It may be at other times when we need to regroup and listen intently.

"Change my attitude with gratitude" is a mantra or affirmation which is catchy and often effective for times when we want to feel better or move out of a negative emotional state. Reminding ourselves of what we feel grateful for can open our hearts and put whatever we were struggling with in perspective. I recommend keeping a gratitude journal or download Gratitude App from iTunes. Begin the day or end the day with writing down at least three ways you feel grateful. On tough days, it may be as simple as "I'm grateful I stayed upright today" or "I'm grateful the sun came out for a few minutes this afternoon." Other days you may be bursting with joy and have many things to record. When we study people who keep grateful journals regularly, they test higher for happiness, stronger immune systems, less stress and anxiety, lower blood pressure and depression. If it was a medicine we could take, it would be a best seller. The other finding is that the more we allow ourselves to feel grateful the easier it is to feel it and the more we feel it. It's like exercising a muscle. It gets stronger with use.

In focusing on gratitude, it is also a good idea to bring awareness to what information we pay attention to. Take a break from Facebook or watching news or other media sources and notice how this affects your mood. Instead of getting caught up in the latest negative news cycle, deliberately turn away and focus on people and news that brings you smiles and joy. Do a detox of ideas and feelings that we don't need to carry around. Just as we push toxins from our body, expel them from our minds and spirits, too.

Tom reminds me of this when he makes fun of medication ads on TV or encountering a sensationalized headline that uses fear as the attention grabber. He says, "There they go again telling us to be afraid, be very, very afraid." And then he laughs. And I do, too.

I write many thank you notes in my head and am so pleased when I actually sit down, select a card, write it and then put in the mail, sending it off with a smile and blessing. I feel the same when someone thanks me or even a stranger shows politeness. It encourages me to do the same. One of the contributions we elders can make is to intentionally teach kindness and hope that the younger generations pass on this legacy.

Meditation

Cathy meditates every day no matter where she is, traveling or at home. When her grandchildren visit or spend the night, they know when she is in her meditation chair to leave her alone or join her by sitting quietly. A former nun, she also practices daily prayer and is active in her Catholic faith.

Meditation involves focused attention or mindfulness, being present to the moment, often using the in and out breath to calm and quiet. Emptying the mind of thoughts and quieting the body, using a mantra or repetitive statement, or toning or chanting or visualizing a place of relaxation and beauty are all techniques used to meditate. Others describe a walk in the woods or swimming laps as their meditation. Practitioners say meditation often leads them into a deeper place of self-acceptance, connection with the Divine and compassion for all beings. They may also enjoy improved health, lower blood pressure, increased immunity and better cardiovascular functioning. For many, meditation is like prayer. Some say prayer is when we speak to God and meditation is when we listen.

Elizabeth Lesser, author of *Broken Open*, shares this story: Buddha was asked, "What have you gained from meditation?" He replied "Nothing. However, let me tell you what I have lost: anger, anxiety, depression, insecurity, fear of old age and death."

Check out types of meditation in resources as well as apps

you can download which give you guided meditations and other suggestions.

Meditation is also bringing awareness to whatever we may be doing, driving to work, folding laundry, doing the dishes, talking a walk, and opening ourselves to the connections in every moment. For example, in our state the car license plates start with letters then followed by numbers. Unless someone has ordered a vanity plate, you get assigned random letters and numbers. I started noticing new license plates with the letters AH then followed by numbers. I noticed that when I saw AH, I automatically took a deep breath and said or thought "Ahhhhhhh!" I started doing this as a practice.

You might decide to find a reminder to take a deep breath and enjoy the moment when you pause at a stoplight, or see a bird out your window, or hear a certain word or hear a time-interval chime from your wall clock. Use pairing like this to bring more awareness to your actions and teach yourself to deep-breathe and relax. Your smart phone may also have an app that you can set up to give you a reminder to deep-breathe during the day.

When I see a red male cardinal, I think of my Dad. When I see a female cardinal, I think of my Mom. My parents loved birds and kept their multiple bird feeders filled. As my father moved into part-time ministry he spent more time gardening, going back to his Iowa farming roots. Now as I work less and play more, I find great enjoyment doing the same. I find that I feel close to Dad as I'm smiling at the zinnias and daisies and when I transplant another hosta which came from his garden. Thanks for the super and ancient clippers, Dad. Sometimes a red cardinal will stay close while I'm working, like Dad's spirit whispering his smiles, too.

Healing Journey

I first learned about meditation through guided visualization when I was diagnosed with cancer while I was pregnant with our third child.

The cancer was found early, and would have been easily treatable if I was not pregnant. The oncologist I was referred to by my obstetrician recommended an immediate hysterectomy. It was unknown how the cancer cells would be affected by the pregnancy hormones. I refused. I was carrying life and I intuitively knew I was going to be OK and so was the baby. However, my worried and loving husband was listening to the oncologist and picturing the worst case scenario of our 6-year-old and 3-year-old sons losing their mom and he his wife. We decided to wait another month and have a second biopsy.

During that time I read research and got a second opinion and also discovered the use of guided visualization and music in self-healing. This was almost 33 years ago in the early days of alternative, wholistic medicine. Not many cancer centers had adopted these techniques. I started meditating every day and visualized the healthy cells replacing the cancer cells. We also felt very supported by knowing we were prob-ably on 100 prayer lists around the country (we both come from large extended families with many church-goers and people of deep faith).

More testing indicated we could progress with the pregnancy, al-lowing me to let go of fear and continue being hopeful. Our daughter was born healthy and strong. The cancer was treated with a less inva-sive procedure and I avoided major surgery, which allowed me to keep nursing our infant. I have no way to measure the effect of the meditation and healing. However, I know this process gave me great comfort and a sense of control.

One of the gifts of this journey into self-healing was to open me into a much deeper connection with my intuition and with my spiritual self. Building on my Judeo-Christian faith tradition, I was guided into studying other traditions, starting with Native American and other indigenous peoples, which led me into learning more about toning and healing chants and the vibra-tional power of music and touch. Meditation continues to be a tool to help me stay connected spiritually and for my health and well-being.

Forgiveness

We know forgiving people are healthier people. They have fewer medical problems, they live longer and have higher satisfaction levels. However, the forgiveness needs to be real — not just empty words or a bypass — to create the health benefits.

How is forgiveness related to couples facing the transition of retirement or for couples already retired? As we get older it is even more important to do an inventory of what hurts we may be storing and what forgiveness we need to practice — for both our health and for our spiritual benefit. We need to start by forgiving ourselves. Then extend the loving kindness of forgiveness to our partners and our loved ones so we can feel freer. I offer this thought: "Forgive not because the other deserves forgiveness, but because you deserve peace."

All of us have experienced pain with hurt and betrayal. For some it is grave. Genuine forgiveness is possible. Whatever the depth, true forgiveness offers transformation, opening our hearts to healing which truly changes us. Deep pain requires deep forgiveness, which brings deep healing. Jack Kornfield, the American Buddhist teacher, writes, "Forgiveness is the invitation to remember the transforming power of our own heart — to remember that no matter where we are and in what situation we find ourselves, freedom of the heart — peace — is possible."

When we've been wronged there is a danger in forgiving too soon. It is important to go through a process of healing. There is a danger in not forgiving. In holding on and obsessing about the hurt and the betrayer, the wrong begins to define our life. My husband and I were affected by an extreme example. A couple we knew lost their son to a street murder when he was a junior in high school. Young people and adults formed long lines at the funeral home. This tragedy defined the parents and they found it impossible to let it go. They had encountered evil in its purest form. They seemed dominated by bitterness and negativity. Serious health concerns added to their misery. This unimaginable loss changed their lives and the lives of their other children and grandchildren forever. Few of us will experience tragedy of such dimension, where the notion of forgiveness seems so foreign.

There are times we can choose not to forgive and still be able to let go and live with an open heart. It requires intention and choice.

Novelist and non-fiction author Anne Lamott, in her books about her faith journey, writes, "Forgiveness is giving up all hope of having had a better past." She also says, "In fact, not forgiving is like drinking rat poison and waiting for the rat to die."

So then, what if the other is not willing to admit he/she is wrong? What if the hurt is denied or minimized or not even acknowledged? In acceptance, one works to let go of the hurt as well as the need for revenge or retribution, not to let the offender off the hook but for our own well-being. It is a program of self-care, a generous and healing gift to oneself, accomplished by the self, for the self and asking nothing of the offender. It involves feeling the pain, and all the emotions with it, then deciding to stop obsessing about the injury and re-engage in life.

Sometimes it involves understanding the offender, framing the behavior in terms of his/her own personal struggles and carefully deciding what kind of relationship we want with the person who hurt us. I see this with my clients who are healing their childhood wounds from abuse or other traumas. I work with them to stop giving the trauma any more energy and to give themselves now what they needed then.

It is very encouraging to me to witness an increase in reconciliation efforts within divorced and blended families, who put aside or work through their own hurts to be more present for their children and grandchildren.

Sue Monk Kidd writes, "There's release in knowing the truth no matter how anguishing it is. You come finally to the irreducible thing, and there's nothing left to do but pick it up and hold it. Then, at last, you can enter the severe mercy of acceptance." In her novel, *The Secret Life of Bees,* her character gives us a model for forgiveness: "In the photograph by my bed my mother is perpetually smiling on me. I guess I have forgiven us both, although sometimes in the night my dreams will take me back to the sadness, and I have to wake up and forgive us again."

In genuine forgiveness, both the hurt one and the offender work to understand their part and hear each other's truths, including the hurt and pain and anger and guilt. They take responsibility. They truly apologize. They work to earn back trust, rebuilding the relationship hopefully to a better, more healthy foundation.

There is a Hawaiian spirituality called H'oponopono of forgiveness. It involves genuinely offering four phrases: "I love you. I'm sorry. Please forgive me. Thank you." This may remind you of a prayer or a tradition you use in your own belief system.

~~~~Reflection~~~~

Offer this very powerful forgiveness practice to each other as a couple. Say the words in a heartfelt way for any general hurt. Try it also for other acts for which you wish to ask forgiveness. See how it feels to go deeper. See how it feels to forgive and be forgiven. Did you notice feeling lighter and freer? Did you notice a release or whoosh of energy?

Faith and Forgiveness

So how does our faith help us in the process of forgiveness? How do we make sense of these hurts, this sorrow and suffering? What is the spiritual guidance for forgiveness? Why is it necessary to forgive now, even if the offense is in the very distant past?

For me it is about personal responsibility and living in intention with Spirit. It is about not getting caught up in the false dualities of right and wrong, good and bad, us/them, you/me, mind/body. There is another false duality in which I believe God loves me if I am being good, but I try to hide from myself and from God when I'm being bad. Forgiveness is receiving and staying in grace. It is an active process of searching and being honest and staying connected to the inner God in me and the inner God in you. You may choose different words to define this spiritual connection, like love, Spirit, Oneness, Source, Allah.

In Native American spirituality all creation is one, all is connected to all living beings. The Jewish Yom Kippur is similar to the Christian version of atonement (at-one-ment). As in Buddhist mindfulness, I believe it is important to set aside times in meditation and prayer where we catch up with ourselves emotionally, do a cleansing of our heart, make amends or be aware of what grudges or hurts we may be holding onto, feel the hurt and then decide when we are ready to let go. In this way we clear the channel for being in alignment with Spirit and being a vessel of loving kindness in our actions in the world.

In many faith traditions, Spirit means breath or wind. The connection to letting go is simply and profoundly our breath. We breathe spirit in and we breathe spirit out. Spirit. Breath. Breathe in. Breathe out.

As you think about the practice of forgiveness, let me also invite you to not overlook the small acts of kindness. Practice forgiving even the small slights, the little irritations. Especially with our loved ones. Kornfield writes, "Do not ignore the effects of each wise action, says the Buddha, thinking this will come to nothing: 'Just as by the gradual fall of raindrops, the water jar is filled, so in time, the wise become filled with the sweetness and goodness of their actions.'" Just let yourself be and remember this human capacity to let go, to meet even difficulty with mercy and kindness. Be sure to extend the kindness to yourself.

Wholehearted Living

Brene Brown, the author of *"Daring Greatly,"* has compiled a list of what she defines as wholehearted living which comes from her research into shame, vulnerability and resilience. "Spirituality emerged as a fundamental guidepost in Wholeheartedness. Not religiosity but the deeply held belief that we are inextricably connected to one another by a force greater than ourselves — a force grounded in love and compassion. For some of us that's

God, for others its nature, art, or even human soulfulness. I believe that owning our worthiness is the act of acknowledging
that we are sacred. Perhaps embracing vulnerability and over-
coming numbness is ultimately about the care and feeding of our
spirits."

Brown defines Wholehearted Living as:

1. Cultivating Authenticity: Letting Go of What People
   Think
2. Cultivating Self-Compassion: Letting Go of Perfection-
   ism
3. Cultivating a Resilient Spirit: Letting Go of Numbing and
   Powerlessness
4. Cultivating Gratitude and Joy: Letting Go of Scarcity and
   Fear of the Dark
5. Cultivating Intuition and Trusting Faith: Letting Go of
   the Need for Certainty
6. Cultivating Creativity: Letting Go of Comparison
7. Cultivating Play and Rest: Letting Go of Exhaustion as a
   Status Symbol and Productivity as Self-Worth
8. Cultivating Calm and Stillness: Letting Go of Anxiety as
   a Lifestyle
9. Cultivating Meaningful Work: Letting Go of Self-Doubt
   and "Supposed To"
10. Cultivating Laughter, Song, Dance: Letting Go of Being
    Cool and "Always Being in Control"

Although this list is for any person of any age, it reads as an
excellent guide for retirees who are wanting to free themselves
to evolve spiritually and have their partner join them on this
wild and exciting ride. The couples we interviewed who were the
happiest displayed many of these qualities of wholehearted living. The list may be more complete if we add Cultivating a Sense
of Death as a Beginning of a New Life: Letting Go of Fear of Death.

~~~~Reflection~~~~

Read the list of wholehearted living with each other and reflect on your relationship. Share your ideas about your spirituality. Listen for changes that may have come over the years of knowing each other and experiencing life events. How have your concepts of spirituality evolved as an individual and as a couple?

I want to end this chapter with a chant, composed by Karen Drucker and taught to me by Susan Lincoln, a singer and teacher known for her interpretations of the works of Hildegard von Bingen, the 12th century visionary. I love to start my day with this song. I always feel uplifted and grounded spiritually. It is for me prayer in song. You can find it on YouTube.

"I start my day with love. When I start my day with love that's what I get more of is love. (Repeat) I choose love, love, love.

I start my day with peace. When I start my day with peace, I feel the sweet release of peace. (Repeat) I choose peace, peace, peace.

I start my day with joy. When I start my day with joy, everything I do is infused with joy. (Repeat) I choose joy, joy, joy.

I start my day with love.

I start my day with peace.

I start my day with joy, I feel that sweet release.

I choose love, love, love."

Oh, yes!

14 - Serious Illness and Facing Death

*"In the end what matters most is
how well did you live,
how well did you love and
how well did you learn to let go."*

— *Viktor Frankl*

In her book, *Through the Dark Forest: Transforming Your Life in the Face of Death*, beloved mystic and visionary teacher Carolyn Conger writes: "The critical moment when death becomes a personal reality — usually when a medical professional delivers the news of an end-stage disease — can be an initiation into a profound and meaningful process of personal transformation. It is a unique opportunity to learn and grow into the essence of one's true self. It is, in some ways, equivalent to a birth announcement. Realizing that we have a finite period of time on this earth, our whole being wakes up. We become mobilized, eager to make our remaining time count, to find meaning and purpose. For many, it is an experience of rebirth and renewal, even with the concurrent feelings of fear."

How we die reflects how we live. How we make plans for our death reflects our ability to cope with our mortality. Facing our own end of life, and our spouse's, is part of planning for our retirement. It becomes one of the most important conversations to have, not just once, but several times for review and update. It is much more fun to talk about travel plans or the next visit to the grandkids than to really dig deep and share about dying. And yet death happens to all of us. And in many instances, not according to our plans.

All of the Wise Married Elder couples we interviewed had been through the "crucial conversation" and knew what each other wanted. They also had filled out the paperwork for advance directives, power of attorney for health care, living wills and "do not resuscitate" instructions to health care providers.

Even so, not all of them were comfortable with the process. It's hard to think of losing a spouse and going it alone. So we include this chapter because preparing our marriages for retirement would not be complete without also preparing our marriages for this eventuality.

The Advanced Directives Conversation

In a survey of 2,015 American adults, asking questions about how they want to die, Consumer Reports found that 86% would want to spend their final days at home, 50% prefer pain management and comfort care over other medical treatments, 61% have never heard of palliative care. Just 47% of people 65-plus have completed an advance directive such as a living will, and 42% have provided end-of-life care for a friend or relative.

We may have an idea about what a "good death" might look like for us. We may have even had the conversations with our spouse and children. However, until we've completed the paperwork and filed it with our health care providers, attorneys and executors, it's only talk and not legally enforceable.

Some have suggested that health care organizations are not set up to provide for all of us baby boomers about to put extra tension on an already stretched and challenged system. A good death may be hard to achieve. According to several sources, the U.S. health care system is inadequately prepared for the number of seniors needing end-of-life care and especially ill equipped to compassionately consider the wishes of terminal patients.

"That's why it's crucial that all Americans think about end-of-life concerns long before the crises arrive," wrote the editors of Consumer Reports. "That thinking should start with an honest talk with your family about the kind of care you want during your final months and days. It should involve creating a living will (advance directive) that specifies what procedures you want and don't want if you have a terminal condition. And you should appoint a health care proxy, someone who knows your desires well and who can make medical decisions for you if you become incapacitated. Having such a plan in place eases the burden on family members and improves the odds that your passing will be under circumstances of your own choosing."

My hope is that all medical clinics take inspiration from an internationally recognized program of advance care planning at Gundersen Health Systems in LaCrosse, WI. The goal to to have every patient in the system at every age register their advanced directives. In a study focusing on Medicare costs the last two years of life, Gundersen patients spent significantly fewer days in the hospital, translating into much lower costs, while still receiving excellent and appropriate medical care at the end of life.

However, if you do not have this guidance, you can do it for yourself. "Five Wishes," designed by Aging with Dignity, is a popular living will because it is written in everyday language and helps start and structure important conversations about care in times of serious illness. It is available on the Aging with Dignity website. I recommend that couples complete this booklet as part of their advance planning, preferably before they actually need it. The five wishes are:

- The person I want to make care decisions for me when I can't.
- The kind of medical treatment I want or don't want.
- How comfortable I want to be.
- How I want people to treat me.
- What I want my loved ones to know.

Fill this out together. Share it with your children or loved ones. Then file it with your will, and give a copy to your physician for your patient record. You can rest assured then. If a medical crisis happens, everyone is more prepared.

~~~~Reflection~~~~

As you read the questions from the "Five Wishes," what feelings do you notice? How does your partner feel? Is it possible that the fears of death and dying might be preventing you from talking this next step? If you have already completed this step, how do you feel about your advance planning directives? Set aside some time to share with each other.

We also recommend watching the 2018 film *Leisure Seekers*, featuring Helen Mirren and Donald Sutherland. It is very touching, with moments of laughter, and an accurate representation of the decisions many older couples (and their families) face.

For more guidance, read *On Being Mortal* by Atul Gawande. As a physician and gerontologist, he writes, "With luck and fastidiousness — eating well, exercising, keeping our blood pressure under control, getting medical help when we need it — people can often live and manage a very long time. But eventually the losses accumulate to the point where life's daily requirements become more than we can physically or mentally manage on our own. As fewer of us are struck dead out of the blue, most of us will spend significant periods of our lives too reduced and debilitated to live independently. We do not like to think about this eventuality. As a result, most of us are unprepared for it "

Social critic Barbara Ehrenreich's book, *Natural Causes: An Epidemic of Wellness, the Certainty of Dying, and Killing Ourselves to Live Longer* encourages us to examine our obsession with trying to control death and dying and let ourselves laugh at the absurdities of trying to control aging. She writes about her own epiphany when she turned 70 and realized she "had lived long enough to die." Ehrenreich looks into the cellular basis of aging, and shows how little control we actually have over it. "We tend to believe we have agency over our bodies, our minds, and even over the manner of our deaths," she writes, "But the latest science shows that the microscopic subunits of our bodies make their own 'decisions,' and not always in our favor." Her message is to focus on "joyously living well at this age" and stage in our lives.

A Change In Health

When I was a therapist in my mid-40s, I remember working with a couple in their mid-50s with a story similar to the one described in *Still Alice*, written by neuroscientist Lisa Genova about a neurolinguistics professor with early onset dementia. Their journey helped educate me and prepare me for other couples struggling with dementia.

Even before Howard retired it was obvious that he was experiencing some cognitive impairment. He had always resembled the "absentminded professor," but it became worrisome when he would lose his place during his lectures, or forget meetings, or completely lose his way around campus. His assistant and his colleagues picked up some of the slack and encouraged him to retire while he could still enjoy life. After further testing, the diagnosis of early onset dementia was confirmed. His wife Gloria, who worked in the Admissions Department at the same college, decided to also retire early, even though it would result in a financial setback. They were not sure how much quality time they had left before the dementia took its toll. Marital therapy focused on adjusting to this "new normal" and helping reduce the stress of increasing limitations.

Illness also affected this next couple's plans:

I first met Anita and Ed when we were at our family cottage in northern Wisconsin. I remember her bright smile the day I brought over welcoming cookies and later when we shared a glass of wine as we watched the sun set over the lake. She shared at that time her desire to retire.

Many years later I interviewed her for this book. Much had happened in her life since our first meeting. She had retired at age 60 a few years before Ed, who retired at 67, both on the faculty of a state university. They enjoyed life in retirement, had planned well and were able to travel extensively, including spending time with their blended families of seven adult children, 11 grandchildren and two great-grandchildren.

Then Ed had a stroke. More symptoms developed, and several tests determined that he suffered from a severe blood-vessel disease which was both degenerative and progressive. After a few years, he was restricted to a wheelchair, and self-care was more challenging.

Now 68, Anita had become 74-year-old Ed's full-time caregiver. At their home in Missouri and when they were at the cottage, she hired a home health worker who came in the morning to help with getting Ed up, showered, dressed and ready for the day. A couple times a year, Ed stayed in a nursing home, which provided respite care so Anita could attend weekend weddings or family events involving cross-country travel.

At the time of our interview, she was going through the painful process of talking with the kids about moving Ed to a nursing home as a full-time resident. The time had come. She hoped Ed's adult children would understand what was involved in the care of their dad. She invited them to stay with him for a weekend so she could travel to attend an extended family reunion. Her own children had been encouraging her to move him much sooner. She did not want rancor. She wanted everyone on board. Anita did not want to fall into the bitterness or martyrdom she had witnessed with some of the spouses from her support group. She was also familiar with the research that indicates that the stress on caregivers often worsens their health and increases the likelihood that they will die before disease takes their loved ones.

When I checked in a few months later, the move had been completed. She visits Ed several times a week. He is comfortable and well cared for, and Anita, free of worry and the stress of 24/7 caregiving, feels younger and healthier. She also speaks to her spiritual faith as a foundation for her care of Ed. She facilitates a local support group for caregivers. Their stories help sustain her.

Since our last update, Ed has passed on. Anita sold their home in Missouri and bought a condo in southern Wisconsin closer to her grandchildren. She continues to spend several months each year at the cottage.

Their story has important lessons for us as we make our own plans to retire. "Do it now. Do not put off anything you want to do," she said. "Complete your bucket list, especially if it involves travel, while you can. Life throws us curves. We have no guarantees of a tomorrow."

Anita and Ed's story also illustrates how important it is to be aware of the stress of being the caregiver for someone with a serious illness, especially our spouse. Illness can rob you of the partner that you knew. It's critical to balance your own needs with their needs and not put your own life completely on hold. This could be a long run, a marathon, not just a sprint. As a family therapist I also appreciate Anita's wisdom in involving the whole family, Ed's children and her own, in making the big decisions about Ed's care. They had lives well lived, a strong second marriage and a loving, if sad, good-bye. Now Anita is planning the next chapter of a very active, vital retirement, grateful for her excellent health, surrounded by friends and family.

In an episode of *Grey's Anatomy*, one of the lead characters, after dealing with a near-death experience, asks the questions: "Did you make the most of this beautiful, terrifying, messed-up life? Did you let go of all the things that held you back so you can hold on to what matters most?" I have witnessed this re-definition of what is most important as we get older and as we embrace our mortality. It is a spiritual and psychological shift which brings the individual and, ideally, the couple to a place of living with more intention, purpose and freedom. We want to pass on our stories, share wisdom and treasures, make peace in our relationships and with our sense of God. We want to know that the loved ones we leave behind when we're gone will be OK. If we can, we want to end our stories on our own terms.

Making The Best Of Bad News

Meredith and Bruce, younger friends of ours, were not considering retirement yet. Bruce, the CEO of his own company which made parts for heavy earth-moving equipment, was at least 10 years away from activating a business succession plan. Then he started experiencing numbness in his arms and difficulty walking. After some false starts, tests finally diagnosed the progression of symptoms as ALS (amyotrophic lateral sclerosis, known as Lou Gehrig's disease). As the disease progressed, rapidly, they worked on adapting their beautiful three-story home to Bruce's anticipated limitations. Their daughter, Maddie, engaged to be married soon, became obsessed with finding innovative or experimental drug treatment trials she wanted her dad to consider.

Six months later, we all dabbed at our tears as we watched Bruce

escort his beautiful daughter down the aisle, the braces on his legs helping him make the walk. Later in the evening, when we told him we
admired how he seemed to still be going strong, he laughed "What
choice do I have? You can wake up in the morning and focus on your
loss or you can wake up and say, 'Thank God, it's another day!' If I start
out with a bad day, then Meredith starts out with a bad day, and that's
not fair to her."

At his son's wedding a few months later, Bruce rolled up the center
aisle in his motorized wheelchair, with Meredith on his lap.

They will not be able to enjoy retirement. Their efforts are focused
on coping with his illness. His spirit is strong and his attitude positive.
The prognosis is uncertain. They don't know how much time they have.

At an ALS Walk, raising funds for research into the disease, more
than 100 people were members of Bruce's team. My husband joined
Bruce's team, walking in tribute to his own father who died at 60 of this
awful disease, which robbed us of his loving presence and made Tom's
mother a widow at 58 with the youngest of their five children still in
high school. We've remarked often over the years how much Tom's father would have enjoyed being a grandfather to our kids. My own father
was aware he was doing double duty.

While he was able, Bruce kept active in his church choir and praise
band, visited with friends and family, and worked with a foundation
which repairs bicycles and teaches bike repair skills to residents of a local homeless shelter. Even as he struggles to hold on to his own life, he
is making a difference in other's lives. Both Meredith and Bruce have
been incredible role models of strength, acceptance and strong faith.
They were overjoyed recently to welcome their first grandchild.

For many, getting a diagnosis like this becomes a call to live
life even more fully focused. For others, it becomes the beginning of the end, "checking out" of living, waiting for the disease
to take its course. For the marriage, such events become the biggest challenge. How are we going to face this together? How will
our lives change? What do we want to do to make the best of
this situation? How do we do the long good-bye while still holding on to hope?

Mim did not get to say good-bye. Her husband, Wally, went on an *errand and never returned, killed instantly in a car accident. A routine errand on a routine day, no preparation, no warning. Mim realized he was gone longer than usual but it was not a concern because Wally would frequently stop to check on elderly neighbors or do errands for others. The realization started to hit her when she answered their front door and encountered the police chaplain who had accompanied the patrol officer to deliver the devastating news. Mim, a retired school social worker, knew what this meant before a word was spoken.*

This beloved man was a popular teacher, father of three and grandfather of four who himself grew up in the community and married a hometown sweetheart. This tragedy deeply affected the whole community. His classmates decided to solicit contributions, build and dedicate a park in his name for their 50th reunion. Mim and Wally raised their three children at the same time we raised ours, members of a parenting support group we called "Mothercare." Wally had retired from teaching at a middle school eight years before his accident. Mim retired several years later. They were thrilled to be retired, fulfilling a dream of Wally's to buy a second home in Florida. He died before he got to enjoy his first winter there. Mim had some consolation knowing she and Wally had been able to do some of the traveling both of them wanted to do in retirement.

Now in her widowhood she's learning how to be alone after 43 years of marriage. One of the hardest adjustments has been to have to make all the decisions without her partner. Her advice to couples planning retirement is "Don't put off your dreams. Take that trip; plant that garden; build that play castle for the grandchildren. Daily I am comforted by memories as varied as trips to foreign lands or country drives for morning coffee. Be certain that both partners possess thorough knowledge of and access to all assets. Find an attorney who specializes in elder law and keep current. This is a gift to self and each other."

I had the privilege of hearing Sue Monk Kidd, author of *The Secret Life of Bees,* deliver the keynote address at a conference as she began her national book tour for her most recent novel, *The Invention of Wings.* She shared the story that as she was writing, her husband was undergoing grueling treatment for cancer. She stopped work on her novel and sat bedside as she watched him struggle. She felt helpless and unable to do anything to lessen his misery. When she pleaded with him to tell her something she could do to help, he told her, "You are helping. You are doing exactly what I need. You are here with me, holding my hand." I remember tearing up and vowing to remind myself of the power of just showing up, just being there. With love and light.

A colleague shared his story as he was dealing with a terminal cancer diagnosis. He had decided to stop treatment. The pain from the chemo and radiation treatments was worse than the pain of surgically removing the tumors. When he asked his wife,"What can I do to make this easier on you?" she replied, "Help me downsize. This house is too big for me to maintain after you are gone." In the time remaining and while he is still able, they are getting her new home ready — one he will not be there to share with her.

The end of life need not be the end of magical moments. I have been very fortunate to work with several families who have used this time to do some powerful healing and reconciliation.

This sacred work creates a legacy which I believe impacts the generations to come as much as for those who have faced their fears and forgiven each other as they said their good-byes.

The Long Good-bye

As my mom's Alzheimer's progressed she became more of her true essence — pure love and light. Everyone who cared for her felt renewed in her presence. Even though the disease took her brain, her huge, open, loving heart prevailed. Then a stroke took away her ability to speak. She would respond when we sang with her, and she seemed particularly soothed when any of her great-grandchildren were present. When she died at 89, she had been in memory care for four years.

When my dad died two-plus years later at age 93, he was embraced by family as we sang him home with his favorite songs. Over a period of several months, Dad's hospice team had called us to his side three times, saying these were his last days. We would all arrive from many hours away. We would pray, sing and tell stories, and he would rally. He continued to express his desire that we be with him when he died. We weren't sure if we would be able to get there at the right time. But we did, and he crossed over the way he, and we, had dreamed he would.

Being at my father's death with my husband and daughter, son and wife was one of the most powerful events of my life. It was sacred. And it was exhausting. To create the container to support his passing and to be so intensely present to his every breath or grimace took enormous energy. I was not fully myself for months afterward. I miss him — his physical presence — every day. Mom, too.

Elizabeth Lesser, director of Omega, a center for spiritual and personal development and author of *Broken Open,* speaks about our fear of death. "Our uneasiness with death is always humming in the background of our consciousness," she writes. "Some people are agitated most by the death of the body and the eternal mystery that follows. Some people do not fear the final death but are more afraid of arriving at the end of life not having fully lived it. Some are most unnerved by the 'ego deaths' we encounter when we experience loss, when we don't get what we want. Whether we fear the big one at the end of life or the little ones in between, our awareness of death causes suffering in our daily existence."

Lesser quotes Thich Nhat Hanh, the Tibetan Buddhist teacher: "Studying death can help each of us become someone with a capacity for being solid, calm, and without fear. ... Even so, we often feel anything but solid and calm when someone we love dies. Death stirs up conflicted feelings in the hearts of those left behind — some of us feel shaky and tender, others are shocked and angry; almost everyone is confused and unsettled. All of these feelings are included in what we call grief."

We have to allow ourselves the full process of grieving with no short cuts — not the fast food version but the slow-cooker, take-as-much-time-as-you-need version which is counter to our culture of quick and easy processes that minimize pain and emotion. I believe that the saying "Time heals all wounds" is a myth.

My work has taught me that healing doesn't wait on time; healing happens when we lean into the grief, allowing the process to come full circle to a place of surrender and acceptance. It hurts. And then it hurts less. Waves of grief come and go and may surprise us with the depth of emotion.

Nancy spoke of her years of grieving and the need for long periods of solitude after the death of her husband Jed. Not necessarily feeling sad or melancholy, but needing to be alone. Rather then being upset when friends mention Jed, she appreciates when they share memories. The stories let her remember the good times; the stories honor their relationship.

In a sermon about grieving, the Rev. Becky Sherwood told her congregation. "First: everyone grieves differently. It is unique to each of us. Do not compare yourself to others who are grieving. Nor should others compare your grief. Some people's tears come quickly, and other people take days or months or years to get to the lake of tears they carry inside." She reminds us, "Another truth about grief and mourning is that it is unpredictable. Sometimes it is the smallest thing that puts us back into our feelings of loss. ... Many people find that music, or certain songs, or hymns can be strong triggers of our grief. And that is normal. ... Grief is not logical. It does not show up as we expect it."

She counsels to talk with our children and grandchildren about death and dying. She assures us that if we do not talk they will not ask us the questions they most assuredly have about our attitudes and fears — and also will not feel free to share about their own. In generations past, as a culture, we were closer to the cycle of life and death. Now we are wise to take more opportunities to have these discussions with our own families, not just once but when life presents the opportunity naturally. Children take their cues from us.

This is not a book about how to grieve. There are several good guides listed in the Notes & Resources. As we age, we experience so many losses. Being healthy includes knowing how to move grief through us and being there for each other. All of it is practice for when we are faced with losing our spouse.

I reassure my clients that feeling grief and sadness is an "in and through" experience. No bypass. There is no way around it but in and through. Getting stuck in the middle is a danger. Sometimes the emotional pain becomes more than we think we can bear. Having support and normalizing the process helps. We can hold on tightly to our partners as the tears flow. We can hope that with this grief and suffering come the gifts of compassion and the promise of renewal.

In her book, *Through the Dark Forest: Transforming Your Life in the Face of Death,* Carolyn Conger focuses on her experiences with people as they are dying. She makes these recommendations for a life well-lived, calling them the principles of wholeness:

- Be yourself.
- Be present.
- Be open to unconditional love and compassion.
- Be of service to others.
- Make each day meaningful.
- Live in gratitude.

Reflection

What does your partner say about his or her fears of death? What are your thoughts? Where are you in the process of facing your own death? How often do you think of it? Is it a backdrop to your everyday life? As our peers age, as we lose our parents to death, as illness strikes and our own bodies break down, how do we encounter our own mortality? What do you think your partner's views are about death and dying? Reflect on these questions. Do some writing if you wish and select a time for discussion followed by a celebration of your life now.

Tom's Note

Growing up, I had very little experience with death. I was either too young or too far away to be involved when a grandparent or family member died. I was in my 20s before I attended a funeral. I was surprised at the amount of laughter that is heard during and after the service, even after so many tears have flowed. The message to me: make good memories so you can share them with friends and loved ones — and their friends — as we take part in and anticipate these final journeys.

Enjoying Retirement

15 - Lifestyles: Do it now!

While writing, I've been watching a couple from the balcony of the condo we rent on Marco Island, FL. They have gone down to the beach at exactly 9 a.m. every day we've been here. They set up their chairs, put up their umbrella, lay out their blanket, take off their coverups to reveal skimpy bikinis and evenly tanned bodies. Then they step off to the north for a long walk. They seem connected by an invisible line at the hip. They move in tandem. When they get back they walk hand-and-hand into the ocean, take a dip and then come out and head south for another long walk. Then back to the ocean. Then back to the chairs. This is repeated for several more hours. It's their couple dance.

This couple illustrates one type of lifestyle in retirement where the couple chooses to do most everything together. Maybe as a couple, maybe with a group of couples. Maybe with their children and grandchildren. Other couples have separate activities and then reconnect at the end of the day.

Nancy called this the base camp idea with their own separate mountains to climb. "Jed and I had very separate interests," she said. "He would read his law journals and still did consultations. I did my own thing and still met with a few clients. It was like we would go climb our separate mountains each day and then return at night to base camp where we would get nourished, connect again as a couple, fill our 'backpacks' and get a good night's sleep for the next day's 'climb.'" In addition to having his own law firm, Jed also piloted his own plane. Nancy didn't fly with him. That was his own time to de-stress, enjoy the beauty of the clouds and work through the details of executing an instrument approach.

After very active successful careers, they retired to the small island of Vieques, just off the southeast coast of Puerto Rico. They spent the exact number of days, about six months, allowed by the government there (to avoid horrendous taxes) and then returned to their home in the Midwest for the rest of the year. Daily lap swimmers, they built a pool with a view of the Caribbean. They started a ritual they called "gratefuls," which they practiced every day as they returned to their "base camp." They met poolside and shared a glass of wine and plate of olives, cheese and crackers and talked about the day's adventures on their "mountains." After suffering two heart attacks, one while on the island, Jed passed away a few years ago. As I interviewed Nancy for the book, I became concerned that I was stirring up too much sadness as I asked about their marriage. She assured me that it was OK and said, "As a widow, no one asks me about Jed anymore. I love talking about our marriage and recalling the memories. Yes, I feel sad, but it also makes me smile. We had so many good times."

The Voyagers

Loy and Linda Williams, 61 and 62 at the time, spent very little time apart for the six years they traveled aboard their 40-foot sailboat from Chicago to the Florida Keys, the Bahamas and the U.S. East Coast. They had played with the idea for years, going on short trips during the summer when Linda had breaks from her school district job and Loy could vacation from his private practice in family therapy. One summer they crewed aboard a sailboat in the Canary Islands and found they loved it. After Linda retired she tried out the idea by being on the crew of a 60-foot sailboat with an all-women crew in the islands of Spain and Greece. She loved it. At home Loy and Linda got some financial consultation, sold their house, downsized to a townhouse and left for what was going to be a two-year sailing adventure. It became six years. Each year they would return, dock their boat on the East Coast for repairs and return to Illinois during the peak of hurricane season. They would come back to their townhouse and visit their son and friends, get their land legs back and plan the next voyage.

When I asked about how retirement affected their marriage, they both laughed and said that learning to sail together and negotiating decisions in dangerous storms was what changed their marriage. There is no room for hedging. Work it out now or it could be never.

They are so grateful for the amazing sights and memories. The experiences are even more precious since they have sold the sailboat and

are now cherishing the time remaining as Linda struggles with conges-
tive pulmonary disorder. She is on oxygen 24/7. They are so glad they
did not wait to embark on their dream voyage. Linda's message for cou-
ples planning to retire: "Discuss your dreams and do them now. Retire
earlier than you planned if possible. Life is unpredictable. Make them
happen sooner rather than later."

Linda's words are even more meaningful since she has since lost
her battle with this disease and has passed on at age 75.

Loy's advice about retirement and marriage is "be friends first,
learn to share values and objectives, help each other with your partner's
problems and projects, share the pleasure of physical contact, and let
the joy of having a partner with whom you have a long history and
whom you can trust absolutely enrich your relationship."

Hitting the Road

Joe and his wife also sold their family home in preparation for
retirement. But instead of downsizing in the town where they
worked and raised their children, they bought a big motor home
and have been touring the national parks for years. They stay
months at a time, volunteering as docents or wherever they are
needed. They get paid a small stipend and are provided free
parking and connections for their motor home. They return occasionally for medical care and visits with family and friends.

Cheri and Terry did something similar when they both retired. They sold their suburban Chicago house, bought a small
motor home and toured the country for a year, scouting out
where they wanted to retire. They had imagined the coast of the
Northwest, maybe Oregon or Washington. When they looked at
property there they were appalled by the prices, especially challenging on their pensions. They knew being by water with a view
was a priority. They were delightfully surprised to find a lovely
and affordable home in Florida, just a block from the Atlantic
Ocean. They have found a very vibrant community of people
with shared interests. Terry supplements their income with a
part-time job, while Cheri explores her artistic side, painting in

various media. Both enjoy practicing meditation and studying Buddhism. Like many couples their age, retirement has included a long ordeal of many trips (back to Ohio) to care for aging parents followed by the phase of grief recovery.

Chuck and Jeanie are the road trip gurus. As a high school teacher, Chuck had summers off. Jeanie could arrange breaks from her administrative corporate job. Now in retirement they love to pack up and hit the road for another excursion. I asked them for pointers. Here are the Naegers' Road Trip Tips:

Learn What You Can

Always be on the lookout for vacation materials. Check out the Travel sections of newspapers. Pay attention to offers for free materials in magazines like Midwest Living or Vacations. Stop at official state welcome centers for maps, travel guides and other brochures of interest. Once you have concrete plans, contact the chambers of commerce of towns nearby and ask them to send information they think will help you.

People often can be your greatest source of information. If you know someone who has recently been on vacation, pick their brain. Or if you are in a new town, and it's almost lunchtime, ask three or four shopkeepers to recommend their personal favorites. The trained expert working behind the desk at the rest center can suggest interesting places on down the road. When you get to your lodging, talk to the people there about places to go and things to do in the area.

One of our most fond vacation memories was the result of a spur-of-the-moment question in Nova Scotia. We had just checked into our B&B when I asked our hostess what she would recommend we do that evening. She sent us off to the town hall of a little, tiny village. There local musicians met every Friday night for an impromptu jam session, playing local folk music. These musicians had so much fun and so did we! One question resulted in a wonderful evening.

How To Save Money

- *If traveling to a famous tourist spot go slightly "off season." You will have almost the same experience as if you visited two weeks earlier, but will pay less money for that experience.*

- *For travel in the US, think spring and fall. You should still have nice weather but miss the crowds swelled by families with school-age children.*

- *Visit legendary spots that everyone wants to go to but stay somewhere else. Last fall we spent a few days along the northern shore of Lake Michigan. High on our list to do was to visit the Grand Hotel on Mackinaw Island. To do so we drove about an hour from where we were staying; took the ferry across to the island; sat in the famous rocking chairs on the porch always pictured in the photos of this legendary place; had lunch feasting on the Grand's amazing buffet; toured much of the island and headed home. By evening we were back at our beautiful inn having had a "Grand" experience while saving lots of money by not paying the outrageous amount the Grand charges for lodging.*

- *If you are going to arrive late and leave early the next morning all you need is a cheaper, clean motel room. Don't pay more for a bunch of extras you don't have time to use.*

- *When booking your lodging think variety. Lodges in state parks are often charming, in scenic spots and cheaper than much of the surrounding lodging. "Old" hotels that dot small Western towns are relatively cheap, beautifully renovated (in many cases) while still maintaining their "Old Wild West" charm.*

- *Plan to picnic along the way. If you are traveling long stretches of scenic highways you may want to consider packing a lunch. Often in these areas, restaurants are few and far between. In addition you may find a nice spot to linger. Many times you eat a large breakfast and only need a little something to tide you over until dinner. Always plan to have a cooler for beverages. Even if you fly and rent a car you can pick up a cheap plastic foam cooler to use during your travels.*

- *If you are traveling to a major city, check out their Groupons for discounts on lodging, dining, and attractions. If you find something of interest, Google to find reviews. Several years ago we met friends for a three-day weekend. Each couple bought a*

Groupon for a lovely modern boutique hotel in the downtown area which also included tickets to the Presidential Library.

- *Seniors need to take advantage of AAA and AARP member discounts whenever available – it never hurts to ask. Buy a senior national parks pass for one-time fee of $80. It generally covers those traveling with you by car. Local attractions generally allow 4 people to enter with one card. Other sites like the Presidential Homes are included. Consider buying membership in Time Travelers or ROAM, North American Reciprocal, which allows entry in several hundred museums and historical sites and discounts in the gift shops.*

- *Lodging places will often have discounts available for local restaurants and attractions. Ask at the desk.*

- *When planning a trip with friends, particularly cruises, you may want to book together with a travel agency like AAA. Most likely you will all get a discount for booking/referring. If someone is a frequent traveler with a cruise line they will get a discount for each person/couple booking from their referral.*

Save Your Body

- *Fly to your vacation area and rent a car. You will save time and aggravation. After all, who wants to drive across Kansas when you could be frolicking in the Rocky Mountains?*

- *Take frequent stretch breaks. Pass the time with audio books or read out loud to each other.*

- *If you are going to drive a long distance, keep in mind that you are retired with a flexible schedule and you are not driving in the Daytona 500. Add couple of days to your trip, drive fewer miles per day and plan to take the time to see sights along the way.*

- *I'm always amazed when I hear someone brag, "We made it to somewhere in X hours by only stopping for gas." I will think to myself, "He's a Civil War buff on vacation, and was within 50 miles of Gettysburg and did not stop. What is he going to do later in life? Drive 600 miles from his home to see the sights* then?"

- Don't be afraid to venture off the planned route. Sometimes the journey can be more fun than the destination.
- Even in this digital age, maps and various states' official travel guides are very useful tools. Sure the GPS will show you how to get where you want to go, but first you have to figure out where you want to go. That old map might remind you that if you got off the superhighway and travel a certain two-lane road the scenery would be prettier, and that state travel guide (put together by experts) might inspire you to stop at that old wooden covered bridge. Using all these tools can result in a drive (and a vacation) that is lots of fun.

There are many other excellent travel guides for seniors. I've included Jeanie and Chuck's Road Trip Tips in this book about loving your marriage in retirement because I find these stories and ideas inspiring. One of the ways to keep the music playing is to change it up, see new sights, break our routines and hit the road for some fun and adventure while not breaking the bank.

Separate Interests

Cath and Del had an unusual style of easing into retirement. Cath had always done a lot of traveling in her corporate training job which left her with an urge to visit parts of the world she had not been able to explore on her own time. Del, seven years older, had little interest in global travel and was content to follow his interest in World War II history. They tried to reach a compromise that would let them pursue their interests together, but couldn't agree.

They boldly decided to pursue their interests separately. Not to separate, but to stay together even more passionately by being apart.

Cath took a trip to the Galapagos Islands with a college roommate who had remained a dear friend and was working through her own grief at losing her husband a few years before.

While away, Cath hatched up the idea to travel by herself or with others for three months at a time and return home to Del and share their adventures while apart. Her next excursion was to visit a friend in a small fishing village in the Yucatan. While Del kept cozy in his northern Michigan study, watching the snow swirl around the backyard bird feeder, Cath toured the ancient Mayan sites. She bought fruit and vegetables at the market. She became expert at preparing feasts of fresh fish. She learned to meditate and discovered a lower gear in contrast to the years of balancing fast pace at work and keeping up with the kids' activities when she was home.

Meanwhile, Del appreciated the long stretches of uninterrupted alone time his introverted self could never get enough of. They Skyped each week and could reach each other for emergencies. They missed each other, but they were having fun on their own terms. When Cath returned in spring, they both felt like newlyweds, eager to reconnect and passionate to share. Cath continued traveling solo to Mexico, Central America, South America, Thailand and Bali. Now 82 and 75, after five years of her solo travel, Cath has stayed home the last several years, grounded by desire to spend more time with her four grandchildren and also because her wanderlust has been satisfied.

Some of their friends have been vocal about their objections to this arrangement. Cath and Del listen to such complaints, nod their heads in acknowledgement, then laugh and say, "Choosing to be apart allowed us to stay together."

Expatriates — Temporarily

Mimi and Nancy have been together for 18 years. Mimi was married when I first met her shortly after my own marriage 46 years ago. She and I were part of the movers and shakers in the early days of feminist activism. We started consciousness-raising groups, helped organize a volunteer advocacy group that worked with rape victims and met to write the first proposal to establish and seek funding for a battered women's shelter to serve our large community. She's been my dear friend as well as an adopted aunt to my three kids. And now Nancy is a dear friend also.

Mimi, the youngest daughter in a large Catholic family, really wanted to be a mom. When she and her husband were not able to conceive and fertility treatments were not successful, they considered adoption. Their name was placed on her doctor's list of couples wanting to adopt. It took three years before their name came up to the top of the list. During that time their marriage disintegrated. As Mimi said, "We were like many couples where infertility either brings them closer or creates a chasm that is nearly impossible to reach across. In our case, our already fragile marriage fell apart. While talking with the doctor, I realized we no longer had a family to bring the baby home to. It was and still is the most difficult decision I have ever had to make."

A few years later, after attempts to repair the marriage failed, Mimi said goodbye to her friends in the area and moved up to Minnesota to be nanny for her older sister's children and try to pick up the pieces of her life. She enjoyed success as a sales representative for several companies. Several years and several men later, Mimi gave up on finding love and gave up on men. Shortly after, a mutual friend introduced Nancy and Mimi. They clicked on many levels and started an adventure which Mimi calls the best chapter of her life. Now that same-sex marriage is legal, they are considering making plans for a wedding.

They share a home in Mexico which Nancy bought 25 years ago when she fell in love with a quaint fishing village close to ancient Mayan archeological sites. After retiring from teaching Spanish at a high school in Minneapolis, she started spending more months in Mexico. Since Mimi retired five years later from her elder care job, they spend more time together. They have established a nonprofit organization that gives aid to mothers and children in the area.

Because their part of Mexico is more conservative and Catholic, and because they live "where the people live, not where the tourists stay," they keep their relationship discreet. They avoid public displays of affection. They are respectful, and do not call attention to being a couple. In contrast, they are "out" to friends where they live in Minnesota. When Mimi moved in with Nancy in a suburb of Minneapolis, she sold her beautiful Queen Anne Victorian and bought a duplex further *north by Lake Superior in Grand Marais, a diverse community welcoming to gays and lesbians. In both communities they feel free to be who they are.*

During our interviews, they raised an issue: "We want to find a retirement community that will be 'gay and lesbian friendly.' If and when this becomes necessary or desirable, we want to live where we are accepted as a loving and committed couple and where we no longer need to hide any aspects of our relationship."

Another couple I interviewed expressed the same desire. This will become increasingly needed as more boomers retire, and as more people declare their sexual orientation. I hope the retirement communities are preparing themselves. Hopefully we are moving toward a more open and accepting world.

Not Retiring From Leadership

For Shelley and Doug, moving to a Florida golf community and choosing not to travel anymore was their plan for retirement. Doug's job had sent them overseas for years at a time. Finally being able to come back to the states and settle in was exciting to them. He plays golf and she volunteers as president of the art center and lay leader at their church.

She does not consider herself "retired," nor does she like the words elder or aging. She'll agree to be called a senior and be appreciated for the wisdom which comes from intentional living. Although she doesn't judge the wives who fill their time with golf, tennis, crafts, shopping and lunches, she chooses to spend her time contributing to the community. When pushed to identify something that bothers her about retired couples, she describes how boring it is to her to hear about their health problems. It's not that she doesn't feel compassion, she just doesn't want to hear about it so much from all the older folks. She also is bothered by the "sunbirds" who come to Florida for part of the year but still consider their home back east or in the Midwest and do nothing to make the place they live six months out of the year a better place for everyone else who lives there year-round.

55-Plus Retirement Villages

Jerry and Connie, both retired, spend most of their year in an over-55 community in Florida called The Villages. The rest of the year they visit friends and their family. The Villages consists of several neighborhoods of predominantly single-family homes, with 11 championship and 32 executive (shorter) golf courses. In 2011 a total of 55,663 Villagers played one or more rounds of golf for a total of 2,546,611 rounds of golf. Each area has its own town square center with many daily activities. The area has every type of fast food and fine dining, several churches and synagogues, a meditation center and a huge fitness club. Connie plays flute in community musical groups and directs the choir at her church. Both of them play golf several times a week as well as entertain their many out-of-state friends who visit. They are good advertisement for this type of retired lifestyle.

Grace and Bernie do not consider themselves retired. Both in their mid-70s, they are very active professionally. They did not have children and have fun "adopting" grandchildren whom they dearly love. They love entertaining friends with potluck dinner parties. Their guest room is almost always full with friends they have met in their travels around the world with Road Scholar and Rick Steves tours.

Volunteering

Volunteering is another attraction for retirees. So many opportunities. Nancy with river clean-up, Sherry with Survivors of Suicide, John with hospice grief group, Larry teaching about raptors, Tom regularly donating platelets at the blood bank with his rare blood type, Cathy singing with Thresholds Choir bedside, Denis with Kiwanis, Jeanie serving as president of Optimist, Jim with a mission group to Haiti, Bruce building bikes, Mary reading to children at the Visiting Nurse Association, Eileen and Lou's Taize services, Anita's Alzheimer's caregiver group, Mark's Parkinson resource group, Jan at the animal shelter, Jean's networking group and George's Meals on Wheels and serving soup at the homeless shelter. Volunteering may be an extension of your work life or allowing you to explore new interests, being available when it fits your schedule.

Many Styles of Retirement

There are as many styles of retirement as there are retired couples. Sharing your expectations of retirement and what you want to get out of the rest of your life will guide you in the planning necessary to maximize success.

What lifestyle you mutually choose, and how you make decisions as you go along, will shape the quality of your life in retirement. Couples who are flexible and keep updating their plans to accommodate changing factors of life seem to be the most resilient. It is important to have a plan and yet be willing to change the plans.

Remember the motto repeated in several places in this book by the Wise Married Elders. Do it now! Don't delay.

~~~~Reflection~~~~

This chapter has many examples of very different approaches to aging and retirement. Which of these stories excite you? Which of these stories do not interest you? Share your thoughts and dreams with each other as you design your own retirement. Revisit this periodically as you experience and explore.

Tom's Note

I've donated blood ever since I was in the Army. My blood bank's records only go back to 1987, but since then I've donated 46 pints of whole blood, four double-units of red cells and 36 batches of platelets. I'm frustrated by how difficult it is for the blood bank to recruit donors. To give a unit of whole blood takes less than half an hour. If you haven't donated for years, you'll be pleasantly surprised at how fast and relatively painless the process has become. Supervisors at our blood center asked me if I would be willing to donate platelets instead — especially because I'm a relatively rare A-negative. So now, every five weeks or so, I spend a couple of hours (including interviews and post-donation refreshments) in a procedure called apheresis, where blood is withdrawn, the platelets are removed, and the rest of the blood returned. There are no negative consequences for me, and the platelets are used — sometimes the same day — by cancer patients whose therapy is destroying their own platelets. Support your local blood center (this has been an unpaid commercial announcement).

16 - The Other Generations

For the mid-life to older couple, caring for the other generations — our elderly parents, our own adult children and our grandchildren — presents the dances of balance and boundaries. Opportunities and possibilities. Headaches and smiles. Tears of joy and depths of sadness. Disappointment and despair, dilemmas and delights. Bubbles, bugs and diapers — both Pampers and Depends.

Part of coming up with the plan for your retirement involves discussing questions about the demands of caring for your elderly parents and their heath needs, as well as how much involvement you want with your grandchildren and adult children.

We have been hearing about the stress on baby boomers, called the Sandwich Generation, caught between the needs of their children (and grandchildren) and the needs of their elderly and often ailing parents. When demands from the other generations are pulling on one or both spouses, nurturing the marriage can get put on hold. If this happens for too long or without attention, the marriage can start to suffer, as well as your health.

For Victoria and Richard, both recently retired, the stress piled on and came to a head during a health crisis which landed her in the hospital, needing weeks to recover, and him with a bad case of shingles. Months earlier a work and child care emergency had sent Victoria out to the West Coast to be with their son's children while Richard flew to the East Coast to assist his mother with her move into a retirement center. Ordinarily they would have done these trips together, but the nature of the emergencies required that they divide up the tasks. The situation worsened in both places, so the separation lasted much longer than originally anticipated. While they were willing and glad to be of service and were appreciated by their family members, their lifelong patterns of putting everyone else's needs first and not attending to their own health took a toll. This awareness became the tipping point for some radical self-care commitments. Their West Coast family made some better decisions about their work schedules and hired childcare, and the East Coast siblings stepped up to do their part in helping Mom move and get the family home ready for sale.

This couple's story typifies the stressors I hear about from the mid-life to older couples I work with. The details of their lives differ, but the issues are similar. How do we show up as caregivers and yet stay balanced and healthy? What can we ask others to do, and what is our reasonable share of the load?

Sharing the load among siblings helps. It took us months of multiple trips to clear out my parents' home when they became impaired and moved into a retirement center. My sibs and I would often say to each other, "It takes a village ... " This included our immense gratitude to the excellent caregivers at the retirement center.

It is my observation that often families have the appointed one who is expected to do the work and respond to the demands, while others are "too busy or not available" or keep themselves uninformed so they can plead ignorance. Some may take more of the financial responsibility, feeling this is enough of a contribution and leaving the other siblings to do the grunt work. This is a fertile ground for resentments to escalate. In some families it becomes an all-out war, with sisters and brothers refusing to speak with each other and cousins estranged or confused.

One of my clients decided that she valued her siblings too much to let this pattern continue and called a family meeting. She asked everyone to come prepared to listen and speak from a place of respect and work together to come up with a plan for their ailing parents' care. She reported to me afterwards that despite some moments of struggle, she felt the meeting was a success. She added that she greatly appreciated her husband's support before and during the meeting. "He gets my family to laugh by his gentle teasing, which we all needed to break the tension," she said.

Family caregiving has many challenges, including time demands, missed work, sibling conflicts, marital distress, financial strain, guilt, emotional overload and burnout. If you decide to become a part-time or full-time caregiver, please be very careful of your own needs. Ask for help. Use your marriage as a refuge.

The AARP book, *Meditations for Caregivers* by Jacobs and Mayer, has excellent ideas. Support groups in your area may help also.

Adult Children Moving Home

If you still have adult children depending on your support, financial or otherwise, who may have moved back in or never moved out, paying attention to your marriage becomes even more essential. It is possible that you have not experienced the return to couple-focus that often happens in response to "empty nest." The nest has not been empty yet. Matter of fact, the adult child's issues or circumstances may have dominated your attention to the exclusion of nurturing your marriage. Maybe you and your spouse disagree on an action plan. You might have different perspectives that impede progress. Often parents express guilt, feeling that their son or daughter's failure to launch is because of bad or ineffective parenting. They blame themselves or each other. Discussing this with each other and offering forgiveness may clear the air and bring resolution.

Sometimes in our attempts to be helpful, we unknowingly miss the window of encouraging our adult children to fly the nest and make it on their own. They may fall and struggle with finding work and ways to support themselves. This happened for one of the couples who sought marriage counseling.

Their two older children were successfully off on their own. Their younger son experienced a terrifying trauma in college and dropped out, coming home to recover. Unfortunately, he got too comfortable, got addicted to video games and started using marijuana nightly. Now they were struggling as a couple to decide how to handle it. Every time they came up with a plan and their son resisted, one of them would give in and not follow through. They were feeling very discouraged and not hopeful. Part of treatment involved helping them detach from controlling the outcome for their son and finding a way to lovingly support his independence and full recovery. It also involved strengthening their own skills to deal with the discomfort of confrontation.

For another couple, a lawyer and a teacher, the care and

handling of their mentally ill adult son has been a huge financial and emotional drain on their marriage before and during retirement. They have wisely set up a trust fund as part of their estate to provide for both their sons and to protect their other son and his family from the stress and responsibility of being in charge of his brother's finances, making decisions and having to be involved in giving permission if his brother becomes unable to manage for himself.

The saving grace in these examples is the ability of these retired couples to put the health of their marriage above all other priorities. They have continued good communication, sharing and talking through these difficult challenges, finding creative solutions and then letting go of attachment to the outcome. Optimism helps.

On the other side, an adult child moving home may be positive, especially if expectations are discussed and chores and private spaces are agreed upon. Having a third person on board to shop and cook and mow the lawn can be a bonus, especially if you also enjoy each other's company.

Blended Families

Blended families may mean multiple sets of grandparents, stepchildren, half siblings, and more complicated family dynamics to be aware of, negotiate and navigate. If this is the result of divorce and remarriage, the family system has already dealt with these complexities on several levels, probably for several years. For the retired couple it may mean trying to figure out where you fit in, what your role is with the adult children and grandchildren and how to "let love lead." In the most ideal settings, for the children it may mean more attention and more hugs. As one 8-year-old told me, "I love all the presents, but I don't love going to four houses on holidays."

The family system also gets stirred up when a death has occurred and it is widows who are remarrying, sometimes to someone who has also lost their partner. Unresolved grief introduces another layer of emotion and confusion for the children, often surfacing as a misplaced sense that the deceased parent is being betrayed. Clearly stating the expectations and the boundaries while lovingly talking through the feelings is important. This letter to "Ask Amy" illustrates this situation.

Amy Dickinson, syndicated columnist and author of two excellent memoirs, gives effective direction in her answer:

*"**Dear Amy:** I was in the same situation as "Baffled Bride" who married a widower, and his adult children rejected her. This happened to me. Both my husband and I lost our spouses. My children accepted him but his children rejected me. They seemed to hold a perception that we were fighting for control of their father. I guess I understand this, but I'll never understand my husband for allowing it. — Sad*

__Dear Sad:__ This rejection seems fairly common. Acceptance definitely takes time, but it should not be presented as optional." (Chicago Tribune, Feb. 14, 2018)

Barry Free, author of *Letters From Home: I Loved Ya Before I Even Met Ya,* writes a powerful memoir about his grief process coming to terms with the sudden death of his beloved wife. His life changed forever, as did the lives of his two adult children and grandchildren. At first, his wife felt as if she just had the flu. Later, Barry felt powerless as the medical staff scrambled to correctly diagnose and then try to treat the rapidly spreading bacterial infection which took her life in just two days. Their two adult children and spouses arrived just in time to say good-bye. His book started as a collection of letters he began writing to his children as a way to record his thoughts and also as a way to begin conversation about how each was feeling over the five years following. The book is a beautiful and courageous tribute to his wife, to their loving marriage and family and to the therapeutic process of grief.

Barry recently started a new chapter, marrying another widow who also came from a loving, beautiful marriage, creating a new blended family. Being clear that they expected their children to support their decision to date and then marry, despite knowing it may take some time to fully accept the choices, has deepened their trust in each other and led the way.

Grandparenting

At a recent gathering of women, I was surprised by the vehemence of the discussion — or perhaps argument — about the proper care of grandchildren. One woman was proclaiming that grandparents should NEVER be expected to provide regular day care for their grandchildren, adding that she resented her son asking her to do so. Another grandmother spoke about how much fun it is for her and her husband to take care of their daughters' little ones once a week while they are in town, since they travel for parts of the year and miss them so much. She would not choose to do regular day care, believing that would change her role from attentive grandmother to disciplinarian, which might spoil the specialness. In contrast, a third woman spoke of how her life has been enriched by caring for her divorced son's three children full-time, even though she can hardly wait till he comes at 5 p.m. to pick them up. "It's a long, long day for me since he drops them off at 6 a.m., but I wouldn't trade it for the world. This is precious time. I can give to his kids what I gave to him growing up. My time to relax will come later."

At a memorial service, a relative confided that since his parents moved out of state they have basically "dropped out of their grandkids' lives. Phone calls, FaceTime and Skype don't cut it. My dad wants to travel up and spend extended times but my mom won't leave Florida. She's afraid to fly, and the car ride is too hard on her. And my dad is too devoted to her to leave her and come by himself. They are missing out and we are missing out. I feel sad and mad, and I don't like how selfish I feel they are being. Mostly I'm sad for my kids because they are missing out on knowing their grandparents."

Because we live a distance from our grandchildren, we can't just pop in for a short visit. We have to plan ahead. Nor can we be of service for sick call or have the pleasure of going to every soccer game or piano recital. When we go we usually stay a few days and do an outing, or sometimes just stay at home and play with all the cool toys.

We appreciate that the other set of grandparents, who live close by and do see them frequently, are sensitive to our needs to spend time alone with our son and his wife and their children even though we also enjoy hanging out with them. We pass that pointer on to you if you are the grandparents who live in town.

Our own experience has taught us to be mindful of our ages and the ages of our grandchildren. We want to maximize the time while we still feel good and our grandchildren are open to spending time with us. For example, when our three children were younger we appreciated my parents gifting us once a year with an escape weekend. We would travel to them and drop off the kids. We would return reconnected and rejuvenated as a couple. My parents got to have time alone with our kids without all the other cousins around. Our children got to have precious time snuggled up to grandma reading books and with grandpa in the garden picking raspberries and hearing stories of growing up on the farm.

However, when my younger siblings had their children my parents were not able to do this anymore. Their health problems and being older did not allow this output of energy. Our response to this awareness is that we crave more time with our grandboys now because we might not be able to do so later. When we're choosing between doing a local event or seeing them, we factor this into the equation.

The Baby Boom Becomes the Grandparent Boom

If my experience in my practice and our interviews, as well as stories from our friends and Facebook are an indication, being a grandparent is a big deal these days. In fact, the baby boom has become the grandparent boom. According to some surveys, there are more grandparents in the U.S. than ever before — some

70 million, according to the latest census. That's a 24 percent increase since 2001. And some suggest that we baby boomers are doing the grandparent gig differently, more focused, maybe more obsessed and more indulgently. However, we also reap the benefits. Hanging out with our grandkids helps strengthen our immune system, have less depression, reduce social isolation and be happier and healthier. And we live longer, too.

What does that mean for you as a couple? It means you need to discuss your expectations with each other and clearly understand what you each desire in relation to your grandchildren. This is especially important if you decide to take on a regular commitment to provide child care. Discuss how it may impact your relationship and your retirement plans. If one of you is still working , how does this fit in? How does it affect your fitness goals or travel, volunteer work or other interests? How will you each cover the other to have the energy and stamina to chase toddlers or rock babies or drive the elementary age children from place to place?

Also explore your ideas about the dynamics of being your grandchild's caregiver. Are you expected to follow Mom and Dad's rules? Are you also the disciplinarian? Will it still be special to hang out with Grandpa? These are opportunities that provide lasting bonds. To be successful you need to commit to regular and open conversation with your spouse and with your adult children. Have an agreement and a trust that you will talk through any issues that arise.

One couple we know has overcommitted to five-day-a-week child care, which is exhausting them. They find it hard to pull away and have not found a way to speak with their daughter and son-in-law about their hesitancy. It shows up in resentment and complaining. They don't enjoy their grandchildren as much because they see them too much. It is affecting their marriage because they are not in agreement about how much child care they want to do. They feel caught in fear of letting their daughter down but concerned for their own health. Each is angry at the other for not resolving this problem.

If it is not a mutual agreement and only one spouse wants to take on the commitment while the other wants to be free to pursue other retirement interests, I recommend that you have an understanding about how to continue to enrich your marriage. Be careful not to let the childcare throw you off balance, in which one of you — or both — feel neglected by the other. Those little ones are precious, but so are you.

Jolene, a retired financial planner, felt strongly that she did not want to do regular daycare for her granddaughters when her son and his wife moved back to the community. Jolene wanted to have the freedom to be with her granddaughters for special outings and occasional babysitting, but did not want to be tied down to a regular schedule. Her son's mother-in-law had provided babysitting several times a week where they used to live. Jolene and her new husband, also recently retired, wanted to continue their plans to travel. Risking disappointing her son, Jolene held fast to what she knew was the right decision for her.

It takes courage to speak our truth. It is not an issue about right and wrong. Each couple has to review their priorities and decide what fits for their relationship.

For Donna and Vern, being full-time day care providers for both of their sons' children matched their desires and goals. "We would not have passed this up for any travel in the world," Donna said. "Our connections are so tight and precious. Our parents helped us out with our little ones, and we are doing the same for our sons."

Phil and Ellen, both retired, have given each of their three children the gift of full-time baby care for the first year, after maternity leave, for each baby, believing that they can give this great start to this new little one and also understanding how difficult and expensive infant day care can be in many communities.

While Lynn was still teaching, Dave, already retired, was able to take care of their grandson every Friday for the first three years of the boy's life. This formed a bond that has stayed precious over the next decade.

My sister, a retired special education teacher and administrator, and her husband, a retired pastor, volunteer one morning a week in each of their grandsons' classrooms doing whatever the teacher needs. They laughed with us as they awaited the background check now done on any volunteer who has contact with students. "I love seeing my grandson's face light up when he sees us coming into his room," she said.

Boundaries, Boundaries, Boundaries

The guiding principle for retired couples with their adult children and grandchildren is boundaries, boundaries and more boundaries. Determine and set yours. Respect theirs.

Mike and Carol spoke of how careful they are when they give advice to their children, especially about their grandchildren. Since Mike is a retired OB-GYN physician and Carol is a retired nurse, they have more than the average expertise in these areas. "We say, 'We understand that you are coming to your own ideas about how to handle this, and we offer these ideas and you are free to take them or leave them. We love you and care about you.'" And then they truly let it go.

Sometimes that's not an easy task. We need to remind ourselves that no matter how good we think our ideas are, our children are finding their way as adults or as parents, and they need to be allowed to make their own mistakes. Their struggles are part of the journey. Even if we believe we can make it easier for them or help them avoid a problem, it's not always wise to do so.

I look back at how careful my own parents were, especially in our early years as young newlyweds and as parents. They were very helpful when we asked them for advice directly. During visits, I'm sure there were many times they chose to keep their thoughts to themselves. I would have loved to hear their conversations in the car ride back home to Wisconsin. They gave us good models. As did my husband's parents.

Pat, 77, is Tom's older sister married to Ken, 78. About 20 years ago, Ken retired from his job designing computerized medical equipment (calculating, for example, the dosage and vectors for administering radiation in cancer treatment). This often involved travel to hospitals around the world: Japan, Italy, Germany, Switzerland. Pat stayed at home with their two sons. Interested in social justice and advocacy for

*children, they felt called to adopt, especially more hard-to-place chil-
dren. Within 10 years, they had adopted another son and four daughters. They had provided short-term foster care for other infants and
youngsters. Their family received the Missouri Family of the Year
Award. Pat's training as a nurse helped her as she managed the needs
of this diverse group. We enjoyed visiting their household which was a
trip into multi-cultural education as they made sure each culture rep-
resented in the family was celebrated.*

*They now are parents of seven adults plus partners, seven grand-
children and two great-grandchildren. Moving into retirement has necessitated good communication about boundaries, or their lives would
be consumed by the requests of all these busy lives. Now in retirement,
their frequent trips abroad (especially to Italy, where they have helped
with olive harvests) or up to their cottage in northern Wisconsin give
them the much-needed respite and couple time to just enjoy and reap
the benefits of their full life. They continue to inspire us as parents who
show up for their very diverse family through all the challenges and delights.*

Enriching the Grandparenting Experience

My father started writing "Grandpa Stories" in his mid-70s and
continued until he was 90. Each story was about 3-4 pages long
and would begin with "Dear Grandchildren, Let me tell you a
story about my life." He included many stories about growing up
on Iowa farms, his school years, college and graduate school
years, ministry, marriage and their worldwide travels, including
visiting all the national parks and every state of the U.S. The 98
stories fit into two looseleaf notebooks. They are a precious legacy.

Several of the Wise Married Elders gave suggestions for enriching the grandparent experience:

- Grandpa cookies and Grandma muffins.
- Share your interests like how to knit or how to cook or
  how to play golf. Make a cookbook of favorite recipes

you've prepared together or a scarf or enter a tournament.

- Volunteer at your grandchild's elementary school.
- Explore the opportunities with Road Scholar or park districts or museums and programs for grandparent-grandchild adventures. Or do your own GramCamp.
- Take a trip with each grandchild alone. Give them a budget. Let them choose where to go and plan it together. Let them navigate. Put a memory book together.
- Write a short story for each grandchild. Let the other grandchildren help you illustrate or add photos.
- Keep your own journal about each child and let them add entries each visit.
- Offer escape weekends or date nights for the parents while you enjoy time alone with the kids.
- Rent a home at the beach or in the mountains or at a resort. Each family kicks in what they can afford. Spend a week together. Take portraits.
- Take a cruise together, maybe to celebrate your 50th wedding anniversary.
- Do a legacy tour of the addresses or places their parents grew up. Include where you grew up.
- Tell stories and show pictures of their parents at the age they are now. Take a picture of them holding the picture or a selfie of all three generations — or four if you have a picture of you at the same age as they are now.
- Choose a place together to volunteer. Do this often enough to teach commitment and reap the rewards of service.

Our friends, Sus and Craig, have designed a nice balance. They are both in their mid-60s and are still active professionally. Because they are self-employed they can set their own schedules. They live close to their daughter and her husband, who both work full time. For the first granddaughter, they put their work projects on a reduced schedule for 4-1/2 years while they took care of her full time. For the second granddaughter, just born last year, they do baby care only in the afternoon and have their mornings free. They do not view this as a sacrifice. Even though it is hard work, they believe they are living out a spiritual mission as well as a hands-on investment in the future.

This beautiful chant is spinning in my mind as I think of all the ways in which we embrace our families in this circle of love:

You are the heart
You are the hands
You are the voice of Spirit on Earth
And who you are
and all you do
Is a blessing to the world. You're a blessing to the world.

— *Karen Drucker, who can be seen on YouTube*

~~~~Reflection~~~~

Close your eyes for a minute, take a deep breath and pull up in your mind a picture of your oldest grandchild (or a child you have a close relationship with if you're not a grandparent). Smile as you imagine his or her face. Think about a memory you have of a special time together. Imagine what words this child would use to describe you. Now do the same for your youngest grandchild. What words would be used to describe you? How do you want to be remembered as a grandparent? Imagine placing those words in your heart. Associate them with a color. Carry this with you in your next encounter.

Tom Note

As a grandparent I can't quite summon the energy that I think I used to have as a parent. I can quickly lose patience with the youngsters when they don't heed my instructions right away (although probably my own children didn't comply so quickly at these ages, either). I have let small things escalate into a shouting match, which does little to solve that small thing (Grandpa needs you to be quiet for 15 more minutes). I try to avoid escalation of anything. I want to be remembered as the cookie baker and "Tickle Monster" who would romp with them. Disciplinary issues that don't involve safety are best left to their parents.

17 - Friendships: Enriching the Quality of Our Lives

My women friends help make my marriage work. Maybe it's because I grew up the oldest daughter with two sisters, two brothers and a very loving mother and father in a close extended family. So as an adult I've re-created my close family by always being in groups: professional consultation, support, study or singing circles. Part of the reason is my commitment to my professional ethics to keep myself tuned and in tune. Some is for my personal growth. Some is just for fun.

I am in a group of five other therapists and educators, Abundia 5, who have been meeting for an annual retreat for 28 years and in another group, Vision Circle, which has been meeting monthly for 18 years. We value each other and have been there through marriages, divorces, serious illness, family issues, job and life changes. It is sacred to meet with friends in an atmosphere of acceptance and trust. We laugh about growing old as we imagine the picture of being in our rocking chairs (or wheelchairs!) in our 90s, telling stories about our great-grandchildren or our newest adventure. We know the time will come when we will attend one of our funerals.

I am also in a singing circle which meets every summer at a retreat center on Lake Michigan. I have been in the group for 16 years and have been joined first by my daughter and then both my sisters and their daughters, and my sons' wives, and some of my dear friends. We bring up Susan Lincoln from Austin, Texas, and we sing our hearts for four days. We study the music and theology of Hildegard of Bingen, a 12th century mystic and visionary and other healing chants. We also stay connected via email all year sending love, light and song. Some of us meet quarterly to get a song boost. If I come home from work dragging and I question if I have the energy to go out again that night, my husband will encourage me. "You know how you will feel after you get all those hugs and sing for a couple hours." I'm grateful he understands.

These groups help my marriage because that's where I do

some of the heavy lifting of sorting through issues and meet my needs for woman-to-woman emotional intimacy. As long as I give the summary version to Tom and we keep up with each other, we're solid. It's a good balance. If I looked to Tom for all that intensity I would disappoint myself and frustrate him. He's not a therapist. He's not hard-wired like that. He's very good with feelings — his own and mine — and with listening, but only to a point and then his let's-move-on signal goes off. Similarly I can only hear so much about golf or football or stand-up comedy or which car has what features, and I'm ready to move on, too.

I also belong to a book club that has enriched my life with new friends and introduces me to books and authors I might not have chosen on my own. We started it nine years ago when three of us were having dinner together and discovered we were each reading the same book, *The Help* by Kathryn Stockett. We had so much fun discussing the book, we decided to start a book club. It could not have been easier. We set a date, picked a place and each invited two or three friends. This many years later, we keep meeting monthly and also have taken field trips related to the books we've read. After we read *Loving Frank,* we toured Taliesin, designed by Frank Lloyd Wright, in Spring Green, Wis. After *Team of Rivals*, we went to the Lincoln Museum in Springfield. We explored the Hudson River Valley after we read a biography of Eleanor Roosevelt. We visited a book club member's new home in Florida. After reading an LBJ biography by Doris Kearns Goodwin, we traveled to Austin, Texas, and toured the LBJ Presidential Library. The next year it was on to Santa Fe, N.M., after reading *Georgia*, about Georgia O'Keefe. All the other book club ladies are retired, except me. It's fun to think of the next place we may travel and the books we read in between.

Differences With Men and Women

One difference between men and women is friendships. For many husbands, their wives are not only their best friend but their only real friend. Their fellow golfers or volunteer buddies are not their confidantes. They might know what cars they drive and what golf courses they've played but not know much more about each other's lives. Sometimes in retirement men now have more time and more interest to develop new friendships with other men. Women, in general, have had more occasion and maybe more need to have long-term relationships with other women, sharing at a soul level about their dreams, concerns, feelings and asking for support. Retirement may offer more leisure to keep nurturing these friendships.

Creative Friend Fun

Socializing with other couple or solo friends is part of the fun of retirement. It might involve traveling together or having breakfast with your retired teachers group or having monthly game night after the Friday Fish Fry. Churches offer a variety of social groups. These relationships are special and enrich the couple life.

Lynn has a group of women called the Winettes who gather at her cottage every year from all parts of the country. They share their lives, have fun, laugh, cry, take the boat out and, of course, drink wine. Lynn's husband, Dave, has a group of guys he meets with every weekday morning at the local coffee shop. They keep track of each other. They call and check in if someone is missing. When Dave went through a serious health scare recently, these fellows were there for him and for his wife.

For Cathy and Denis, members of their primary social group live in the same communities all year around. Six months in Illinois and six months in Arizona, with shorter trips in between for each of the couples to visit families out of state and visit timeshares in Cozumel and other places.

Jackie and Leslie enjoyed making friends with other RV folks in their campgrounds as they traveled the country scouting out retirement locales. They still stay in touch with some folks while others were fun to meet, swap supplies, and share stories and s'mores over a campfire on a full-moon night, knowing they most likely wouldn't cross paths again down the road.

The internet now has given us several opportunities to connect and meet virtual friends via social media, blogs and chat rooms through websites dedicated to our age group. Check out AARP/ healthy living, Senior planet.org and others.

Retired couples who have active social lives live longer. With the elder couples I interviewed, having good friends was listed as one of the rewards of retirement and contributed to the health of the marriage.

Although it might be tempting to "veg out" on the couch and catch up with your recorded TV programs or watch the live stream of that movie you've been waiting for, be careful not to isolate yourselves as a couple. Allow a good balance of time spent with other couples you enjoy. Invite some of the single widows or widowers to join you, too. It's great to spend time with your children and grandchildren, but also include building friendships as part of your couple enrichment program.

One of the book club members, Phyllis, makes sure she also includes younger friends in her close circle. "I enjoy how they think, and it makes me feel younger," she said.

On a recent New Year's Eve a group of us gathered in the hours before midnight. We collected magazines and had big poster boards, scissors, glue sticks and markers. We put on some meditative music and quieted ourselves. We did a guided visualization reviewing the year and imagined what we wanted to keep in our lives moving forward and what we wanted to let go of from the past. We imagined what we wanted more of in the new year and what we wanted to have less of. We imagined how we wanted to feel at this time next year. After some moments of silence, we opened our eyes and began to flip through the magazines to find images and words to create our vision collage for the new year. We kept the music playing and worked in silence with an occasional chuckle. After an hour or so, those who wished began to share, showing the others their visions for the new year. We had such a good time we decided to make this a ritual. My vision collage has been my companion in my home office as I finished this book, the powerful images reminding me of my purpose when I needed inspiration, courage or motivation.

This gathering happened to be with my extended family. My sisters, brother, nieces and nephew sat around the big dining room table. I've also done this with gatherings of friends. Using the art images, photos, colors and designs can be fun and also profoundly touching, sometimes in a surprising way. You may think about the groups you are in and wonder if this exercise might enhance your experience together.

Friendship Circles Shrink

As we get older our social circles may get smaller. When we retire we don't have the built-in interactions that work presents. We have to work harder at keeping up contacts. Friends and family members may move away for work or not even live in our same area. Old friends may move away to retirement communities or sadly, become ill and pass away.

Several of the Wise Married Elders we interviewed spoke both of how much they valued their friends and how difficult it is to make new friends at this age.

As we discussed in the health and wellness chapter, loneliness may be a health issue contributing to impairment. Although married people over age 65 report less loneliness, being married is not foolproof protection. I have interviewed many husbands and wives over the years who are suffering in their loneliness. Let's make a distinction. Someone can be married and surrounded by friends, and still feel lonely.

Loneliness is defined as feeling alone, whereas social isolation is measured by the number of relationships and social contacts someone has. Some people are socially isolated and not lonely. In contrast, some people are lonely, even if they have a lot of social contacts. So as you look at how you are aging as an individual and as a couple, addressing loneliness and friendship is essential.

We know that there are health benefits to social connection. The research studying the "SuperAgers," those living to 100 and beyond, have found that social connection is significantly correlated with daily contact with friends and family. Like the Beatles song, "We get by with a little help from our friends ... "

After she and her husband moved to a new community after they retired, Gwen, 72, was very intentional in finding a church that had several social options for her age group. She knew her husband would not be joining her. He chose to worship on Sunday mornings on the golf course and was not interested in meeting new friends. Being outgoing and very busy at her former church, she knew this would help combat feelings of loneliness and help her make new friends. She found a church that welcomed her with open arms. Her pineapple upside down cake became a fast favorite at the potlucks and funeral luncheons.

The effects of social media, especially Facebook and texting, complicate matters. Are we more socially isolated because we are connecting more on social media, or do we interact less face to face because we connect on social media? Reading what others are doing on FaceBook becomes a replacement for the real deal.The most recent research suggests that we need to strive for a balance of social media and actual face-to-face time with our friends and family.

Don and Nancy started a couples support group at their church for elders to share about issues related to aging. Jean and George also started a similar group who have been meeting regularly for years. Members of the group take turns co-leading and organizing which helps the group stay active and vital. They also have started a monthly supper club in every community they have lived over their 49 years together. When they were younger and raising their babies it met weekly. Five to six families would gather once a week, each taking a turn preparing the meal. This same group would also do a monthly Saturday work day at each other's homes, painting a room or cleaning a garage or doing a chore together. Some watched the little ones while everyone else pitched in to complete the task getting done faster and maybe with more merriment. Both of these couples are profiled in Chapter 4, The Wise Married Elders Speak.

Friends As Lifesavers

Friends are also the ones who shovel our walk or bring our news-paper up from the driveway. They not only enhance the quality of life but may also be life-savers in time of need, or help if we get stressed with life events.

Maria was still working when Juan, retired, had a heart attack. She didn't have enough sick and personal days to take off work to drive him to his rehab sessions. Friends took shifts to help them out, and provided meals as well. They were returning the favors this generous couple had given to their friends and neighbors over the years.

In a weather emergency, our friends came through:

In 1996, 14,000 homes in our area were damaged in a bizarre weather system that dumped 18 inches of rain in 24 hours. The water had no place to go, exacerbated by construction in areas that used to be cornfields. In the early hours of the night, our son, whose bedroom was in the finished basement, started hearing a popping sound. It was the mortar in the cement-block foundation. Fortunately he ran upstairs to alert us just as the basement wall collapsed. Soon the basement was filled with seven feet of muddy water. We fled for safer ground. After our house was secured, the hard work of removing the damaged items, re-building the basement walls and replacing furnace, water heater and appliances took months. We felt more fortunate than some whose homes sustained more damage. Our friends whose homes were not damaged became our lifelines, doing laundry, providing meals, salvaging pre-cious pictures from soaked photo albums and most importantly, help-ing us laugh. We're not in touch with the worry and the extreme fatigue we felt during that time, but we do remember the wonderful friends who helped us out.

My hunch is you have your own stories similar to ours. You have been married a long time and have helped and been helped by your friends over the years. It takes a village ... and we are grateful.

I enjoyed this essay in AARP newsletter, called "Better Than

Sex" by Suzanne Braun Levine, author of *How We Love Now: Women Talk About Intimacy After Fifty.*

"There comes a time when remembering a name is better than having an orgasm. Which is not to denigrate orgasms, just to acknowledge a pattern that comes to the fore around the same time as forgetting names. It is inelegantly called downsizing, and many aspects of older people's lives are, like lust, diminished. But in my experience, the process is also about upgrading. What is left is all the more precious because of its quality. For some, the downsizing applies to sex, ... but the upgrading is expanding horizons of sensuality and intimacy. In my case, the discovery that my feet are an erogenous zone has suggested wondrous possibilities.

The territory of love, once so closely tied to sex, is also expanding. Friends experience ecstatic bonding with grandchildren. ('When I'm expecting a call from my granddaughter, my heart beats as if I were awaiting a call from a lover,' one told me.) I don't have grandkids, but I have felt a surge of love for my girlfriends and my husband of over 40 years. Earlier on, my friendships with women were important, but there was an out-of-sight, out-of-mind quality to them. So much else was going on. Now, I simply can't imagine getting older without my girlfriends. And I wouldn't have said that my husband provided that 'girlfriend' kind of support before; but that is changing — because we are changing. He and I have downsized our expectations of each other and upgraded our appreciation. These few carefully selected and tended people always know just what I mean, and they can make me laugh. Laughter may be the one experience that need not be either downsized or upgraded. So it is reassuring to learn that a good belly laugh is physiologically a lot like an orgasm. And almost as satisfying as remembering a name."

In a Harvard University study, following graduates for more than 80 years, the researchers found that close relationships more than anything else, including money and health, keep people happy. Nurturing relationships with friends, family and community helps people through difficult situations. Researchers also found that those with strong social support experienced less mental deterioration as they aged.

"The surprising finding is that our relationships and how happy

we are in our relationships have a powerful influence on our health," said Robert Waldinger, director of the study and a professor of psychiatry at Harvard Medical School. "Taking care of your body is important, but tending to your relationships is a form of self-care too. That, I think, is the revelation."

"When we gathered together everything we knew about them at age 50, it wasn't their middle-age cholesterol levels that predicted how they were going to grow old. It was how satisfied they were in their relationships. The people who were the most satisfied in their relationships at age 50 were the healthiest at age 80."

For more about the research and his ideas about living and aging well, check out Dr. Waldinger's popular TED Talk called *What Makes a Good Life? Lessons from the Longest Study on Happiness.*

Friends are part of keeping the music playing for us married folks who are loving our marriages in retirement.

~~~~Reflection~~~~

How are you with friends? How lonely are you? What ideas do you have as a couple to make or sustain the friendships you have?

18 - Retirement Choices: Plan, But Be Flexible

Marilyn, a trust attorney, is contemplating retiring, but worries that as soon as she retires, she will just watch TV and turn into a blob — which is what she feels she does on her days off. I explained that she probably does that because she is so exhausted from her job, which requires weekly travel around the U.S. When she is home, she goes into recovery mode and just wants to rest and "veg." She feels unmotivated. I wondered with her what might happen if she slowed down, went to part-time and started building more self-care into her schedule. What might happen if she had some days of doing nothing, with no agenda, no schedule, no plane to catch? What might happen if she allowed herself to have several uninterrupted days? Not vacation days but self-care, exploration days. Learning how to relax and "let go" days.

What she uncovered as she tried to imagine this was an underlying fear many people feel: "Who am I if I'm not doing what I've been doing? Who am I if I'm not the trust attorney? Mother? Wife? What's my value if I don't have a title, if I do nothing?" She felt immediately relieved when I explained this retirement phenomenon and how common it is. I encouraged her to imagine what she might discover about herself, her own interests, what makes her tick deep down inside when she allows herself to not be so busy and task-oriented. She quoted a common myth about retirement that if you don't have something to retire to you'll just dry up and die. That has not been my experience with the couples I work with or interview.

Build In Unstructured Time

As you transition into retirement, it is recommended that you spend some time — a good amount of time, maybe several months to a year — unscheduled and unbooked. This serves at least three purposes: 1. It allows you to learn how to relax. 2. It allows you to explore how you want to spend your time in retirement without pressure. 3. It makes more time available for your marriage.

If you find unstructured time unsettling, I recommend that you sit with the discomfort long enough to allow the deeper self to bubble up through the years of work and busyness. If someone harasses you and asks what are you retiring to, you can say, "I'm retiring to the adventure of discovering me, who am I when I'm not working."

My husband promised himself that he was not going to commit to anything for at least six months after retiring from his job as news editor of the local daily newspaper. After four-plus decades of deadlines, it was glorious for him to go to sleep when he wanted to and sleep as long as his mind would allow, trying to reset his body clock after years of shift work. As Tom's retirement date approached he was alternately amused and annoyed with how often other people wanted to plan his time or sign him up for lifelong learning classes for seniors or volunteering at the food pantry or the homeless shelter or at church. Instead, he enjoyed feeling free of a to-do list or any "oughta-woulda-shoulda-couldas." He enjoyed "putzing" and taking all day to do the laundry or plan and prepare the evening meal or catch a luxurious nap without guilt. It was a pretty good deal for me too, since I came home from my day at the office to a happier, rested husband, completed household tasks and a new recipe on the table.

Like Tom, Lynn was also clear with her husband who had retired five years earlier. She did not want to schedule her time after she retired for at least six months, including travel. After 30 years of teaching elementary school, she enjoyed sleeping late and taking her time with her morning coffee and the newspaper. The one exception to the travel ban was a trip she and her husband planned to coincide with the beginning of the school year. Like many teachers, from preschool to college, the academic calendar is in their blood. Fall means the end of summer vacation and back to the very long days of lesson plans, instruction, grading homework, conferences with parents and staff and doing it all again the next day. Many teachers, especially those who felt ambivalent about leaving the profession they dearly love, speak of how hard it was to get through the first week of the new school year after they retired. For Lynn, planning to be away, traveling to be with the comfort of friends in The Villages of Florida and playtime at Disney World was a creative way to deal with the transition and set the stage for their new life in retirement.

For Larry, retirement without a plan sounded like his idea of hell. He could hardly wait to start on the list of projects he had been accumulating for years. Caught in a boring job which he could barely endure, he looked forward to being his own boss and getting things done on his own timetable. The idea of sitting still, quietly contemplating the reason for his existence, did not appeal to him. He didn't slow down until years later when a back injury finally grounded him and he was forced to find enjoyment in more sedentary activities until he recovered. His wife June appreciated the slower version of her husband and asked that they continue some of the newly discovered couple activities even after his back was healed.

A year before Mary retired, she started keeping a list of all the things she wanted to do after she retired. She discovered it years later. She hadn't needed it. However, in the months leading up to her last day of work, it gave her comfort to record her ideas during the pre-retirement phase.

When And How To Retire

For some people planning retirement, easing into the final date by cutting to part-time or reducing the workload helps with the transition as well as the financial management. For others, the time to retire becomes clear when certain changes happen at work which create obstacles they don't want to tackle. People reassure me, "You know when you're done." Retirees explained that it is ideal if the actual date to leave can come shortly after this awareness — with proper notice. They recommend if you need to stay longer, you can use the additional time to get more clear about how and when you want to leave your job.

For Chuck it was when the school system adopted new computer software. He just didn't want to learn it. He knew it was time to retire. Don wanted to hold on two more years as an accountant for a major manufacturing company because of his financial plan. When it was announced that the firm was moving to new offices an hour away, he moved his retirement date up a year. The job wasn't worth a two-hour-a-day commute.

For Mike, an OB/GYN physician, retirement was well planned. He had the date in mind and had a 10-year plan. First he stopped doing on-call hospital service, then he no longer did surgery or baby deliveries. Then he resigned from all the hospital and clinic committees and went to part-time. By the time he retired completely he was adjusted and eager to begin his new life. His wife Carol, retired from nursing years before, was grateful for the easy, spaced-out transition. Used to years of raising their children and doing volunteer work at church, she said she would not have been ready for him to be at work one day and home full time the next. They used the careful plan to adjust their expectations and renegotiate their relationship. During that time, they also sold the home where they raised their children and downsized into a much smaller condo with access to a bike path from their backyard. With no outdoor maintenance, they just lock the door and leave to visit their grandchildren around the country.

Mike said, "One of the most helpful things we planned was to leave town a month after we retired and travel around Europe. We were gone for six weeks. When we returned, life had already changed. There were no routines to fall back into. We had to create anew, from scratch, how we wanted to be with each other and how we wanted to spend time now that our life work was over and we were now free to pursue other interests."

Between visits to grandchildren, Mike takes long walks, mentors younger colleagues, and four times a year comes down to Chicago to conduct architecture tours, a long-term interest of his. Carol loves volunteering at her church. For this highly educated, cerebral couple, investing in this long-range planning helped ensure a smooth transition.

Not all of us can afford to travel around the world, but the idea of planning an event to mark the retirement date is a good one. Maybe you have a retirement party as a send-off or go on an affordable excursion so when you return it feels different than coming back from a short vacation.

Life Interferes

Other couples may have had a similar long-range plans, but life threw curves that necessitated quick responses. It sometimes felt like a high stakes game of dodgeball.

Grace and Michael had a plan for retirement, too. Then Grace, director of a large county health department, suffered a heart attack. She recovered well and actually went back to work in a reduced, more manageable role. Just as they thought they were back on track for their financial plans to retire, Michael got laid off from his job as a research chemist. He did not see it coming and admits that it really threw him into a tailspin. "I was devastated that they would treat me so unkindly after so many years, and then I got angry," he said. "I had worked hard for them for decades. They changed management, and the new guys really didn't care. It was all about the bottom dollar. They could bring in someone younger and cheaper. I felt lost for awhile." Michael tried to bounce back, and explored other ways to use his education and experience. Teaching high school chemistry was not a good fit. He found his niche teaching chemistry at two local community colleges. They finally eased into full-time retirement five years later.

Grace's advice to younger couples is to mind the finances very closely. Have a financial plan, and do it together as a couple. She advises to stay informed all the way. Even if one spouse manages the finances, make sure the other spouse is on board and knows where everything is.

Grace and Michael are also good examples of getting squeezed in the middle by caring for elderly friends as well as helping relieve stressors that affected both their adult children and families. They are grateful they were able to be there for their loved ones, both financially and emotionally. They are also grateful that things have calmed down and they can look forward to more time together traveling — and relaxing in their tranquil backyard.

Abrupt Health Changes

The advice to plan when you can and stay resilient and flexible when you can't is helpful guidance. It's a good reminder that our best intentions can be challenged by life's changes in a heartbeat. Our investment in our psychological and physical health and strength pays off at these times when we need to be flexible and resilient. We need to prepare ourselves, just to keep our heads above water and not be swept away by the strong current or roaring waves.

This happened to our good friends, Jeanette and Ken. Their lives changed in a matter of hours.

Jeanette, 70, a psychotherapist, planned to retire in a few months so they could take their long dreamed for six-month cruise around the world. She had stopped taking new clients and had begun referring or completing the work with her current clients. Their children and grandchildren, who all lived nearby, were starting to adjust to the idea of the long separation, knowing they could communicate by FaceTime and Skype while their loved ones were on another continent oceans away. And then Ken, 75, who had retired 10 years before from IBM, had a stroke.

Jeanette came out of her home office to find Ken speaking with a friend on the phone, not being able to feel the right side of his body, just not feeling right. Living five minutes from a hospital, Jeannette wasted no time driving him there. He was admitted after doctors diagnosed that he had indeed had a stroke affecting his right side and his vision. Two days later, he suffered a second stroke. He was transferred to a rehabilitation center, where he began a course of physical, occupational, optical and speech therapy several times a day to retrain his brain to "work around" the damaged places. After other medical complications and hard work, he is well on the way to a partial recovery. They are both grateful for their family's assistance, especially bringing meals and revamping their way of life. They decided to sell their home of 47 years and move to a retirement community nearby. Their adult children and grandchildren helped tremendously to get the house ready to sell while Jeanette assisted Ken in his recovery. Fortunately, they were able to get a refund of their cruise money. They are navigating a very different journey now.

Anyone reading this book has similar stories of their friends or relatives — or maybe even closer to home with your spouse or parent or child. We hold each other tighter and fill our hearts with gratitude for this moment. We may say a prayer and send a blessing and remind each other how precious we are to each other and our loved ones. And to not take even a moment for granted.

The Tim McGraw song *Live Like You Were Dying* is a good reminder. The poignant lyrics go like this: " ... I asked him 'When it sank in that this might really be the real end, how's it hit you when you get that kind of news? Man, what'd you do?' He said, 'I went skydiving. I went Rocky Mountain climbing. I went 2.7 seconds on a bull named Fumanchu. And I loved deeper. And I spoke sweeter. And I gave forgiveness I'd been denying.' And he said, 'Someday I hope you get the chance to live like you were dying. Like tomorrow was a gift.'"

So plan when you can and be resilient when you can't. What are ways we can increase our ability to be resilient? Chapters 3, 11, 13 on aging and resilience, on health and wellness, and on spirituality give more ideas about increasing your resilience skills and building your strength. You may already be doing many of the strategies recommended. Feel validated that you are on the right track and commit to trying some of the others.

Retire Together?

Deciding whether both husband and wife should retire at the same time takes a lot of conversation, especially about expectations. It is often the case that both are not ready at the same time to retire together. It is sometimes referred to as "in-sync" where the couple retires at the same time or "out-of-sync" where one retires before the other. There are pros and cons with each option. Age, money, health, and job satisfaction are big factors.

This disparity is often the case for wives who may have spent time out of the workforce raising the children and are now enjoying a career and are not ready yet to retire. The wife may also be younger then her husband who may be ready to retire as soon as he turns 66 and can collect full Social Security. Some considerations are:

- Schedule. If one is working and the other is not, when will you see each other? Will you share meals? Will you go to bed and wake up at similar times? Same questions apply if you retire at the same time.

- Money. Does one need to work longer because of health insurance coverage or needing the income for daily expenses or to build the "nest egg" for retirement, or do you have enough money now to support both of you retiring?

- Job satisfaction. How do you both feel about your career goals? Is work fulfilling? How will those needs be met in retirement? Or not?

- Health. How is your health being affected by your jobs?

- Retirement dreams. Are you "in-sync" with each other for what you want to do and when you want to do it? Does it require both of you retiring at the same time? Is there a way to allow one to still work part-time while the other retires, without losing track of your joint "bucket list?"

It is important to remember to stay close and keep checking in with each other about the decisions related to retirement. These discussions can help head off potential problems. If expectations are different and are unexpressed, dissatisfaction with each other can flare up easily. We each respond to transitions differently. Some take change in stride and their natural optimism guides them through bumpy patches. Others feel change is threatening or disturbing and may feel off balance or discombobulated. Do not judge each other. Keep talking and supporting each other through these decisions and transitions.

Spend time envisioning your own ideas about retirement and then hearing your spouse's ideas and designing a joint plan. It's OK if you disagree. It's very likely that your visions may not sync up. You might actually find that you are far apart in your ideas about a perfect day or a perfect week in retirement. One of you may dream about being on the road traveling the country while the other can hardly wait to be available 24/7 for the grandkids. One of you may look forward to spending many hours a day together whereas the other may have dreams that do not often include their spouse. One of you may be afraid that your money will run out more sooner than later, while the other has expensive plans for a home remodel and worldwide travel.

Dick owned a sporting goods company. He was several years older than wife, Francie, in second marriages for both. He asked her to sell her home inspection business so they could retire together. She agreed with some hesitancy, and then became disappointed when it took him a lot longer to shorten his work day. Although they had more time together, she missed being the boss and having her own business and income. When they did both finally retire they discovered their mutual bucket lists were closely in agreement and they started checking off the things they wanted to do and where they wanted to go, free of their respective jobs.

For Lorraine and Pat, who owned a business together, planning for retirement also involved the complication of the sale of the company. For family-owned businesses where relatives are in the line of succession, disputes can complicate the process, sometimes requiring a consultant or arbitrator who can assess the needs of the company and the specific skills of the family employees and owners.

For some women who have been at home for some years — whether they retired earlier or were stay-at-home moms who never entered the workforce — it may take a huge adjustment to have hubby home. One of the biggest complaints from wives is called the Velcro effect: "He is at my side constantly. I'm used to being alone for hours. Now he follows me around the house, talking nonstop, reloading the dishwasher or commenting on my routines. Or he goes with me to the grocery store and questions the brands I select or the things I put in the cart. Before he retired, he never used to pay any attention to these tasks. I'm ready to bash his head in or go to work myself."

Where To Live

There are so many factors influencing where to live in retirement. If you're not retiring at the same time, it makes sense to stay where you are until both of you are free to consider a move. However, I have encountered several cases recently where one spouse, age 55-60 plus, gets a work promotion or relocation to another state, which prompts the other spouse to retire earlier then planned or consider a new job in the new area.

My husband and I enjoy reading the articles in AARP and other publications geared to the baby boomers entitled "Ten Best Cities to Retire." We read them and fantasize about our life there and then remind ourselves how far we'd have to travel to see our family. That's one of our big factors. We also thought we might downsize to a smaller home or even buy or rent a condo. Then we ran the numbers and discovered we are financially better off staying where we are for the time being. Plus we have enough room when everyone comes home for holidays and we have plenty of garden space in the backyard. So, as long as we are able and it makes sense, we'll stay put and dream about life somewhere else and be grateful for what we have here.

We know of a couple where the husband is retired and the wife still has five years on her contract. They did the numbers with their accountant and decided to sell their home and buy an independent living condo in a retirement village nearby. Even though they are only in their mid-60s and well under the age of most of the other residents, this decision fits their lifestyle of travel part of the year and low-cost home maintenance. Paying the monthly fee is a good deal and they have guarantees of health care at every level for their remaining years.

Whether or where you might want to relocate is an important part of designing your retirement plan. Knowing your interests, values and budget will help set the parameters. Do you want to live in the city, country or suburb? By water or mountains or bike paths or golf courses? Do you need to be near health care facilities? Do you want theater, live music, sporting events close by? How close to family? What's your budget for rent or mortgage? What is the cost of living at possible relocation sites? Several lifestyle options are presented in Chapter 15.

If you are both retiring and only one of you wants to move to a new area, how do you make the choice? Talk about it. Listen to each other's views on what you need and the impact of each option.

For one of the WME couples, the husband's job had kept them several states away from the wife's extended family. They had to travel a long distance every time they came for reunions of her family, whereas his relatives lived close by. Over the years, they came to a decision that when he was ready to retire they would move to her state and find a place closer to her family. He was willing to give up being closer to his own family. The wife was younger so when he retired, it meant that she retired early with the idea she might find work in the new area or not if they both decided to retire together. They decided that even though money might be tighter they looked forward to settling into their new location and spending more time together while they were both in good health. In the years that followed their children also relocated to be closer to them.

Bucket List — Mine? Yours? Ours

Have some fun dreaming about what you might do with your time when you are free from work demands and schedules. Come up with a bucket list. The things you want to do or see before you "kick the bucket." In the feel-good movie *The Bucket List*, Morgan Freeman and Jack Nicholson take off from the cancer ward to discover what more life has to offer. The message to us is to do it now and do it with intention. To have even more fun coming up with your bucket list, brainstorm the first one with no thought to your budget. If money was not an issue, what would be on your bucket list? Then go back and make another one within budget. You may surprise yourself and each other.

About The Money ...

What about finances? If you are a typical almost-retiree, you have been inundated with invitations to investment seminars. After listening about investments, insurance, annuities, wills and trusts, you are likely to emerge feeling poor. You may feel that you haven't saved enough, or have spent too much. The free dinner doesn't sit too well either.

You're in good company. The people we interviewed were all in agreement about planning for what you need when you retire: save early, save often, save as much as you can. Start Social Security as late as you can. Be careful how you spend. Expect to outlast your money.

Financial strategies are beyond the scope of this book. We will trust you to find a good resource among the many available. In the meantime, discuss your financial plan and retirement with each other until you find agreement so that it is not one of the obstacles in your relationship. Most likely if you handled money well in your marriage up to this point, you will continue to do so in retirement. If not, you may want to seek professional financial counseling.

What is within the scope of this book is a discussion about the underlying values, attitudes, fears and myths we may carry about our relationship with money. For all of us, this goes back to our childhoods.

A self-identified workaholic, sociologist Sarah felt a disproportionate amount of panic when she contemplated her retirement from teaching and research at an East Coast College. Her husband, Ted, also calls himself a workaholic. He was on the faculty at the same college in the economics department. Ethical and political issues in both of their departments forced them to decide to retire before their planned date. The panic she felt about this decision was out of proportion to her usual calm state of being. It felt abnormal. She knew she needed to sort it out in a professional setting. She made a psychotherapy appointment.

Her therapist helped her uncover a fear which dated back to her youth. She remembered having heard as a pre-teen about a painful se-cret involving her father and the shame he carried at losing the family savings before she was born. He had decided to leave a good job, moved his young family to the big city to pursue a dream, but the would-be partner in this venture absconded with all the money. Her father was forced to return to his prior employer and beg for his old job back. He remained loyal to that employer for the whole of his working life. Since this traumatic episode was never discussed in her home, some buried understanding for Sarah was the unexplained terrible cost of leaving one's job.

Being able to retrieve this story and tell it out loud helped her feel the effect of the trauma and its role in fears she unconsciously carried about giving up her own job. She was able to get hold of the financial reality of her own retirement. Her healthy pension—and circumstances very different from her parents—allowed her to let go of the panic. How-ever, the crisis which provoked their mutual early retirement caused both Sarah and Ted to leave their long, successful careers with consid-erable resentment. Needing to work through the pain and sudden loss of their professional roles put a strain on their relationship for some time. The support of their friends and their church community helped get them through. Now they are using their many gifts as volunteers, Sarah as a lay pastoral counselor and writing poetry and Ted as a com-munity organizer and leader of an environmental political movement in his area.

The bottom line is not to let money or lack of it interfere with what is most important for you. Whether living on a limited budget or unlimited wealth, couples can be healthy and happy. It is up to you to decide how you want to live and what your val-ues are. What is imperative is that you do not let discouragement — or regret that you didn't save more earlier — get in the way of having a plan now. Work with what you have. Getting consumed with what you don't have can immobilize you and keep you stuck in the same patterns that resulted in your financial condition. We tend to avoid thinking about what we feel badly about. Even though we might wish for better circumstances, being grateful for what we do have can bring us back to feeling more positive and ready to make plans.

Downsizing and Decluttering

Clearing out our space and reallocating all our stuff is big business for baby boomers and the services that advertise to us. It also occupies space in the conversations with our friends and our adult children. Tom and I have promised our children we will not leave them with the task of decluttering our home like we had to do with my folks. I hear this promise echoed frequently. We as a generation have acquired more possessions than previous generations. We now have the task of decluttering and re-purposing. We are witness to the storage lockers dotting our countrysides, filling the spaces once occupied by cornfields, or around shuttered factories in cities, now holding all the stuff that won't fit in our crammed-wall-to-wall basements and three-car garages.

It is such a glorious feeling to drop off bags of still good clean clothing and coats and furniture to Goodwill or the local homeless shelter. Shredding the files with confidential information and recycling the rest clears space. Boxing up books I'll never open again for the local used bookstore or library takes longer because I open one and sit down to re-read a passage I had forgotten or I reminiscence about the time in my life when I acquired the book. It's all good.

Deciding what is an heirloom to keep and pass on some day and what to donate can stir up good memories. A client who had to move to a much smaller place and could not take many possessions shared a suggestion her aunt had given her years before. Take pictures of what is valuable to you. Capture the memory. Then pass the object on. Another friend told about a place she learned about that takes donated office supplies and recycles them to teachers for classrooms or to new entrepreneurs on a limited budget. We pass on the good wishes for success, too.

As I was decluttering in a closet which had become a neglected collection site, I found a jewelry box that belonged to my husband's mother. I had forgotten that it had found its way to our house after she was dividing up her things as she moved into a retirement center. I lifted the lid and was flooded by precious memories of "Happy" (her nickname since she was a child). I passed the box on to our daughter who can decide what she wants to keep and use and save for her children. In the meantime, I get to see the brooch or necklace worn by our daughter who cherishes this connection with her grandmother, whom she misses dearly. I share this story to remind myself that decluttering is more than just getting rid of the stuff. It is also a valuing of our connections. It is worth all the attention we're giving it. It is revisiting a life well-lived. And giving new life to the precious and useful that can be passed on. And saving our landfills.

Designing Your Retirement Plan

The following chapter helps you build your own custom retirement plan. Answer the questions for yourself and share your responses with each other. Plan on several sessions. Keep revising as you go along. Even if life throws you a curve and you don't get to follow your ideal plan, the research you've done and the discussions you've had will lay the groundwork to help ensure a more successful retirement.

Tom's Note

However much money you have, spend a little of it to be free of the daily worry about money. When you go out to eat, don't feel obligated to order from the bottom of the menu. Order something that really sounds good at the moment. Save the extra few dollars somewhere else. (For golfers, there are great deals out there for seniors. In our area, my friend and I have played more than a dozen courses, rarely paying more than $29 — with cart! And we enjoy the game every bit as much as people who pay tens of thousands to join a private club.) As Porgy sings in Porgy and Bess, "Folks wid plenty o' plenty, they got a lock on the door, 'fraid somebody's a-goin' to rob 'em while dey's out a makin' more. What for?" You've worked a long time to — at least for a while — have the privilege of not worrying about your money.

19 - Designing Your Retirement Plan: Be Proactive, Starting Now

The strongest suggestion from the couples interviewed was to plan for your retirement. When you are in your 50s, talk with each other about expectations: when, where, how. As the time approaches, have more discussion and redefine or refine or update those expectations. Review changes in your health, attitudes or circumstances. Keep updated about your finances. Review where you are emotionally and psychologically with regard to work, marriage and relationships with friends or adult children.

Here is a list of questions we recommend you answer together as part of coming up with your plan for retirement. Set aside some time to complete the process. You might want to plan a couple's retreat getaway specifically for this purpose and follow the outline suggested. However and whenever you decide, start planning, discussing, dreaming soon and then stay with it until you have some answers. You can always change your mind. Or life might change it for you.

Ideally, if you have a date in mind, a few months before, set aside a day or several hours to be together to focus and review your plan. Remember you might not know some of the answers. Or your answers might change as you get closer to the date or start to experience the changes associated with retiring.

Follow the set of questions below. You might want to prepare by spending some time answering the questions yourself before you begin sharing with your partner. Notice which questions stir up feelings of fear, anxiety and excitement. Trust your intuition.

Questions For Your Retirement Plan

1. When do you plan to retire? Retire at same time? Different times? How might this affect plans?
2. What factors influence this decision?

3. What are your expectations of retirement? What does retirement look like? What feelings do you each have about retirement? Fears? Excitement? Concerns?

4. What ideas do you have about how to spend your time?

5. Do you want to work part-time? Have paid employment? Volunteer? Retire from what you are doing now and do something else?

6. What is your time line? Do you want to leave work by a certain date? Do you want to ease into retirement by going to part-time or reducing hours over a period of time?

7. What do you want to do immediately after you retire? Do you want to plan a period of rest and exploration before committing to any other work or volunteering or obligations?

8. How do you want to spend time together? Apart? Separate interests? Shared interests?

9. How do you want to divide household chores and car, yard and home maintenance?

10. Where do you want to live? Same home? Same location? Somewhere else? Downsize? Sell? Have two homes? Two locations? Live on a boat? Buy an RV?

11. How do you decide where to settle? Close to the children and grandchildren? What if they are spread out? What if you move close to them and then they are transferred?

12. What are short-term plans? Long-term? What's on your bucket lists? Her list? His list? Joint list?

13. Travel? Road trips? Air and train? Overseas? Tour? Cost? When? How much?

14. How much money do you have? What is the plan for making it last? What limitations do you have?

15. How much time do you want to spend with your adult children and grandchildren? Do you want to do regular grandchild care?

16. What about care for parents or other loved ones?

17. What do you want your sex life to be like? Satisfied now? More passion? Light the fire? Reignite the fire?

18. What are your health concerns? What are plans for healthy living?

19. What are plans to do regular couple check-in to sustain and nurture your relationship?

20. What about friends and social life?

21. Looking at life now: What do you want less of? What do you want more of? How might retirement affect this?

22. What annoying habits do you want to change? Start with awareness of self and then ask of your partner.

23. What is your sense of spirituality? As a person? As a couple? How important is a daily practice or attending fellowship or church, synagogue, temple, mosque or other place of worship?

24. If you have serious health issues, what are your long-term plans? Long-term care insurance? Have you executed the needed documents: power of attorney for healthcare, power of attorney for property, advanced health directives?

25. End-of-life issues? Burial or cremation? Funeral or memorial service? Do your loved ones know your wishes, and know where they are written down? Wills, trusts and bequests?

26. Do you have positive models for retirement? Who do you know who you admire in retirement? How might you emulate them? Do you need a retirement mentor?

27. What else needs to be included in your retirement plan?

Congratulate yourself on getting to the bottom of this very long list of questions. It is a huge task to read, consider and discuss all of these with your partner. Hopefully you feel it has been time and energy well spent.

Tom's Note

If you have more than you need — money, property, cars, books, music, sports equipment, bicycles, yard and garden equipment, whatever — have you tried the joy of giving it away rather than storing it or moving it around? There are bound to be people and organizations who would be glad to accept some or all of it, and put everything to good use. First, of course, let loved ones and family members choose what they want, now or later. But ... when in doubt, move it out. After you're gone somebody else will be faced with all those decisions.

20 - Grow Old Along With Me

I'm watching my husband weed, rake and try to make a path through the jungle in the back of our yard. The very wet spring and then the hot May and June have made everything grow quickly. We have tomatoes and cucumbers coming and basil and kale and beans galore. I promise him that I will join him when I'm done editing this chapter, after I put a lot of mosquito goop on.

In writing this book I've come to even more deeply appreciate Tom's cooperative spirit and his work ethic. We make a good team. I feel good about how we raised our children as co-parents with two careers and active lives. I love how gentle we are with each other, when either one of us is struggling with a wave of guilt or an attack of oughta-woulda-shoulda-coulda, we hug and commiserate. Get a drink of water for the other and say, "Breathe." We may laugh at something we saw on Facebook about our grandsons or remind ourselves of a memory or an event coming up we're looking forward to. We put on some music. Our mood has lifted. Soon, we're feeling better.

So, I just reread that paragraph and I think I just summarized the message of the book. I want to add a thought about being gentle with yourself, too. We all know that life is messy. So are relationships. It takes commitment and courage to stay married and to make our marriage even more satisfying and fun. We all have good moments and some others that are forgettable. Hopefully not unforgivable. The good news is that we are in there with each other day by day, trying to figure it out, just like everyone else.

I am most comfortable with collaboration. As a wife, I'm side by side with my husband. In writing this book together we are author and editor and contributor. As a therapist, I'm working with the client to come up with solutions. As a singer, I love doing duets, quartets or singing in groups, harmonizing, rather than doing solos. As the author of this book, I imagine being in dialogue with you, the reader.

One of our precious memories is singing in worship as a family, all five of us, as a quintet. I often felt moved and almost couldn't hold my alto voice steady as my daughter's soprano voice soared on the melody and each son, bass and baritone, supported Tom as he sang tenor. I had terrific fun when my daughter and my niece joined me on the healing chant CD we recorded called *Spirit Song*. Making music together is one of the ways I literally keep the music playing in my life. What are the ways you keep the music playing in your life?

We are inspired by couples who create together. Our friends, Ina and Jim Heup, husband and wife, sang at our wedding, almost 47 years ago. They sang at Wally's memorial service (Chapter 14). The fine arts, especially making music, are central to their lives. Another couple, Susan Lincoln and her husband Craig Toungate (Chapter 16) are an amazing singer, songwriter, composer, arranger duo whose songs are deeply moving. Their anthem *Let Love Lead*, written as witness after the 2016 election, reminds me of how I felt when I first heard the Quincy Jones song *We Are the World*. I use their song *Breathe Love* in daily meditation.

In Chapter 3 we quote the John Lennon song, *Grow Old With Me,* which he wrote with his wife, Yoko Ono, believed to be the last song he recorded. They were both inspired by the works of husband and wife, Robert Browning and Elizabeth Barrett Browning. They based the song on the opening stanza "Grow old along with me, the best is yet to be," from the poem *Rabbi ben Ezra,* and Barrett Browning's famous sonnet whose opening lines are "How do I love thee? Let me count the ways. I love thee to the depth and breadth and height my soul can reach." She ends the sonnet with, ... "I love thee with the breath, smiles, tears of all my life; and, if God choose, I shall but love thee better after death."

A jazz combo we enjoy when they are in town is the Judy Roberts Quartet. They winter in Phoenix; they return to Chicago for summer. Judy is a exquisite pianist and singer. Her husband, Greg is an amazing musician, playing saxophone, clarinet, flute, vibes and other instruments. He is also 20 years younger. We love to watch how they pass the melody and harmony, rhythm and song back and forth into seamless and playful dialogue, a couples' dance.

We shared the lyrics of *How Do You Keep The Music Playing?"* written by Marilyn and Alan Bergman in Chapter 1 and throughout the book. This husband, 93, and wife, 89, have been writing songs together for as long as they've been married, 60 years — plus the two years before. When asked how they work together all these years, Alan uses a baseball analogy of pitcher and catcher and Marilyn uses the example of the potter molding the clay, back and forth. They explained that it is about communication, starting with the meaning of the song, combined with the melody and then involving sometimes long periods of silence where they are both thinking about the composition. Marilyn says, "When we're working on composing the lyrics, often we will go into silence at the same time and sit for awhile, maybe several minutes, and then at the same time, come out of the silence and often thinking the same thought or saying the same word." Watching their interviews, I am inspired by how much they are in sync. They seem to be the best of friends, just like their lyric from the song which inspired our title.

As we conclude this book, I want to leave you with two parts from two poems. The first is by William Martin, from *The Couple's Tao Te Ching:*

" ... *If you could speak but fifty words*
each day to your beloved,
only that and no more,
what would be your words today?"

And from John O'Donohue's poem, "For Old Age", in *To Bless the Space Between Us*:

> *"May you be blessed;*
> *And may you find a wonderful love*
> *In your self for your self."*

It is a privilege to meet you through this book and share some of the stories and ideas as we journey through this retirement transition. This journey continues. But first I'm going to take a nap. Maybe Tom will join me. ... Mmmmm. ... Oh, wait, I was supposed to weed the garden.

~~~~Reflection~~~~

Imagine Your Marriage In Retirement

Chapter 2 concluded with a guided visualization. This is the conclusion of Chapter 20, the conclusion of the book. It may be interesting to take yourself on the same guided visualization now that you've traveled through the book. You might compare the experiences.

Set aside 15-30 minutes and do the following guided visualization. You can find a recording of this script on the website www.sallystrosahl.com. Pick a quiet time where you won't be interrupted. Put on some relaxing music if you choose. Have a notepad and pen ready. Or a voice recorder. Get comfortable. Take a few deep breaths, exhaling completely. Bring yourself into the moment. Close your eyes and get a picture of you and your spouse in a place of beauty and relaxation. Now visualize your retirement. Create a picture or a vision in your mind's eye. What does it look like? Where are you? What are the sights and sounds, the sensations, tastes and smells of this place of beauty and adventure? How do you feel? What are you wearing? What is your spouse wearing? What do you notice around you? Heighten the experience by making all your senses more vivid. See the colors brighter. Feel the sensations sharper. Turn up the volume. Use your imagination to flesh out this vision of retirement.

Enjoy the vision. When you are ready, take another deep breath and return to here and now, this time and place. Take a few moments to write down this vision and record your experience.

Now, read what you've written or recorded. Write a list of five things you need to do to make this vision a reality. Now write five things your partner needs to do to make this happen.

If you choose, share this experience with each other. See how close (or far apart) your visions are. Discuss. Repeat as you choose. It's your imagination. It's your creation. You are in charge of the manifestation.

Acknowledgements

Writing a book is so much more than I could have imagined! There have been so many people who have helped us, supported us, cheered us on through these five years to get to a book in our hands. YAY!

To my clients, thank you for the privilege of being invited into your life, the honor of your trust and for being my teacher. I have the best seat in the house, front seat to miracles of hope and transformation.

To the many couples who shared their stories either in interviews as Wise Married Elders or in other settings, I am so grateful for your time and courage. I especially want to thank Lynn and Dave Elko, Meredith and Bruce Lindgren, Cathy and Denis Haggerty, Nancy Mickelson, Sherry Bryant and John Urlich, Jim and Leslie Friedrich, Pat and Lorraine Dillon, Mabel and Bud Feldhausen, Connie and Jerry Emory, Anita and Ed Metzen, Eileen and Lou Parker, Susan Lincoln and Craig Toungate, Leonard Slovinski and Ira Epstein, Shelley and Doug Donaldson, Cath and Del Cooper, Cheri Erdman and Terry Jones, Chuck and Jean Naeger, Mimi Telfer and Nancy Wrobel, Loy and Linda Williams, Mike and Carol Mader, Faith and Don Smith, Pat and Ken Krippner, Barb Heyl and Bill Rau, Nancy and Don Tubesing, and Jean and George Palmer. And to my older brother Mark and his wife Barb — and their family — who have never been far from our thoughts as we observe how you continue each day to live your bucket list despite the ravages of Parkinson's. You are an inspiration.

To the first readers who gave us encouragement and helpful feedback — and told us to keep going: Marty Deming, Mitzi Beno, Allen Roberts, Mary Speers, Amanda Strosahl and Jack Udell, Polly Strosahl, Marilyn Marchetti, Cheri Erdman. To Chuck and Jean Naeger, our Road Trip Tip Gurus and fellow grandparents: it's fun to share your wonderful daughter and our amazing grandboys.

For being such supportive cheerleaders, I want to do a

shout-out to my Book Club: Phyllis Kramer, Kerry Proczko, Georgette Prisco, Mim Smith and Mary Speers, and to my Vision Circle: Marcia Gerzan, Cathy Haggerty, Jeanette Zweifel and Jacqui Neurauter, and to my Abundia Goddesses: Sue Ross, Barb Spaulding, Jeanette Zweifel and Cheri Erdman. To this great group I also add Allen Roberts, Deb and Mark Gauldin, Francie Quast-Hayden, Karen Turk, Mary Acton, Cindy Fischer, Jan Livene, Jan Vollmer, Renee Wood, Cathy Leoni, Kathy and Don Pilmer, Becky Sherwood, Megan Cook, Barry Free, Clif and Mary TeBeau, Dr. Diane Goodman, Maureen McKane, Loretta Lescelius, Beverly Miller, Denise Crosby, Dr. Dileep Borra. To Mary Faydash, thank you for the use of your beautiful home on Lake Michigan for a writing retreat. And to my younger brother, Phil Strosahl, for being such a good friend to us both. All of you asked us how we were doing. You heard the play-by-play, the excitement, the doubts, the frustrations and the delights. You kept the vision for us when we couldn't see the next step.

To my healing team, Anne Elementi, Ann O'Malley, Dr. Sharon Ollee, Barbara Blount, Jean Reddemann, Isabel Andrews, Sus Lincoln, Gahana Bonnington, Colleen Gorman, Karen McGuire and the Midwest Hilde Song Sisters. To my niece, Dr. Claire Strosahl Udell, who was my writing buddy while she finished her doctoral dissertation and I finished one more draft and countless rewrites of paragraphs and chapters.

To our publishing team, starting with Nancy and Don Tubesing and adding Julie Oleszek and Sue Becker, who showed us the way; Nancy Vedder-Schultz, who validated the path; and Linda Schwartz, who insisted we get endorsements. To Dr. Carolyn Conger, Dr. Jeanette Zweifel and Dr. Cheri Erdman for your endorsements and expert coaching. To Stephanie Warner, our graphic artist and cover designer. To Donnell Collins for making our photography session actually fun. To Laura Slivinski for her developmental editing, Kim Williams, our copy editor, and format technician Kevin Moriarity, who is actually a midwife by a different name.

To the inner circle of birthing this project: Marty Deming,

who taught me the 80-20 rule; my sisters, Amanda and Polly Strosahl, and my mentor Cheri Erdman. This book would not have come out of the womb had you not kept reminding me who and what and why.

To our sons Andrew and Kyle, and their wives Jen and Alisha: Your support for this writing project is deeply appreciated. It has meant some sacrifice. Your words of humor, interest and encouragement have helped me when I've needed it most. And to our daughter Kate, who has heard more than her share of angst and who reminded me in a moment of complete doubt when I was ready to shelve this whole time-consuming project, "That's why it's called a first draft, Momma." Thanks for your daily affirmations and joining me in starting our days with love, peace and joy in song and dance, even when we are many miles apart. This journey has also allowed Dad and me to reminisce about many precious family times. We are so grateful.

And to our grandchildren, Evan and Owen, and those little ones yet to join us, who teach us every day. "Where are you, Nama?," asked Evan, on the phone, when he was 3 years old and Papa Tom went down to visit by himself. "At the lake," I told him. "What are you doing?" he asked. "I'm writing a book." "Why?, he said in an accusatory voice, In other words, "Nama, why aren't you down here with me playing dinosaurs?" Yes, Evan. Why? is a really good question to keep asking ourselves always. It helps keep us on track — most of the time.

To my father Stan Strosahl, who taught so many pastors and their wives in so many retirement workshops over the years. I have all of your handouts. And to my mother Phyllis, who would pack his Thermos of coffee, sandwich and homemade treat, and send him off with a hug and kiss.

And to my precious loved one, Tom, editor-in-chief and chef-in-chief and main go-to guy for everything, and who keeps my effect and my affect straight, who blesses me every day, and who took on this project even though he IS retired. I promise, we can now retire from writing this book about retirement.

Notes & Resources

Chapter 1

Bergman, Alan and Marilyn, *The Bergman SongBook,* particularly *How Do You Keep the Music Playing?* Copyright material used with permission of Alfred Music

Research support for spike in divorce with "empty nest" and at retirement see pewreasearch.org, "gray divorce"; see also New York Times, Oct 30, 2015, "After full lives together, more older couples divorce", Abby Ellin

Eastman, Richard M., *Style: Writing as the Discovery of Outlook,* Oxford University Press, 1971

Thomas, Marlo, *It Ain't Over ... Till It's Over,* Atria Books, 2014

Satir, Virginia, *Making Contact*

Chapter 2

All of the worksheets for *Reflections* are available as download or in a workbook on our website: www.sallystrosahl.com

Select your own music, if you wish, as background for guided visualization. Check out *Inner Sanctum* on *Heartistry,* a CD by Carolyn Gahana Bonnington and Beckie Forsyth or Steve Halpern's *Starborn Suite.*

Chapter 3

John Lennon wrote the song, *Grow Old With Me,* with his wife, Yoko Ono, believed to be the last song he recorded. He captured it on a tape player with the idea of working out an arrangement to be recorded later in the studio. He never got the chance. They were both inspired by the works of husband and wife, Robert

Browning and Elizabeth Barrett Browning. They based this song on the opening stanza "Grow old along with me, the best is yet to be," from the poem *Rabbi ben Ezra,* and Barrett Browning's famous sonnet whose opening lines are "How do I love thee? Let me count the ways." Yoko Ono wrote a song with the same title.

Loverde, Joy, *Who Will Take Care of Me When I'm Old?: Plan Now to Safeguard Your health and Happiness in Old Age.* DaCapo Lifelong Books, 2017

Bette Davis is most often cited as the one who said "Getting old ain't for sissies."

Barbara Ehrenreich, *Natural Causes*, presents the science of aging. Worth the read.

Check out the website www.boombycindyjoseph.com. Cindy Joseph has a pro-aging philosophy which she writes about in her blog and also carries skin products that use natural ingredients. Her positive spirit shines. She says, "Crows feet, wrinkles, age spots are the badges we earn as we age."

Bill O' Hanlon presents the "Four Energies: Do we feel Bliss? Blessed? Pissed? Or Dissed?" in his videos called RESET about making changes. Check out his website www.billohanlon.com and https://possibilities.mykajabi.com/p/bills-RESET-opt-in

Arrien, Angeles, *The Second Half of Life*, Sounds True, 2005

Arrien, Angeles, *The Four-Fold Way*, Harper SanFrancisco, 1993

Holy Bible, Ecclesiastes 3:1-8 NRSV

Chapter 5

Stern, Robin, *The Gaslight Effect,* Harmony Books, 2007

Behary, Wendy, *Disarming the Narcissist*, 2008

Anonymous, *The Big Book: Twelve Steps and Twelve Traditions,1939*

Mason, Paul, *Stop Walking on Eggshells*, New Harbinger Press, 2010

Gottman, John M., and Silver, Nan, *The Seven Principles for Making Marriage Work,* Three Rivers Press, 1999

Oliver, Mary, *The Journey, From Devotions: The Selected Poems of Mary Oliver, 2017*

Chapter 6

Northrup, Christiane, *The Secret Pleasures of Menopause*, 2008

Gray, John, *Men Are From Mars, Women Are From Venus*, 1992

Brown, Brene, *The Gifts of Imperfection*, Hazeldon, 2010

This reference to Ho'oponopono (ho-o-pono-pono) is inspired by training I received in this method, an Hawaiian practice of reconciliation and forgiveness. "I Love You, I'm Sorry, Forgive Me, Thank You." For several articles on the ho'oponopono process, see the official ho'oponopono website. Even if you are skeptical, consider giving this simple healing method a try to see what happens.

"If you can fall in love..." quotation is from *Notes from Universe Calendar,* August 27.

Chapman, Gary. The Five Love Languages, Moody Publishers,1995.

Hendrix, Harville, *Getting the Love You Want*, Henry Holt, 1988

Chapter 8

Lerner, Harriet, *The Dance of Connection,* HarperCollins, 2001

See also the I Corinthians 13:4-8 passage in *Messages* by Eugene Peterson. The modern language gives it new meaning and the interpretation.

Davidson, Peter, *Marital Advice to My Grandson, Joel,* Sweet Memories Publishing, 2018

Moriarty, Kevin, *Reset Your Expectation, Improve Your Life,* on website *The Voice of Gloom and Doom.* Used with permission of author

Robinson, Jonathan, *Communication Miracles,* 2012

Gottman, John M., and Silver, Nan, *The Seven Principles for Making Marriage Work,* Three Rivers Press, 1999

Hendrix, Harville and LaKelly Hunt, Helen, *Making Marriage Simple,* Harmony, 2013, Copyright material used with permission of authors

Chapter 9

Hafiz, *The Gift: Poems by Hafiz,* The Great Sufi Master

Allen, Woody and Brickman, Marshall, *Annie Hall,* United Artists, 1977

Herman, Mark (screenplay) and Webb, Charles (novel), *Hope Springs,* MGM, 2012

Northrup, Christiane, *The Secret Pleasures of Menopause,* 2008 Printed with permission

The AARP survey of 8,000 people 50 years or older was conducted by Northrup, Schwartz and Witte, and reported in AARP Magazine. This same article quoted Dr. Marty Klein and Dr. Ken Haslam, a retired anesthesiologist who teaches workshops on sex and aging. AARP.org. Check out all the information available on the website. Use the Search feature.

Kauffman, Marta and Morris, Howard et. al., *Grace and Frankie*, Netflix, 2015-2018

A Woman's Touch Sexuality Resource Center is operated by a physician and a sex educator with both online and retail store.

Price, Joan, *Naked at Our Age: Talking Out Loud About Senior Sex*, Seal Press, 2011. Copyright material used with permission of author. www.NakedAtOurAge.com.

Interesting study on safe positions after joint replacement surgery. Certainly check with your doctor. Check out peerwell.com for discussion of safe sex positions. "Sexual Function improves Significantly After Primary Total Hip and Knee Arthroplasty: A Prospective Study by Rathod,MD, Deshmukh, MD, Ranawat, MD and Rodriguez, MD. presented at American Association of Orthopeadic Surgeons, Conference, 2013

Hammerstein, Oscar, *I Cain't Say No*, from Oklahoma, 1955

Gross, Zenith Henkin, *Seasons of the Heart*, New World Library, 2000

Streicher, Lauren, *Love Sex Again*, HarperCollins, 2014. This resource is very helpful with both medical and practical information.

Chapter 10

Mintz, Laurie B., *A Tired Woman's Guide to Passionate Sex*, Adams

Media, 2009

Spring, Janis Abrahms, *After the Affair*, HarperCollins, 2012

Spring, Janis Abrahms, *How Can I Forgive You?* HarperCollins, 2005

DeMore, Melanie, *Sending You Light*, Apple Music

Chapter 11

Cain, Susan, *Quiet,* Crown Publishing Group, 2012

Myers-Briggs Type Indicator www.mbtionline.com

Hagerty, Barbara Bradley, *Life Reimagined: The Science, Art and Opportunity of Midlife,* Riverhead Books, 2016   Copyright material used with permission of author

Stone, Hal and Sidra, *Embracing Ourselves,* New World Publishing, 1993

Zweifel, Jeanette C., *Will the Real Me Please Stand Up?,* Nell Thurber Press, 2002. Copyright material used with permission of author

Zorn, Eric, column from The Chicago Tribune, January 2018

Chapter 12

Northrup, Christiane, *The Secret Pleasures of Menopause*, 2008 Printed with permission

Holden, Lee, *Qi Gong for Seniors*, DVD

Check out websites drnorthrup.com, aarp.org/health/healthy-living and seniorplanet.org. As with any information, put it through your own truth filter and your own sense of what is in your best health interest. Always check with your doctor if you have a doubt. No one knows you better than you.

Normal memory loss vs. signs of dementia, see www.aarp.org/dementia; https://www.nia.nih.gov/health/do-memory-problems-always-mean-alzheimers-disease; also google normal memory loss with aging.

Loneliness and aging: see Aspen Institute, 2017- Epidemic of Loneliness; see also aarp.org/loneliness; see also https://www.nia.nih.gov/health/loneliness

Erdman, Cheri, *Live Large!,* HarperCollins, 1997. Copyright material used with permission of author

Strosahl, Kirk, and Robinson, Patricia, *In This Moment*, New Harbinger, 2015. Copyright material used with permission of author

Dillard, James, *The Chronic Pain Solution*, Bantam Books, 2002

Anthony, Karl, *Every Little Cell in My Body Is Happy*, Rainbow Songs, 2014

Chapter 13

Martin, William, *The Sage's Tao Te Ching,* Da Capo Press, 2000

Zukav, Gary, *Soul Stories,* Simon and Schuster, 2000

Lesser, Elizabeth, *Broken Open: How Difficult Times Can Make Us Grow,* 2012
Copyright material used with permission of author

Meditation is focused attention. It helps to use attention to the breath or to have your own mantra which bring you back to focus, such as "Breathe in... Breathe out." I also love using song in meditation , like "Breathe Love" by Susan Lincoln and Craig

Toungate. www.susanlincoln.com

Harris, Dan, *10% Happier,* HarperCollins, 2015. I love recommending this book to folks who feel they are failures at meditation and have given up. His second book, *Meditation for the Fidgety Skeptic* is good also. Remember learning to meditate is a lifelong task not something you can do in a weekend or five minutes.

Lamott, Anne, *Traveling Mercies: Some Thoughts on Faith,* Anchor Books, 1999

Kidd, Sue Monk, *The Secret Life of Bees,* Penguin, 2001

Brown, Brene, *Daring Greatly,* Avery, 2012. Copyright material used with permission of author

Drucker, Karen. *Songs of the Spirit III,* Audio CD

Chapter 14

Frankl, Viktor, *Man's Search for Meaning,* Beacon Press, 1946
As I researched the citation for this quotation to make sure I was giving the correct attribution, I found several authors given credit including Jack Kornfield and the Dalia Lama. Frankl, an Austrian neurologist and psychiatrist was also a Holocaust survivor. There is also a wonderful Threshold Choir chant using this poem.

Survey of 2,015 American adults about how we want to die, Consumer Reports Magazine, December 2014

According to a September 2014 report from the Institute of Medicine, the health arm of the National Academy of Sciences, the U.S. health care system "is poorly designed to deal with end-of-life concerns, particularly when it comes to considering the wishes of terminal patients."

See Gundersen Health Systems, "Making Choices" Advanced Care Planning at gundersenhealth.org

"Five Wishes" Aging with dignity.org

Virzi, Paolo, *The Leisure Seeker,* Sony Pictures, 2018

Gawande, Atul, *Being Mortal: Medicine and What Matters in the End,* 2014

Ehrenreich, Barbara, *Natural Causes,* Twelve, 2018

Genova, Lisa, *Still Alice,* Pocket Books, 2009

Various writers, *Grey's Anatomy,* ABC-TV, 2005-2018

Kidd, Sue Monk, *The Invention of Wings,* (promotional tour) 2015

Lesser, Elizabeth, *Broken Open: How Difficult Times Can Make Us Grow,* 2012. Copyright material used with permission of author

Conger, Carolyn, *Through the Dark Forest: Transforming Your Life in the Face of Death,* Penguin, 2014 Copyright material used with permission of author

There are many excellent resources for grief and grieving. Here are some of my favorites: *Good Grief* by Dr. Granger Westberg; *On Death and Dying* By Elizabeth Kubler-Ross; *Don't Take My Grief Away* by Doug Manning; *Letters From Home,* by Barry Free; *Option B* by Sheryl Sandberg; *I Wasn't Ready To Say Good-bye* by Brook Noel and Pamela Blair; *Through the Dark Forest* by Carolyn Conger; *A Grief Observed* by C.S. Lewis; *Please Be Patient, I'm Grieving* by Gary Roe; *Tear Soup* by Pat Schwiebert; *When Bad Things Happen To Good People* by Harold Kushner.

Chapter 16

Jacobs, Barry J. and Mayer, Julia L., *Meditations for Caregivers,* Da Capo Press, 2016. This is one of the many books with AARP sponsorship. Excellent resource

Dickinson, Amy, *Ask Amy,* Syndicated Column, Chicago Tribune, Feb. 14, 2018. Copyright material used with permission of author.

Free, Barry K., *Letters From Home,* Self-published, 2017. Copyright material used with permission of author

From AARP Bulletin, June 2018, Vol 59 No 5. More generational households in America share adults living with another generation; highest since 1950. "In 2016 64 million people or 20% of the US population lived with multiple generations under one roof according to Pew Research Center." AARP.org

Drucker, Karen, *Songs of the Spirit II,* 2001 TayToones Music, 2001

Chapter 17

Levine, Suzanne Braun, *How We Love Now: Women Talk About Intimacy After Fifty.* Copyright material used with permission.

Waldinger, Robert, *What Makes a Good Life: Lessons from the Longest Study on Happiness.* TED talk. Director of study on aging conducted by Harvard Medical School, where he is professor of psychiatry.

TED Conferences, LLC is a media organization that posts talks online for free distribution, under the slogan "ideas worth spreading". TED was founded in February 1984 as a conference, which has been held annually since 1990. Wikipedia. It's my new go to for fun.

Chapter 18

McGraw, Tim, *Live Like You Were Dying,* title track from album released in 2004.

There are many resources in AARP Magazine, AARP Bulletin and AARP website

See other websites like "The joy of retirement", Retirement Rocks.org

When you retire is more complicated than just if you want to leave your job. It may also affect your heath. A study at Cornell University shows a striking correlation between Social Security claims for early taker and a jump in mortality, especially for men. See article in Bloomberg by Christopher Cordon. December 19, 2017. There are so many factors to consider, including your state of health.

Chapter 20

Marilyn and Alan Bergman You Tube video interview at University of North Carolina, Chapel Hill and You Tube video by Film Music Foundation.

Check out www.judyroberts.com for a list of recordings and dates and locations of performances of her quartet.

Martin, Willam, *The Couple's Tao Te Ching,* Da Capo Press, 2000. Consider using this excerpt from The Couple's Tao Te Ching by William Martin as an exercise.Try doing this for a few days in a row, write down the 50 words you speak, and your partners reactions.

> " ... If you could speak but fifty words
> each day to your beloved,
> only that and no more,
> what would be your words today?"

O'Donohue, John. *To Bless The Space Between Us: A Book of Blessings,* Doubleday, 2008

Bibliography

Allen, Woody and Brickman, Marshall, *Annie Hall,* United Artists, 1977

Anderson, George and Barone, Andrew, *Walking in the Garden of Souls,* Berkley, 2002

Anonymous, The Big Book: *Twelve Steps and Twelve Traditions,1939*

Anthony, Karl, *Every Little Cell in My Body Is Happy,* Rainbow Songs, 2014

Arp, David and Claudia, with Stanley, Markman and Blumberg, *Fighting for Your Empty Nest Marriage,* Jossey-Bass, 2000

Arrien, Angeles, *The Four-Fold Way,* HarperSanFrancisco, 1993

Arrien, Angeles, *The Second Half of Life,* Sounds True, 2005

Barks, Coleman, with John Moyne, *The Essential Rumi,* HarperCollins, 1995

Barron, Renee, and Elizabeth Wagele, *The Enneagram Made Easy,* HarperCollins, 1994

Behary, Wendy, *Disarming the Narcissist,* 2008

Berg, Elizabeth, *Escaping into the Open: The Art of Writing True,* Perennial, 1999

Bergman, Alan and Marilyn, *The Bergman SongBook,* particularly *How Do You Keep the Music Playing?*

Borkoski, Jeff, *The Sex-Starved Husband's Guide,* Self-Published, 2016

Brody, Steve, and Brody, Cathy, *Renew Your Marriage at Midlife,* Perigee Relationships, 1999

Block, Ira, *Dying Well: Peace and Possibilities at the End of Life,* Riverhead Books, 1997

Bonnington, Carolyn Gahana and Forsyth, Beckie, *Inner Sanctum. Heartistry,* CD, HeartistrySoundbath.com

Brach, Tara, *Radical Acceptance*

Brown, Brene, *Braving the Wilderness,* Random House, 2017

Brown, Brene, *Daring Greatly,* Avery, 2012

Brown, Brene, *The Gifts of Imperfection,* Hazeldon, 2010

Brown, Brene, *Rising Strong,* Random House, 2015

Cain, Susan, *Quiet,* Crown Publishing Group, 2012

Chapman, Gary. *The Five Love Languages,* Moody Publishers, 1995.

Chimsky, Mark Evan (editor), *65 Things To Do When You Retire,* 2013

Chodron, Pema, *Living Beautifully With Uncertainty and Change,* Shambhala, 2012

Coleman, Barks, *The Essential Rumi,* Harper SanFrancisco, 1995

Conger, Carolyn, *Through the Dark Forest: Transforming Your Life in the Face of Death,* Penguin, 2014

Dalai Lama, *The Book of Joy: Lasting Happiness in a Changing World*

Davidson, Peter, *Marital Advice to My Grandson, Joel,* Sweet Memories Publishing, 2018

Delamontague, Robert, *Honey, I'm Home: How to Prevent or Resolve Marriage Conflicts Caused by Retirement,* 2011

DeMore, Melanie, *Sending You Light,* Apple Music

Dickinson, Amy, *Ask Amy,* Syndicated Column, Chicago Tribune, Feb. 14, 2018

Dickinson, Amy, *The Mighty Queens of Freeville,* Hachette Book Group, 2010

Dickinson, *Strangers Tend To Tell Me Things,* Hachette Book Group, 2018

Dillard, James, *The Chronic Pain Solution,* Bantam Books, 2002

Drucker, Karen, *Songs of the Spirit II,* TayToones Music, 2001 Audio CD

Drucker, Karen, *Songs of the Spirit III,* TayToones Music, 2001 Audio CD

Eastman, Richard M., *Style: Writing as the Discovery of Outlook,* Oxford University Press, 1971

Ellis, Albert and Velten, Emmett, *Optimal Aging,* Open Court, 1998

Ehrenreich, Barbara, *Natural Causes,* Twelve, 2018

Erdman, Cheri, *Live Large!,* HarperCollins, 1997

Erdman, Cheri, *Nothing to Lose,* HarperCollins, 1995

Free, Barry K., *Letters From Home,* Self-published, 2017

Floyd, Mary Louise, *Retired With Husband: Superwoman's New Challenge,* VanderWyck & Burnham, 2006

Gawande, Atul, *On Being Mortal: Medicine and What Matters in the End,* Henry Holt, 2014

Genova, Lisa, *Still Alice,* Pocket Books, 2009

Gottman, John M., and Silver, Nan, *The Seven Principles for Making Marriage Work,* Three Rivers Press, 1999

Graham, Linda, *Bouncing Back: Rewiring Your Brain For Maximum Resilience and Well-Being,* New World Library, *2013*

Gray, John, *Men Are From Mars, Women Are From Venus,* Harper-Collins, 1992

Gross, Zenith Henkin, *Seasons of the Heart,* New World Library, 2000

Hafiz, *The Gift: Poems by Hafiz, The Great Sufi Master*

Hagerty, Barbara Bradley, *Life Reimagined: The Science, Art and Opportunity of Midlife,* Riverhead Books, 2016

Hall, Nora R., *Survive Your Husband's Retirement,* Self-Published, 2017

Hammerstein, Oscar, *I Cain't Say No,* from *Oklahoma,* 1955

Hanson, Waverly, *How to Divorce-Proof Your Marriage,* 2015

Harris, Dan, *Meditation for the Fidgety Skeptic,* Penguin Random House, 2017

Harris, Dan, *10% Happier,* HarperCollins, 2015

Hay, Louise et. al., *Loving Yourself to Great Health,* 2014

Heitler, Susan, *The Power of Two,* New Harbinger, 1997

Hendrix, Harville, *Getting the Love You Want,* Henry Holt, 1988

Hendrix, Harville and LaKelly Hunt, Helen, *Making Marriage Simple,* Harmony, 2013

Herman, Mark (screenplay) and Webb, Charles (novel), *Hope Springs,* MGM, 2012

Holden, Lee, *Qi Gong for Seniors,* DVD

Holy Bible, NRSV

Jacobs, Barry J. and Mayer, Julia L., *Meditations for Caregivers,* Da Capo Press, 2016

Jameson, Marni, *Downsizing the Family Home,* AARP Real Possibilities, Sterling, 2015

Jenkinson, Stephen, *Die Wise: A Manifesto for Sanity and Soul,* North Atlantic Books, 2014

Johnson, Sue, *Hold Me Tight,* Hachette, 2008

Kabot-Zinn, Jon. *Wherever You Go There You Are,* Hachette, 2005

Kauffman, Marta and Morris, Howard et. al., *Grace and Frankie,* Netflix, 2015-2018

Kelly, Rob, *The Complete Guide to a Creative Retirement,* 2003

Kidd, Sue Monk, *The Invention of Wings,* Penguin, 2014, (promotional tour)

Kidd, Sue Monk, *The Secret Life of Bees,* Penguin, 2003

Kidd, Sue Monk. *When the Heart Waits,* Harper & Row, 1990

Kiersey, David, and Marilyn Bates, *Please Understand Me: Character and Temperament Types,* Prometheus Nemesis,1984

Kornfield, Jack, *The Art of Forgiveness, Lovingkindness,and Peace,* Random House, 2002

Kornfield, Jack, *The Wise Heart,* Random House, 2009

Krasnow, Iris, *Sex After: Women Share How Intimacy Changes as Life Changes,* Gotham Books, 2014

Kushner, Harold. *When Bad Things Happen To Good People,* Penguin Random House, 1981

Lamott, Anne, *Bird By Bird: Some Instructions on Writing and Life,* Anchor Books, 1995

Lamott, Anne, *Help Thanks Wow: The Three Essential Prayers,* Riverhead Books, 2002

Lamott, Anne, *Traveling Mercies: Some Thoughts on Faith,* Anchor Books, 1999

Law, Rick L. and Hesselbaum, Zachary, *Cruising Through Retirement,* Word Association Publishers, 2015

Lerner, Harriet, *The Dance of Connection,* HarperCollins, 2001

Lerner, Harriet, *Marriage Rules,* Gotham Books, 2012

Lesser, Elizabeth, *Broken Open: How Difficult Times Can Make Us Grow,* Penguin, 2012

Levine, Stephen, *A Year to Live,* Three Rivers Press, 1997

Levine, Suzanne Braun, *How We Love Now: Women Talk About Intimacy After Fifty,* Plume Books, 2013

Lincoln, Susan. *Mother Heart: Songs for the Sacred Feminine by Hildegard of Bingen,* CD

Lincoln, Susan, *Breathe Love* and *Let Love Lead. www.susanlincoln.com*

Loverde, Joy, *Who Will Take Care of Me When I'm Old?,* DaCapo Lifelong Books, 2017

Lynn, Dorree, *Sex for Grownups,* Health Communications, 2010

Martin, William, *The Sage's Tao Te Ching,* Da Capo Press, 2000

Martin, Willam, *The Couple's Tao Te Ching,* Da Capo Press, 2000

Mason, Paul, *Stop Walking on Eggshells*, New Harbinger Press, 2010

McCarthy, Barry and Emily, *Rekindling Desire: A Step-By-Step Program to Help Low-Sex and No-Sex Marriages,* Routledge, Taylor & Francis, 2003

McGraw, Tim, *Live Like You Were Dying,* title track from album released in 2004.

Mewes, Gail, *Tips and Tricks for Boomer Chicks,* Self-Published, 2014

Mintz, Laurie B., *A Tired Woman's Guide to Passionate Sex,* Adams Media, 2009

Moriarty, Kevin, *Reset Your Expectation, Improve Your Life,* on website *The Voice of Gloom and Doom*

Morelan, Bill, *Married for Life,* Concerned Communications, 2004

Nelson, Marcia Z., *Come and Sit: A Week Inside Meditation Centers,* 2001

Northrup, Christiane, *The Secret Pleasures of Menopause,* Hay House, 2008

O'Donohue, John. *To Bless The Space Between Us: A Book of Blessings,* Doubleday, 2008

O'Hanlon, Bill, *Do One Thing Different,* HarperCollins, 1999

Oliver, Mary, *The Journey, From Devotions: The Selected Poems of Mary Oliver, 2017*

Palmer, Parker, *Let Your Life Speak: Listening for the Voice of Vocation,* Jossey-Bass, 1999

Palmer, Parker, *On the Brink of Everything,* Berrett-Koehler, 2018

Pascale, Rob; Primavera, Louis H. and Roach, Rip, *The Retirement Maze: What You Should Know Before and After You Retire,* Rowman & Littlefield, 2012

Peterson, Eugene, *The Message: The Bible in Contemporary Language,* Navpress, 2002

Pevny, Ron, *Conscious Living, Conscious Aging,* Atria Paperback, 2014

Pillemer, Karl, *30 Lessons for Loving,* Hudson Street Press, 2015

Price, Joan, *Naked at Our Age: Talking Out Loud About Senior Sex,* Seal Press, 2011

Price, Joan, *The Ultimate Guide to Sex After 50,* Cleis Press, 2014

Real, Terrence, *The New Rules of Marriage,* Penguin Random House, 2008

Robinson, Jonathan, *Communication Miracles,* Conari Press, 2012

Satir, Virginia, *Making Contact,* Celestial Arts

Satir, Virginia. *People-Making,* Condor Books, 1972

Satir, Virginia, *Self-Esteem,* Celestial Arts, 1975

Schachter-Shalomi, Zalman and Miller, Ronald S., *From Age-ing to Sage-ing,* Warner Books, 1995

Schnarch, David, *Passionate Marriage,* Norton, 2009

Schwiebert, Pat and DeKlyven, Chuck, *Tear Soup: a Recipe for Healing After Loss,* Grief Watch, 1999

Sellers, Ronnie (editor), *Sixty Things To Do When You Turn Sixty,* 2006

Solin, Daniel R., *The Smartest Retirement Book You'll Ever Read,* Penguin Group, 2009

Spring, Janis Abrahms, *After the Affair,* HarperCollins, 2012

Spring, Janis Abrahms, *How Can I Forgive You?* HarperCollins, 2005

Smith, Marion Roach, *The Memoir Project*, Hachette, 2011

Stern, Robin, *The Gaslight Effect,* Harmony Books, 2007

Streicher, Lauren, *Love Sex Again,* Harper Collins, 2014

Stone, Hal and Sidra, *Embracing Ourselves,* New World Publishing, 1993

Strosahl, Kirk, and Robinson, Patricia, *In This Moment,* New Harbinger, 2015

Strosahl, Sally and Kate Strosahl-Johnson. *Spirit Song: Chants For Healing, Inspiration and Fun.* Audio CD. www.sallystrosahl.com.

Strosahl, Sally, www.sallystrosahl.com

Taylor, Barbara Brown, *An Altar in the World: A Geography of Faith,* HarperCollins, 2009

Taylor, Roberta K. and Mintzer, Dorian, *The Couple's Retirement Puzzle,* Lincoln Street Press, 2011

TED Talks, www.tedtalks.com

Thomas, Marlo, *It Ain't Over ... Till It's Over,* Atria Books, 2014

Thomas, William H., *What Are Old People For?,* VanderWyck & Burnham, 2004

Tubesing, Donald, *Kicking Your Stress Habits,* Whole Person Associates, 1997

Vedder-Shults, Nancy, *The World is Your Oracle*, Quarto Press, 2017

Walzer, Robyn D. and Westrup, Darrah, *The Mindful Couple,* New Harbinger, 2009

Waldinger, Robert, *What Makes a Good Life: Lessons from the Longest Study on Happiness.* TED talk. Director of study on aging conducted by Harvard Medical School, where he is professor of psychiatry.

Wehrenberg, Margaret, *The 10 Best-Ever Anxiety Management Techniques*, Norton, 2008

Westheimer, Ruth, *Dr. Ruth's Sex After 50*, Quill Driver Books, 2005

Wolfelt, Alan D., *Understanding Your Grief*, Companion Press, 2003

Wright, Judith and Wright, Bob, *The Heart of the Fight*, New Harbinger, 2016

Yogev, Sara, *A Couple's Guide to Happy Retirement and Aging*, Familius, 2018

Yogev, Sara, *For Better or for Worse, but Not for Lunch: Making Marriage Work in Retirement*, Contemporary Books, 2002

Zeig, Jeffrey K. and Kulbatski, Tami, *For Couples: Ten Commandments for Every Aspect of Your Relationship Journey*, Zieg, Tucker & Theisen, 2013

Zelinski, Ernie J., *How to Retire Happy, Wild and Free*, VIP Books, 2010

Zorn, Eric, column from The Chicago Tribune, January 2018

Zukav, Gary, *Soul Stories*, Simon and Schuster, 2000

Zweifel, Jeanette C., *Will the Real Me Please Stand Up?*, Nell Thurber Press, 2002

About the Authors

Sally Strosahl, M.A., LCPC, has her master's degree in clinical psychology and several years of advanced training. She is a licensed clinical professional counselor, in private practice for more than four decades providing individual, couple and family therapy. She is known as the "therapist's therapist." Sally often receives referrals of couples who have tried several other places and are willing to try one more time. In addition to regular office appointments, Sally offers to work with couples in a more intensive setting, for several hours over several days.

Sally grew up in Wisconsin, graduated from North Central College (1973) with majors in psychology and sociology. Her graduate degree is from Roosevelt University. Her other interests, in addition to being Mom and Grandma, include reading, nutrition, spirituality, music, travel and being in nature.

Her biggest credential for this book is her 46-year marriage to Tom Johnson, retired newspaper editor. They are the parents of three adult children and grandparents of two. The experiences of caring for their own parents, who have now all passed on, enrich the stories in this book and provide compassion for others in similar situations. Since Tom is retired and Sally is not, this difference adds to the authenticity of the examples in the book. We are "walking the talk" of the transition into retirement and the effects on our marriage. www.sallystrosahl.com.

About the Contributor

Tom Johnson grew up in Minneapolis and in the North Dakota cities of Grand Forks and Minot. He graduated from North Central College (1968) with majors in English and political science, and was in graduate school when he was drafted into the Army during the Vietnam War. His 34 months on active duty were spent stateside. He met Sally at North Central's Homecoming in 1970, and leaped into action, lining up their first date six weeks later. They were married Jan. 8, 1972. In the fall of 1971, he started as a reporter for The Beacon-News in Aurora, Ill., and worked there for more than 40 years in a variety of editorial positions, retiring as news editor in 2012. His biggest delight is being the parent of Andy, Kyle and Kate, and "Papa Tom" to grandsons Evan and Owen. His interests include golf, biographies, aviation and a wide variety of music.

CPSIA information can be obtained
at www.ICGtesting.com
Printed in the USA
BVHW042324011218
534560BV00018B/560/P

9 780692 163207